# Comments on *And That's the Way It Is(n't)*

"Ever since our media stars began admitting that they are, on average, well to the left of most Americans, the problem has been to prove that this bias contaminates their 'news' -- something they hotly deny. Now, thanks to the wonders of computerization, plus a lot of sweat and persistence, the job has been done at last. This volume lays out the statistical proof of the media's distortion of the news in overwhelming quantity, neatly organized by topics, lavishly supported with names and quotations, and crisply illustrated with simple bar graphs. How will the media respond? My guess is that they will try hard to ignore it. For this book not only settles their hash -- it cooks their goose." -- *William Rusher, former publisher of* National Review.

"It should be required reading in every 'Media and Society' course. Those on the left might argue that any particular study is methodologically flawed or refutable, but the impact of the whole, like row upon row of soldiers assaulting a tenaciously defended but inherently flimsy position, is overwhelming. If I were using the book, I would not assign it to be read all at once -- that's like watching all the episodes of *Friday the 13th* or some other horror movie back-to-back." -- *Dr. Marvin Olasky, professor of journalism, University of Texas.*

"The people at the Media Research Center don't rant about media bias. They study it -- methodically, comprehensively, without blinking. Their new book makes a case for liberal bias that no honest journalist can easily dismiss." -- *Dan Griswold,* Colorado Springs Gazette Telegraph *editorial page editor.*

"The biggest con job perpetuated on the American people in the 1980s was the media didn't have an ideological axe to grind. *And That's the Way It Is(n't)* blows the lid off the dominant media culture and exposes its 'nobody here but us apolitical observers' claim for the lie it is." -- *Rep. Robert K. Dornan (R-CA).*

"Settles once and for all the question of media bias in America....Well, it should settle the question, since it is virtually bursting with studies, compilations, and quotes proving the liberal bias of Big Media beyond any shadow or hint of doubt. But it won't. It won't because the men and women who are the subject of this book adamantly refuse to acknowledge their bias." -- *Mona Charen, syndicated columnist and former speechwriter for President Reagan.*

"A great resource. Will be a real eye-opener to some, a confirmation to others. Voluminously documents and analyzes the unmistakingly one-sided, liberal bias of the media. Should be required reading in every journalism class in the country. It won't be." -- *Michael Rosen, talkshow host, KOA Radio, Denver.*

"Are the media biased? They sure are. Will the media enjoy this book? They sure won't. Is that a good reason to read and learn from this book? It sure is." -- *William Murchison,* Dallas Morning News *editorial page editor and Heritage Features columnist.*

"In the information age, 'truth in labeling' is just as important for news as it is for nutrition. With this guide to understanding our journalistic daily diet, the Media Research Center has done wonders for the health of our national democracy. And unlike the low-sodium diet books that crowd our shelves, their findings suggest we should take our media with a grain of salt." -- *Congressman Chris Cox (R-CA).*

"*And That's the Way It Is(n't)* is the ultimate truth in labeling. The question of left-wing bias has been debated for years. This volume ought to end the discussion." -- *Dick Williams,* Atlanta Journal *columnist.*

"Indispensable reading. This extraordinary book provides irrefutable proof of the liberal bias of the mass media. For too long, the media have hidden behind the veil of 'objectivity' to refute criticisms of bias. No longer. *And That's The Way It Is(n't)* is the best tool in America for ensuring our free press is accountable to the public it serves." -- *Congressman Bob McEwen (R-OH).*

"Current complaints about the 'unaccountable power' of America's media, their ingrained political bias and indifference to accusations of arrogance, as a rule, fall short of remedial suggestions. So cowed is the public that nobody even dares remind the nation's schools of journalism of their professional obligation to monitor and critique the 'Teflon Estate,' and of their failure to perform this essential function. *And That's The Way It Is(n't)* contains all the facts and figures, means and modes needed by journalism teachers to regain their confidence and roles as media critics vital for the cultural health of America." -- *H. Joachim Maitre, Dean, Boston University College of Communication.*

# AND THAT'S THE WAY IT IS(N'T)

## A Reference Guide to Media Bias

### Edited by L. Brent Bozell III and Brent H. Baker

Media Research Center   •   Alexandria, Virginia

Dedicated to the memory of
Dr. Harold Walter Siebens
1905-1989

Media Research Center
111 S. Columbus Street
Alexandria, VA 22314


Copyright © 1990 by the Media Research Center

ISBN 0-9627348-0-2




Printed in the United States of America
**First Edition**
Second Printing, September, 1990

# Table of Contents

# About the Publisher: the Media Research Center

The Media Research Center (MRC) is a non-profit educational foundation. Organized in 1987 to document liberal media bias and distribute this research to the public, the MRC records and maintains a tape library of all ABC, CBS and NBC news programs along with selected CNN and PBS news and public affairs shows. Each day the MRC updates a computer data base that tracks the content of these news shows, enabling researchers to locate stories by topic or individual reporter. In addition, MRC analysts monitor the content of *Time, Newsweek*, and *U.S. News & World Report* as well as numerous major newspapers.

The Center publishes *Media Watch*, a monthly newsletter that reviews news coverage of political and current events, and *Notable Quotables*, a bi-weekly compilation of the latest noteworthy, sometimes humorous, quotes in the liberal media.

In 1989 the Center expanded its scope, launching an effort to document the liberal policies and values promoted by the entertainment community. *TV etc.*, a bi-monthly newsletter, examines the liberal issue agenda permeating prime time television, current cinematic fare and record releases and catalogues the off-screen political activities of the Hollywood Left.

# About the Editors

**L. Brent Bozell III** established the Media Research Center (MRC) in April, 1987, and serves as the Chairman of the Board of Directors and President. He is the Publisher of the MRC's monthly newsletter *MediaWatch*, its bi-weekly *Notable Quotables*, and *TV etc.*, a bi-monthly review of the entertainment industry.

Before founding the MRC, Bozell was Executive Director of the National Conservative Foundation where he served as Publisher of the newsletter *Newswatch* until 1987.

Bozell frequently discusses media bias on radio talk shows across the country. He has been interviewed on many television news shows, including CNN's *Crossfire, Inside Politics, Newswatch* and Headline News; C-SPAN viewer call-in shows; *Entertainment Tonight;* and ABC, CBS and NBC news programs. His articles have appeared in *The Wall Street Journal, Washington Times, Washington Post, Detroit News, Providence Journal* and *National Review.*

Bozell is a graduate of the University of Dallas in Irving, Texas, where he received a Bachelor of Arts degree in history. He resides with his wife, Norma, and their four children in Alexandria, Virginia.

**Brent H. Baker** has served as Executive Director of the Media Research Center (MRC) since its founding in 1987. He is the Editor of the MRC's *Media-Watch* and *Notable Quotables* newsletters. He was previously Editor of *Newswatch*, a newsletter published by the National Conservative Foundation. During college he edited a conservative student newspaper.

Baker's articles analyzing media coverage of current and political events have appeared in numerous newspapers, including the *Colorado Springs Gazette-Telegraph, Union Leader* (Manchester, N.H.), *The Orange County Register, Wheeling Intelligencer, Panama City News Herald* and *Human Events*. In addition, Baker has written pieces for *USA Today* magazine, *Journalism Quarterly* and *Vista*, the Hispanic Sunday newspaper supplement.

Baker received a Bachelor of Arts degree with special honors in political science from George Washington University in Washington, D.C.

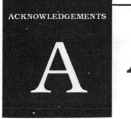

# Acknowledgements

The purpose of this book is to demonstrate that there is no such thing as an "objective" national news media. Indeed, many media analysts have made this point in their unique studies of the press, and their contributions have been indispensable to our examination. In 1984, Bill Adams developed the guidelines to analyze political party conventions; we emulated his methodology in our own analysis four years later. Michael Robinson (who disagrees with many of our views) has in recent years published several fascinating studies which he generously allowed us to reproduce. Robert and Linda Lichter, most famous for their groundbreaking 1981 analysis on the liberal attitude of the media elite have published many studies, and we thank them for letting us reprint their work. And Ted J. Smith III not only produced two fabulous studies which we've summarized, but also gave us invaluable advice as we prepared this book.

The Media Research Center (MRC) staff of media analysts, past and present, deserve credit as well. Tim Graham spearheaded the study which looked at media foundation grants and oversaw the MRC's studies over the past year or so. Dorothy Warner coordinated the study on the media labeling in the abortion debate. Others who performed yeoman's work to gather the exhaustive research that went into the MRC's studies include Kimberly Bellissimo, Richard Marois, Gerry Scimeca and Stewart Verdery.

We recognize the specific contributions of Marc Ryan who provided much of the research and direction on the chapters dealing with foreign policy; of Steven Allen who made the meaning, importance and ways to measure media bias so clear in this book's introduction; and of Patricia Bozell, who plodded through all of this and caught all of our grammatical errors and made our convoluted sentences much more succinct.

Some labored long hours to turn mountains of raw data into a published work. Jim Heiser spent months working on layout software to turn typed copy into what you see here. Kristin Kelly, and before her Cindy Bulman, coordinated the 10,000 administrative details we overlooked (or delicately ignored). Susan Estrella produced the graphs and tables while Paul Hebert designed the book's cover which Joseph Borzotta illustrated. Richard Kimble and Lawrence Gourlay identified the grants to fund MRC research, while Leif Noren oversaw the fiscal management of the project.

We appreciate the cooperation of those who let us reprint work from their publications: Frank Quine of the *Washington Journalism Review*, Karlyn Keene of the American Enterprise Institute, Barbara Bernstein of Ablex Publishing and Ann Merriman of the *Richmond News Leader*.

We thank those whose gentle words of encouragement and advice continue to fuel this enterprise. In particular, we cite the MRC's Board of Directors, Burton Yale Pines, Harold C. Simmons and William A. Rusher; to that list we add Ed Capano and Vic Gold, two who will probably never fully know the degree to which they've helped the Center.

Finally, and most importantly, we thank the supporters of the Media Research Center for their faith in and contributions to our work.

*-- L. Brent Bozell III and Brent H. Baker*
*March 29, 1990*

# F by *Jeane Kirkpatrick*
*Former U.S. Ambassador to the United Nations*

With regard to a good many fundamental principles of political philosophy, I am a liberal. We in the United States were founded in the 18th century on what are classically liberal assumptions. Almost all of the most fundamental assumptions that inspirit, not only the Declaration of Independence, but the Constitution as well, are liberal principles. The overriding concern that's reflected both in the Declaration of Independence and in the Constitution is with controlling arbitrary power.

After all, our national experience is grounded in the effort to control arbitrary power, which we thought King George was exercising over us in arbitrary, unreasonable, and unlawful ways. The Founding Fathers, in the Articles of Confederation and later in the Constitution, were concerned not only with establishing a government, but also with establishing a government that would be responsive to "the people" -- the American people -- and which would be able to be controlled collectively. One of the authors of *The Federalist Papers* wrote that we must first enable government to control the people and, second, it must be required to control itself.

This whole problem of controlling arbitrary power is, in short, one that has been with us throughout our national life. It inspirits all our basic documents and our political culture. We developed the whole notion of separation of power as the response to the desire to control arbitrary power over our lives and times and national affairs. Popular government itself is regarded by our Constitution and by democratic theory in general as the most effective means of controlling arbitrary power, on the grounds that if government can be kept responsive to citizens, and rulers can be forced to be accountable to the people whom they rule, then we will truly have government by the consent and control of the governed.

---

*Adapted by Ambassador Kirkpatrick from an address delivered in 1983.*

What's the point? Obviously, the point is that we have always sought to control (not to destroy, but to control) important, significant powers that small groups can exercise over ourselves and our society. Government structure is a monument to the proposition of the need to control arbitrary power. The application of our laws in the economic sphere, beginning in the late nineteenth century, from 1890 through the New Deal period, reflects the determination to bring the arbitrary power of "big business" under control.

New powers have arisen: among them, the power of the media. Some people believe, and I am among them, that the power of the media today constitutes the most significant exercise of *unaccountable* power in our society. It is unaccountable to anyone, except for those who exercise the power. I believe that the domain of culture is as important as the domain of government or the economy. My view is that the domain of culture is *more* important than that of economics or government. It conditions the economy and it conditions government. When we talk about what comes first, the chicken or the egg, I believe that it's the chicken. Whether economics controls ideology and culture, or whether ideology and culture control economics -- and I believe that it is ideology and culture.

Our ideas about what is true, what is good, what is important, what causes what, what's worth doing, what's legitimate -- those are the very essence of our culture, and they shape our behavior in the economic and the governmental sphere. No domain is more important than the domain in which the media operate.

I believe that it is terribly important that the same principles that concern limitations of arbitrary power apply to the media and in the domain of culture. It is very important to realize that the electronic media, which provide mass audiences, have made our culture much more manipulable than it ever was in the past. Typically, historically, cultures have been slow to change. Ideas about what's real, what's important, and what causes what, change very slowly in history. They are grounded in the experience of peoples, and respond only to additional, cumulative experiences of peoples.

With the rise of electronic media, the possibility of deliberate manipulation of culture has been magnified ten zillion fold. The first step in that direction was the printing press. The importance of the printed word as an instrument for the manipulation of culture is illustrated in the mass literacy campaigns that we see undertaken in societies where there is a desire to transform the culture.

Let me hasten to say that I am not against mass literacy campaigns -- but I am in favor of mass literacy campaigns that are used simply for the purpose of teaching people to read, not for the purpose of controlling and transforming their views. I don't know whether you have looked at any of the literacy materials from Cuba. When Fidel Castro came to power, he organized a mass literacy campaign and used it, as have his Nicaraguan friends, to transmit his new, radical Marxist/Leninist notions about the nature of the world. If you've looked at any of the literacy teaching materials out of the Nicaraguan campaign, or the Cuban or Chinese, or a lot of others before that, you would see how useful mass literacy can be as an instrument for cultural transformation.

The electronic media are many times more useful because they manipulate images as well as ideas. Images are very easily manipulated -- pictures speak a thousand words and all that. People are more readily manipulated through images than just with words.

In the theory of a free press in a liberal society, the competition within the press can produce competing versions of reality in some kind of marketplace of ideas. Oliver Wendell Holmes talks about this; John Stuart Mill talks about it. And what they say is classical liberal theory, that in the clash of opinion and ideas and interpretation, is a discipline. Karl Popper talks about it in a very sophisticated way. Science is kept responsible by being submitted to public criticism. Science is kept responsible and progressive by being "public" where it is open to criticism.

In the early decades of this century, enormous, monopolistic concentrations of power developed with regard to the media. These constitute a great obstacle to the marketplace of ideas and interpretations functioning in the way that was anticipated in classical liberal theory. We do have multiple papers and magazines, and that's an awful lot better than having single sources. I don't ever want to suggest that the press in our society is not a free press. It *is* a free press. Nor do I want to suggest that it is not vastly superior -- morally, politically and intellectually -- to the press in controlled societies. It is vastly superior in all those ways. Nevertheless, there have developed in our times, these colossal concentrations of media power. They weren't planned any more than monopolistic practices that developed in the economy. They just grew. The one-newspaper town developed, and news wire services developed, and the networks developed. Then the network power was extended, and another interesting thing happened in our society. Culture classes developed: we developed a culture class struggle with some very significant divisions between the culture of some of our political and social classes and some other political and social classes.

I've had a little personal experience with these culture classes in universities. The media being what they are, you only read about some of my experiences -- at Berkeley and Minnesota and Smith and Barnard. You didn't read about my experiences at Puget Sound or at the University of Oklahoma or St. Johns University in New York or at Bethany College in West Virginia, and several other places where I was received warmly.

As I reflect on my experiences, it seems remarkable to me that I had become so unacceptable in those kinds of elite institutions in which I had been a student and at which I had taught. Furthermore, I was unacceptable for the offense of energetically articulating the policies of the President of the United States. Now, the President was elected by a majority of American people and is a legitimate ruler who governs constitutionally. We do not break laws in this administration. President Reagan is serious about the law and respects it. He proceeds only within the constraint of law, and I proceed only within the constraints of law. Despite the fact that he was relatively recently elected by the majority of Americans and is very likely to be reelected by a majority of Americans, his policies are so unpalatable to some that his representatives may encounter stiff going in some of the strongholds of that other culture class.

Of course, elite universities are not the only strongholds of the other culture class. The big media are also a major stronghold. That culture class has been described by a lot of people, in colorful language. It is a fairly homogenous elite culture class whose views are reflected in our elite media by the networks and the prestige newspapers. We have a very hard time, as a government, getting fair play from our media as a consequence of this concentration of power. We all know the ways we think the news gets distorted. We in this government do not want a media which is slavish, or supine, or always agrees with us, or always approves of our behavior. We *would* like a media which we felt gave us a fair shake at least half of the time. I think that happens with a good many of our policies, and doesn't happen with others. For example, I don't think our Central America policy gets fair treatment from our media. I don't think the President's economic policies get fair play from the media. I don't think a good many of the social policies of the administration get fair play. I don't think his arms control policies get fair play. By which I mean they don't get described, reported, analyzed in non-prejudicial ways -- objective ways -- half the time.

Abraham Lincoln told a marvelous story about objectivity and neutrality. He said that if a woman was standing in the door of her cabin at the edge of the woods, watching her husband locked in mortal combat with a grizzly bear, it was not necessary for her to shout alternately, "come on husband, come on bear," in order to see how the fight was going. We don't expect anybody to be neutral with regard to administration policies. We do wish that we could get a good fair description of how the fight's going more often.

I think that a kind of self-indulgence has arisen in our media along with the concentration of media power, and that the self-indulgence relates especially to the use of anonymous informants -- "highly placed sources," "officials," "well-informed persons," "diplomats," "State Department officials," -- all those anonymous categories of people whom we read quoted day in and day out. They are not accountable for the accuracy or inaccuracy of what they say either, but somehow the cumulative impact of the accounts of all of these very self-interested, anonymous persons is very large, shaping the conception of political reality, which in turn shapes the responses of American voters.

The problem about politics is that politics is removed from the everyday experiences of people, so they don't have the opportunity for reality testing. If you are a housewife doing the family's clothes, you can read about soaps that take the ring out of the collar, and you can buy a box and you can try it and you can see whether it takes the ring out of the collar in the promised way. If you're thinking about Central American policy, there just is no kind of immediate, personal mechanism for reality testing available for citizens. You have to wait for a long time to see how much of Southeast Asia falls along with Vietnam, how many people are herded into forced labor camps, how many are tortured, how many flee, how many die, and what kind of government emerges. By that time, most people will have forgotten the argument they made about the case anyway.

So, the power of the media is much greater with regard to politics than with regard to experiences that are more subject to reality testing. We rely heavily on what Walter Lippmann called reference groups and reference figures. For most people those are newscasters and newspapers and bishops. Media are not the only source of opinions by which we are influenced -- they're not our only reference groups -- but they are important.

I think that democratic government depends on an enlightened citizenry, and we cannot have that except as we have accounts of reality -- what is good, what is true, and what causes what -- that are reasonably reliable. I keep talking about what causes what, and that's not only an important dimension of culture, it's also a matter of frustration to me with regard to our Central American policy. I think that the United States and most of Western Europe have succumbed to some myths about what causes guerrilla insurrections. It is said that poverty causes revolt, as in El Salvador. I was just in France where I heard the argument that, what could we Americans expect? That after all, there is terrible poverty in Central America; terrible disparities of wealth. It was only natural that people should revolt and become Marxists-Leninists or something.

Nobody thinks, by the way, that poverty is causing revolt in Nicaragua. Nobody thinks poverty is causing revolt in Poland, but everybody is *sure* that poverty is the fundamental cause of something that in our time is called revolution. Revolution usually turns out to be a small band of armed men who are merciless in the use of violence as an instrument of political change. Poverty is a terrible ill, because it causes human misery. It is not terrible because it causes Marxist-Leninist revolts, because it does not cause Marxist-Leninist revolts. Political action causes Marxist-Leninist revolts -- and arms, and guerrillas, and careful training, and theories of guerrilla warfare cause Marxist-Leninist revolts.

But we hear on all our media -- our networks and our prestige papers -- arguments that assume that whatever problems occur in Central America are rooted in social injustice and poverty.

What can we do about it? I think more competition should be introduced in the marketplace of ideas. I think it is very important to be able to present alternative and more accurate conceptions of reality.

But let's leave the accuracy out of it and just talk about alternative conceptions of reality -- alternative notions of what's good, and what's true, and what causes what. We hope that if there is a wider range of those versions of reality presented, some of them *will* be true and will reflect more accurately the totality of human experience and American values.

# I

# The Search for the Smoking Gun

Writers, editors, and producers of the national news media claim to be objective. They contend that they "just report the truth," arguing that a person's personal political philosophy has no more effect on the work of journalists than on the work of scientists and engineers.

But to report on abortion or taxes or national defense is not like counting the clicks on a Geiger counter or calculating the distance to the moon. Journalism is inherently subjective; a journalist's approach to a story invariably reflects his opinions.

No one would accept the statement of a Ku Klux Klansman, in line for a judgeship, that he was capable of applying the civil rights laws objectively, without regard to his personal opinions. Yet the argument is advanced by members of the media that a reporter can cover George Bush fairly even if he believes that Bush is a tool of fascist warmongers and racist plutocrats.

In days past, the biases of individual journalists mattered less because the journalistic profession allowed for a greater diversity of views.

Though the first two television networks with news, CBS and NBC, offered little variety in the 1950s, then and earlier most towns had at least two newspapers that served to act as a check on each other. If there were a strike at the local steel mill, the *Daily Democrat* would blame it on money-grubbing capitalists and the *Daily Republican* would blame it on radical out-of-town labor agitators. A reader could pick the paper that reflected his philosophy -- or he could read both papers and figure out what was *really* happening.

Today, most cities have only one daily newspaper. Few radio stations cover local news other than car wrecks and shootings, and most local TV stations hire news personnel more for their looks than for their reporting ability.

Today too, it's acceptable for journalists in the news media -- television or newspapers that claim to be objective and balanced -- to add their own opinions to a story. Late in 1988, for example, *Time* magazine began to encourage its reporters to inject their personal opinions into their stories. But even before the green light was given, reporters were doing as much, though in a more subtle way. By emphasizing this or that aspect of a news story, highlighting this or that interpretation on what the event means in the hope that other aspects will be ignored, reporters frequently add "spin" to a story. As Professor Michael Robinson puts it in a study in this book, "spin involves tone, the part of the reporting that extends beyond hard news." Robinson provides an illustration from the 1984 campaign: "Ronald Reagan's train trip through western Ohio was hard news. But when Dan Rather chose to label the ride 'a photo-opportunity train trip, chock full of symbolism and trading on Harry Truman's old turf,' Rather added 'spin.'"

### What Constitutes "Big Media"

Most coverage of national news comes from a few sources, referred to as "Big Media" throughout this book -- *The New York Times*, *The Washington Post* (which also publishes *Newsweek*), *The Wall Street Journal*, Gannett (which publishes *USA Today* and other papers), *Time*, AP and UPI, ABC, NBC, CBS, PBS, and the Cable News Network (CNN). Roughly the same political attitudes are held by reporters, editors, and producers for the national news media. Exceptions are rare. Virtually every newspaper gets national news stories off the AP and UPI wire machines. In addition, both *The New York Times* and *The Washington Post* own news services that distribute their stories across the country.

Sometimes it is obvious where a story originates, as when national news stories in a local paper carry a *Washington Post* or AP byline. Sometimes it is not so obvious, as when a local newspaper, reporting on the local congressman, uses the States News Service -- which is distributed by *The New York Times*.

Often, though, it's more indirect. Every morning network producers, reporters, and wire service editors read *The New York Times* and *The Washington Post* to decide what news is important. Every night newspaper editors watch to learn what the network newscasts find significant. Once one Big Media outlet decides a story is worth reporting, the others are bound to follow in lockstep. More important, many editors will ignore a national or international story unless it has received the blessing of a network or *The New York Times*. In 1988 *Los Angeles Times* media reporter David Shaw dedicated a series of stories to the media's Eastern tilt. "Indeed," Shaw wrote, "some reporters have grown so frustrated with this syndrome that they have deliberately leaked stories to reporter friends at *The New York Times*, knowing that publication of the stories in the *Times* might be the quickest way to get their own, otherwise uninterested editors, suddenly interested in the story."

However a national news story is credited, wherever it appears, it almost certainly originated at one of a handful of news organizations based in Washington and New York.

As a result, the American people get a slanted picture of their country and the world. That's why we are so often surprised by the course of events -- for example, by Jimmy Carter's failures, Ronald Reagan's successes, and the crisis in world communism. In each case, the media told us to expect the opposite.

Conservatives, of course, foresaw Carter's failures, Reagan's successes and communism's decline, as well as the evil of the Ayatollah Khomeini, the drug-running dictatorship of Manuel Noriega, the malignant growth of the welfare state, the ethical lapses of Jim Wright and his cronies -- all of which took the national news media by surprise. But conservatives weren't selecting the stories to cover; they weren't picking the experts to quote; they weren't even present in the newsrooms when those decisions were made. The events seemed to come with no warning. Continuing befuddlement is the price we pay for the absence of conservatives in most of the major national media.

But though bias in the media exists, it is rarely a conscious attempt to distort the news. It stems from the fact that most members of the media elite have little contact with conservatives and make little effort to understand the conservative viewpoint. Their friends are liberals, their sources are liberals, what they read and hear is written by liberals. This helps explain why policies considered "liberal" by the public are seen as "mainstream" by reporters and editors.

Conservatives are as rare in the nation's newsrooms as blacks and women once were (and, in some cases, still are). They're rare for much the same reason: Editors and producers, like all bosses, tend to hire people like themselves.

For decades, the media denied that they discriminated against blacks and women. When they finally recognized the problem, they began slowly to solve it. Likewise, if media bias is to be corrected, the first step is to acknowledge that the problem exists.

That is the reason for this book. In the following chapters, documented studies show that media bias is real, that it is prevalent, and that it obscures the reality that the journalistic profession has sworn to report.

### Ways to Measure Media Bias
It should be noted that, in the case of media bias, there is no "smoking gun" -- no single piece of evidence so incriminating that the defendant breaks down on the witness stand and confesses. Over the years, however, the Media Research Center and other organizations have developed methods of demonstrating media bias. Some methods are objective, like fingerprints on a murder weapon. Others are subjective, like eyewitness testimony. Taken as a whole, the studies in this book make a compelling case against the media, contradicting their claims of fairness and balance.

The studies in this book utilize one or more of the following methods to quantify the media's bias:

## 1) Surveys of the political attitudes of journalists, particularly members of the media elite, and of journalism students.

These are conducted in the same way as opinion surveys of any group. A random sample is selected from the members of the group being studied. They are asked to respond to a series of questions regarding their attitudes about various political leaders and ideas. They are asked, for example, how they voted in recent elections, whether they consider themselves liberal or conservative, and which "experts" (liberal or conservative) they turn to for reliable information.

The results of the surveys in these pages show that journalists as a group are very liberal -- more liberal than the general public and more liberal than others with similar backgrounds. They are more likely to vote liberal, more likely to consider themselves liberals, and more likely to select a liberal instead of a conservative as a credible expert on a given subject. Journalism students, the future members of the media elite, are even more liberal than their elders.

## 2) Studies of journalists' previous professional connections.

The studies presented here demonstrate that when members of the media elite engage in politics, their candidates or causes are usually liberal or Democratic. Conversely, the vast majority of former political activists currently working in the media have had professional ties to liberals and Democrats. In fact, every major national media outlet has reporters and executives who were previously professionally associated with liberals, e.g., Gary Hart's press secretary is now the Political Editor for CBS News, a Jimmy Carter speechwriter is now an Associate Editor of *U.S. News & World Report*, and an aide to Mario Cuomo is now Washington Bureau Chief for NBC News. A relatively small number of journalists have had associations with conservatives or Republicans.

## 3) Collections of quotations in which prominent journalists reveal their beliefs about politics and/or about the proper role of their profession.

In unguarded moments -- as when they grant interviews to friendly publications or speak to friendly audiences -- prominent journalists often admit that they are liberals, or hold liberal views, or even promote a liberal political agenda. Walter Cronkite, for example, once declared, "I think most newspapermen by definition have to be liberal. If they're not liberal, by my definition of it, then they can hardly be good newspapermen."

## 4) Word-use analysis.

Using the Nexis ® computer system, researchers can isolate newspaper and magazine articles based on particular words or combinations of words. A researcher seeking articles in which Jesse Jackson was called anti-Semitic could ask the computer for all articles in which Reverend Jackson's name appeared within fifty words of the words "anti-Semitic," "anti-Semitism," "Farrakhan," "Hymietown," "Israel," or "Koch."

With this method, it was possible to determine, for example, how often in a given period *The Washington Post* called Senator Jesse Helms "ultraconservative" and Ted Kennedy "ultraliberal," or how often *The New York Times* mentioned "Reaganomics" in good economic times versus bad.

As it turned out, conservatives were far more likely than liberals to be painted as ideologues and extremists. Moreover, when derogatory labels ceased to be derogatory the media stopped using them. For instance, the media used the term "Reaganomics" to describe President Reagan's supply-side economic policies during the 1982 recession, but gave it up when the economy improved.

This type of word and topic analysis also allows researchers to determine how much coverage the media gave a particular subject. The following pages show that news contradicting liberal ideology, such as the murder of millions of people in communist Cambodia, was often ignored, sometimes for years or decades. And when and if such news was reported, the role of the perpetrator -- communism in the case of Cambodia -- was usually played down or ignored. In another instance, charges made by conservatives that Jim Wright was corrupt were initially written off as the product of paranoia. Specifically, when conservative Congressman Newt Gingrich suggested in 1987 that the House ethics committee investigate the Speaker's financial dealings, Big Media ignored him. But when Common Cause, a liberal lobbying group, questioned Wright's ethics, the national news outlets decided to make it a big story.

### 5) Studies of policies recommended in news stories.

These studies show that when reporters list possible solutions to society's problems, the solutions are almost always those of the Left -- "raise taxes," "cut defense," "have taxpayers pay for abortions."

In the past, most news stories were content to relate a sequence of events, but recently an increasing number mix reporting with specific recommendations for government policy. *Time* magazine's "Planet of the Year" story at the end of 1988 included, as examples of the actions government "must" take to avoid ecological catastrophe, a wish list of liberal and ultraliberal ideas. "Raising the federal gasoline tax by 50 cents per gallon, from 9 cents to 59 cents, over the next 5 years would renew drivers' interest in fuel conservation," was one solution *Time* proposed

By compiling lists of policy recommendations, we can determine how often the media endorsed conservative or liberal proposals. In this book, for example, studies demonstrate the media consistently see higher taxes as the answer to federal budget problems. If spending must be cut, journalists prefer to trim defense rather than social programs. Moreover, when conservative economic policies are successful, they will track down any available hardship case to dampen the impact.

### 6) Comparisons of the agenda of the news media with the agendas of political candidates or organizations.

In this method, researchers count the number of seconds or lines given to controversial issues to determine which ones are given the greatest play. The issues are ranked, then the list is compared with the agendas of, say, the opposing parties in a political campaign. For example, Reagan's age was an issue on the agenda of the Democrats in 1984, and Geraldine Ferraro's finances were an issue on the Republican agenda. Which issue got more coverage?

The studies in this book reveal a pattern of playing up items on the liberal/Democratic agenda and playing down items on the conservative/Republican agenda.

### 7) Positive/negative coverage analysis.

This method involves two steps: first, classifying news stories and/or comments within news stories in respect to the subject as follows: "favorable," "unfavorable," "neutral," or "ambiguous." Second, analysts measure the relative number of stories, comments, or words that fall in each category. Most such studies simply count the number of transcribed lines or seconds of reporting that fall into each classification.

This is one of the more subjective techniques for measuring bias. Some stories are obviously negative or positive; a story about Richard Nixon that mentions Watergate in every line would unquestionably be negative toward Nixon, while a story about Jimmy Carter that concentrates on the Camp David Accord would just as clearly be positive toward Carter. In other cases, however, reasonable people could differ about whether some statements are favorable or unfavorable. This at times depends on the context: "Senator Phogbound admits he's homosexual" might be an unfavorable story in the *Moral Majority Report* but a favorable report in the *Gay Community News*.

But, as the following pages show, in most cases the ratio of positive-to-negative stories, comments, and total words favors the Left beyond reasonable doubt. One study in this book finds, for instance, that during one period President Reagan's coverage in the national media was negative by a ratio of 20-to-one. Even if the researchers had an error rate of 10 to 20 percent, the ratio would still be overwhelming.

### Why Does Media Bias Matter?

What difference does it make if the media are biased? After all, the media attacked Ronald Reagan constantly from the moment he entered politics and they couldn't stop him from being elected and reelected Governor of California and President of the United States.

No, they don't win every time, but they *do* win most of the time. As a wise man once said, the battle goes not always to the strong nor the race to the swift, but that's the way to bet.

By exercising control over the nation's agenda -- picking and choosing which issues are fit for public debate, which news is "fit to print" -- the news media can greatly influence the political direction of the country. They can ignore or ridicule some ideas and promote others. They can wreck a politician's career by taking a quote or two out of context or by spotlighting a weakness in his background. They can make winners look like losers and vice versa, knowing that, in the political world, appearance easily supplants reality.

Consider what happens in a political campaign. An able candidate will concentrate on gaining control of the agenda. If he has a pleasing personality and his opponent is a jerk, he will try to have the election decided on the basis of personality. If he is philosophically in tune with the district and his opponent is not, he will attempt to see that the election is decided on philosophical terms. The key factor may be race, religion, geography, economic class, party affiliation, or something else, but whichever, the winning candidate is typically the one who sets the agenda -- picks the correct key factor -- and puts his opponent on the defensive.

Now, envision American politics as a sort of permanent campaign in which one side almost always gets to set the agenda. That's the power the media give to the Left. For example:

- The media charge that conservatives are out of the political mainstream, that they can't get elected except in unusual circumstances or in backwater districts. As a result, some conservatives are discouraged from running for office. Some adopt more liberal positions to satisfy what the media present as the proper and popular view. Others run as conservatives anyway but can't raise sufficient funds because potential contributors think they "can't win", and then, of course, they don't. How many potential Ronald Reagans never got to first base in politics because of media bias?

- The media want greater government regulation and less individual choice, higher taxes and less take-home pay. A newspaper can win a Pulitzer Prize for advocating tax hikes and the Robert F. Kennedy Prize for advocating an expansion of the bureaucracy. There are no prizes for seeking to restore power to neighborhoods and to families. What price have working people and small business people paid for the massive expansion of government power fueled by this particular bias of the media?

- The media generally ignore atrocities in communist countries (unless, as in the Tienanmen Square Massacre, the atrocities occur within camera range). For forty years, the media depicted communism as the wave of the future in the Third World. They characterized anticommunists as threats to world peace. During the Vietnam War, they pictured the communists as nationalist reformers, valiant underdogs struggling against the imperialist United States. How long did the media prolong the Cold War, and how many people died as a result?

- The media treat technology as a fearsome thing. They aggravate people's natural fear of nuclear power, never pointing out its safety compared to power derived from fossil fuels. They publicize the adverse side effects of drugs, but, except in the cases of AIDS treatment, they ignore the suffering and death that result from unnecessary delays in the approval of new drugs. They mockingly label space-based defense "Star Wars" in an effort to kill it, never mentioning the alternative -- Mutual Assured Destruction, a suicide pact with the Soviets. How successful have the media been in their efforts to impede the technological progress that would improve our standard of living, make us healthier, and help prevent war?

We all pay a price for media bias. As long as an autocratic orthodoxy rules the major national news organizations, the media will continue to defend the political status quo and turn a blind eye to corruption, even as they pride themselves on their independence and incorruptibility.

News people, being human, judge the virtue of ideas by the degree to which those ideas match their own beliefs and prejudices. Until conservatives are given fair access to the newsrooms of this country, and until the American people demand to see and hear both sides of the argument on the major issues of the day, the news media will continue to serve less as a referee than as a cheerleader for one side.

Still not convinced that media bias can influence how you perceive news events, persuade you who is right or wrong, point convincingly to the good guy and the bad guy? Then read through these examples. The quotes in column A are actual statements taken directly from reporters and TV anchors. They reflect the media's liberal bias. Column B reverses the bias of the quote. The media elite would quite properly reject Column B for its conservative bias and political advocacy. But if the Column B quotes are too one-sided for broadcast or publication in a news story, why are Column A quotes acceptable?

## COLUMN A

"[Elliott] Abrams, a vigorous proponent of the Contra war, and [Jim] Wright, a champion of the Central American peace process, have clashed in the past." -- *Washington Post* reporters Tom Kenworthy and Joe Pichirallo, September 21, 1988.

"Bush broke a tie vote in the Senate to confirm Appeals Court Judge Daniel Manion, an obscure conservative opposed by the deans of 44 major law schools. Dukakis, as Governor of Massachusetts, used a non-partisan advisory commission on naming judges, and says he would do the same as President." -- NBC's Carl Stern, October 10, 1988.

"It's this kind of rhetoric [Bush on the Pledge of Allegiance] that leads some to recall Samuel Johnson's observation that patriotism is the last refuge of a scoundrel." -- NBC reporter Lisa Myers, September 20, 1988.

"And so we choose Betty Friedan [as Person of the Week] because she had the ability and the sensitivity to articulate the needs of women, which means that she did us all a favor." -- Peter Jennings on ABC's *World News Tonight*, February 19, 1988.

## COLUMN B

"[Elliott] Abrams, a champion of peace and freedom in Central American, and [Jim] Wright a supporter of the Nicaraguan dictatorship, have clashed in the past."

"Bush promises to appoint conservative judges, as Reagan did. Dukakis surrounds himself with fellow members of the ACLU...which believes that drugs and pornography should be legalized, that the death penalty and the life sentence should be abolished, and that gays have a Constitutional right to participate in 'Big Brother' programs."

"It's this kind of rhetoric [Dukakis on the Pledge of Allegiance] defending himself from the charges that he is not sufficiently patriotic, that leads some to say he 'doth protest too much.'"

"And so we choose Phyllis Schlafly [as Person of the Week] because she had the courage to fight, and beat, the ERA -- a victory not just for women, but for every family in America."

"There is, in Cuba, government intrusion into everyone's life, from the moment he is born until the day he dies. The reasoning is that the government wants to better the lives of its citizens and keep them from exploiting or hurting one another...on a sunny day in a park in the old city of Havana it is difficult to see anything that is sinister." -- NBC reporter Ed Rabel on *Sunday Today*, February 28, 1988.

"There is, in Cuba, government intrusion into everyone's life, from the moment he is born until the day he dies. The reasoning is that the government wants to better the lives of its citizens and keep them from exploiting or hurting one another...Of course that was Hitler's reasoning. That's not the only parallel between Nazi Germany and Castro's Cuba."

"Once the Kremlin was the home of czars. Today it belongs to the people... Atheist though the state may be, freedom to worship is enshrined in the Soviet Constitution." -- from the TBS program *Portrait of the Soviet Union*, March 1988.

"The Kremlin, once the home of czars, now belongs to the party elite...Freedom to worship is enshrined in the Soviet Constitution, but the gulag is full of those who took that guarantee seriously."

"George Bush wants to convince voters that Michael Dukakis is a big spender who will raise taxes, coddle criminals and disarm America. In other words, a 'liberal.' But does the dreaded 'L' word stick to Dukakis? Probably not." -- *Newsweek*, July 4, 1988.

"The fact is Michael Dukakis is a big spender who will raise taxes, coddle criminals and disarm America. In other words, a 'liberal.' But will George Bush stick the dreaded 'L' word to Dukakis? Only if he wants to win."

"Dukakis is a centrist." -- *Los Angeles Times* reporter Robert Scheer on *The McLaughlin Group*, June 11, 1988.

"Dukakis is more liberal than McGovern."

"When he entered the race nearly a year ago he [Bruce Babbitt] had the courage to say that as President he would probably have to raise taxes. And he never recovered from his courage." -- Peter Jennings, ABC's *World News Tonight*, February 18, 1988.

"When he entered the race nearly a year ago he [Jack Kemp] had the courage to say that Reagan did not go far enough to cut taxes. And he never recovered from his courage."

"*Today*'s Jane Pauley...arose for work at 4 a.m. as usual, after having stayed up until the wee hours. The compelling draw to keep her out late Tuesday night? Visiting the [Democratic] convention. 'I'm a Jesse [Jackson] fan,' she says." -- *USA Today*, July 21, 1988.

"*Today*'s Jane Pauley...arose for work at 4 a.m. as usual, after having stayed up until the wee hours. The compelling draw to keep her out late Tuesday night? Visiting the [Republican] convention. 'I'm a Jesse [Helms] fan,' she says."

"He's against outlawing abortions, he's against President Reagan's Star Wars defense, he worries about the poor and the homeless...Nine delegates to this convention describe themselves as liberals...Harold Fergiss: a lonely, rather brave figure out there on Canal Street. Symbol of the kind of Republican that once was, but almost isn't anymore." -- Charles Kuralt on CBS, August 17, 1988.

"He's against abortion-on-demand, he's for a strong defense, he worries about the middle class...Nine delegates to this convention describe themselves as conservative...Harold Fergiss: a lonely, rather brave figure out there on Peachtree Street. Symbol of the kind of Democrat that once was, but almost isn't anymore."

"Personally, I think the Contras are worthless." -- CBS News producer/reporter Lucy Spiegel, quoted by David Brock in the *American Spectator*, January 1987.

"Personally, I think the Contras are heroes."

"Now half of the Cuban population is under the age of 25, mostly Spanish speaking, and all have benefitted from Castro's Cuba, where their health and their education are priorities." -- Kathleen Sullivan, *CBS This Morning*, December 9, 1988.

"Now half of the Cuban population is under the age of 25, mostly Spanish speaking, and all have suffered from Castro's Cuba, a corrupt, drug-running military dictatorship."

"How well I remember the fall day in 1980 when Ronald Reagan was elected...Once the outcome was clear, I walked the streets until dawn, sure that the world would come to an end." -- Former CBS News assignment editor Jamie Stiehm, in the *Christian Science Monitor*, January 19, 1989.

"How well I remember the fall day in 1980 when Ronald Reagan was elected...Once the outcome was clear, I walked the streets until dawn, celebrating."

"Gorbachev is helping the West by showing that the Soviet threat isn't what it used to be -- and what's more, that it never was." -- *Time* magazine's Strobe Talbott, January 1, 1990.

"Reagan is helping the West by showing that the Soviet threat was always great -- and what's more, that it had to be countered."

"Taxes are very much at the heart of what all our potential solutions are. How long can both sides pretend that a hike's not needed?" -- *Today* co-host Bryant Gumbel, January 31, 1990.

"Budget cuts are very much at the heart of what all our potential solutions are. How long can Democrats pretend that federal spending cuts are not needed?"

"Ah yes. The dreaded federal deficit, created, for the most part, by the most massive peacetime military buildup in America's history." -- Reporter Jim Wooten on ABC's *Nightline*, January 29, 1990.

"Ah yes. The dreaded federal deficit, created, for the most part, by the most massive federal social spending drive in America's history."

"By 'selling the sizzle' of Reagan, as his aide Michael Deaver put it, the administration spun the nation out of its torpor with such fantasies as supply-side economics, the nuclear weapons 'window of vulnerability,' and the Strategic Defense Inititiative." -- Harrison Rainie, Senior Editor of *U.S. News & World Report*, December 25, 1989.

"By 'publicizing the essence' of Reagan, as his aide Michael Deaver put it, the administration spun the nation out of its Carter era malaise with such vibrant and successful policies as supply-side economics, Pershing II deployment, and the Strategic Defense Initiative."

"George Mitchell talks about the record of legislation the Senate Democrats are building, the substantive progress on issues from oil spills to rural development, which so often gets overlooked in the day to day political analysis of 'up or down, winner or loser.' His logic is crisp, unassailable, his manner far removed from the thrust and parry of contemporary politics. He is the soul of judiciousness, highminded in his concern for governance." -- *New York Times* reporter Robin Toner, October 17, 1989.

"Jesse Helms talks about the record of legislation the Senate Republicans are building, the substantive progress on issues from child pornography to government deregulation, which so often gets overlooked in the day to day political analysis of 'up or down, winner or loser.' His logic is crisp, unassailable, his manner far removed from the thrust and parry of contemporary politics. He is the soul of judiciousness, highminded in his concern for governance."

"Politics didn't just turn ugly. It evolved from a nasty presidential campaign that featured the GOP's famous Willie Horton ad." -- Reporter Eric Engberg on the *CBS Evening News* when House Speaker Jim Wright resigned, May 29, 1989.

"Politics didn't just turn ugly. It evolved from a nasty Democratic smear campaign against Attorney General Ed Meese."

"And if [Jim Wright's] moving speech today does not restore those decencies he so wistfully remembered today, then perhaps history will remember that at least he tried." -- Reporter Jim Wooten on Wright's resignation announcement, ABC's *World News Tonight*, May 31, 1989.

"And if [Ed Meese's] moving speech today does not restore those decencies he so wistfully remembered today, then perhaps history will remember that at least he tried."

"I read *Mother Jones* carefully and look forward to every issue. After all, stories that started out in *Mother Jones* have wound up on *60 Minutes*." -- CBS' Mike Wallace in subscription letter for the liberal magazine.

"I read *National Review* carefully and look forward to every issue. After all, stories that started out in *National Review* have wound up on *60 Minutes*."

"Largely as a result of the policies and priorities of the Reagan Administration, more people are becoming poor and staying poor in this country than at any time since World War II." -- *Today* co-host Bryant Gumbel, July 17, 1989.

"Largely as a result of the policies and priorities of the Democratic Congress, more people are becoming poor and staying poor in this country than at any time since World War II."

"In just seven weeks, the '80s will be behind us. It was a decade dominated in politics and in style by the Reagans....While the wealthy got most of the attention, those who needed it most were often ignored. More homeless, less spending on housing. The gap between the top and the bottom grew in the '80s." -- *CBS This Morning* co-host Kathleen Sullivan, November 13, 1989.

"In just seven weeks, the '80s will be behind us. It was a decade dominated in politics and in style by the Reagans....The working people burdened by government taxes and regulation got most of the attention. Lower taxes, almost no inflation, more jobs. The poor also got plenty of attention -- the rich paid a higher percentage of taxes collected by the federal government, so the poor paid less in the '80s."

Again: The real quotes are in column A. But of course that's obvious. And that's the point.

*-- Introduction by Steven Allen*

# 1 *What Do Reporters Believe?*

Reporters should keep their personal opinions from influencing the news stories they write and produce. But journalists are only human. A reporter's political outlook is bound to sway the judgments he or she makes each day, such as what events are newsworthy and on whom to rely for information. It is therefore essential to know which political philosophy most members of the press espouse in order to understand how media bias occurs.

Are Big Media reporters, editors, producers and executives moderates and conservatives? Or, as conservatives contend, are they actually far more liberal than their readers and viewers?

This chapter presents the results of nine polls which substantiate the conservatives' thesis -- that the vast majority of those working for major national news outlets are liberal.

---

## CHAPTER ONE, STUDY 1

## "Media and Business Elites"

### OVERVIEW

In 1981, S. Robert Lichter, then with George Washington University, and Stanley Rothman of Smith College released the results of their survey on the political attitudes and voting patterns of reporters. Lichter and Rothman interviewed 240 journalists for several major outlets comprising the "media elite," including *The New York Times*, *The Washington Post* and the three television networks.

At first, the study went little noticed as media figures dismissed its significance, claiming their personal opinions never enter news stories.

But within a few years, as conservatives continued to refer to it as evidence of what they had been asserting for years, it became the most widely quoted media study of the 1980s.

## KEY FINDINGS

- No less than 81 percent of the press interviewed voted for the Democratic presidential candidate in every election between 1964 and 1976.

- 90 percent favored abortion.

- 80 percent supported affirmative action.

- Most believed the U.S. caused Third World poverty.

## STUDY EXCERPT

**Media and Business Elites** by S. Robert Lichter and Stanley Rothman. From *Public Opinion*, October/November 1981.

Yesteryear's ragtag muckrakers, who tirelessly championed the little guy against powerful insiders, have become insiders themselves. Newsmen have long cherished the vantage point of the outsiders who keep the insiders straight. But now, leading journalists are courted by politicians, studied by scholars and known to millions through their bylines and televised images. In short, the needs of a society increasingly hungry for information have contributed to the rise of a national news network -- the new media elite.

As part of a larger study on elites, we surveyed members of the national media elite during 1979 and 1980. We wanted to discover their backgrounds, attitudes, and outlooks toward American society and their own profession. We conducted hour-long interviews with 240 journalists and broadcasters at the most influential media outlets, including *The New York Times*, *The Washington Post*, *The Wall Street Journal*, the magazines *Time*, *Newsweek*, *U.S. News & World Report*, and the news departments at CBS, NBC, ABC and PBS, along with major public broadcasting stations.

Within each organization, we selected individuals randomly from among those responsible for news content. In the print medium we interviewed reporters, columnists, department heads, bureau chiefs, editors and executives responsible for news content. In the broadcast medium we selected correspondents, anchormen, producers, film editors, and news executives. A very high proportion of those contacted, 76 percent, completed the interview. The response rate was high enough to insure that our findings would provide insight into the composition and perspective of this new elite.

Ideologically, a majority of leading journalists described themselves as liberals. Fifty-four percent placed themselves to the left of center, compared to only 19 percent who chose the right side of the spectrum. When they rated their fellow workers, even greater differences emerged. Fifty-six percent said the people they worked with were mostly on the left, and only 8 percent on the right -- a margin of seven-to-one.

### *Vote for Democrats*

These subjective ratings were borne out by their voting records in presidential elections since 1964. (The interviews were conducted before the 1980 elections, so our most recent data are for 1976.) Of those who said they voted, the proportion of leading journalists who supported the Democratic presidential candidate never dropped below 80 percent [See Graph 1A]. In 1972, when 62 percent of the electorate chose Nixon, 81

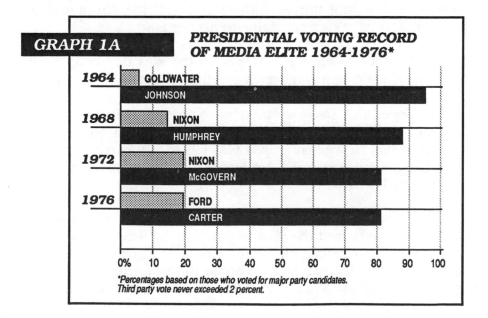

**GRAPH 1A**

**PRESIDENTIAL VOTING RECORD OF MEDIA ELITE 1964-1976\***

*1964* GOLDWATER / JOHNSON

*1968* NIXON / HUMPHREY

*1972* NIXON / McGOVERN

*1976* FORD / CARTER

0%  10  20  30  40  50  60  70  80  90  100

*\*Percentages based on those who voted for major party candidates.
Third party vote never exceeded 2 percent.*

percent of the media elite voted for McGovern. This does not appear to reflect any particular personal aversion to Nixon, despite the well-publicized tensions between the press and his administration. Four years later, leading journalists preferred Carter over Ford by exactly the same margin. In fact, in the Democratic landslide of 1964, media leaders picked Johnson over Goldwater by the staggering margin of 16-to-one, or 94 to 6 percent.

Most significant, though, is the long-term trend. Over the entire 16-year period, less than one-fifth of the media elite supported any Republican presidential candidate. In an era when presidential elections are often settled by a swing vote of 5 to 10 percent, the Democratic margin among elite journalists has been 30 to 50 percent greater than among the entire electorate.

### Liberal Across the Board

These presidential choices were consistent with the media elite's liberal views on a wide range of social and political issues [see Table 1B]. They showed a strong preference for welfare capitalism, pressing for assistance to the poor in the form of income redistribution and guaranteed employment. Few are outright socialists. For example, they overwhelmingly rejected the proposition that major corporations should be publicly owned. Only one in eight would agree to public ownership of corporations, and two-thirds declared themselves strongly opposed. Moreover, very few sympathized with Marx's doctrine, "from each according to his ability, to each according to his needs."

Instead, they overwhelmingly supported the idea that people with greater ability should earn higher wages than those with less ability. Eighty-six percent agreed with this fundamental tenet of capitalism. Most also believed that free enterprise gave workers a fair shake, and that deregulation of business would be good for the country. Seventy percent agreed that private enterprise was fair to working people, and almost as many, 63 percent, said that less regulation of business would serve the national interest.

Despite this basic support for private enterprise, we should not expect the media elite to lead the cheering section for Reagan's economic policies. Leading journalists may subscribe to a capitalist economic framework, but they are equally committed to the welfare state. Sixty-eight percent, about the same proportion that praised the fairness of private enterprise, also agreed that the government should substantially reduce the income gap between the rich and the poor. They were almost evenly divided over the issue of guaranteed employment. Forty-eight percent believed the government should guarantee a job to anyone who wanted one, while a slight majority of 52 percent opposed this principle of entitlement.

Of course, there is no necessary contradiction between praise for private enterprise and calls for government action to aid the poor and jobless. These attitudes mirror the traditional perspective of American liberals who -- unlike many European social democrats -- accept an essentially capitalistic economic framework, even as they press for expansion of the welfare state.

Despite their acceptance of the economic order, many leading journalists voiced a general discontent with the social system. Virtually half, 49 percent, agreed with the statement, "the very structure of our society causes people to feel alienated." A substantial minority would like to overhaul the entire system. Twenty-eight percent agreed that America needed a "complete restructuring of its basic institutions." The same proportion generalized their criticism to include all modern states. They held that all political systems were repressive because they concentrated power and authority in a few hands.

It seems that a substantial portion of the media elite accept the current economic order, yet remain dissatisfied with the social system. Indeed, it is today's divisive "social issues" that bring their liberalism to the fore. Leading journalists emerged from our survey as strong supporters of environmental protection, affirmative action, women's rights, homosexual rights, and sexual freedom in general.

Fewer than one in five assented to the statement, "our environmental problems are not as serious as people have been led to believe." Only one percent strongly agreed that environmental problems were overrated, while a majority of 54 percent strongly disagreed. They were nearly as vehement in their support for affirmative action, an issue that has split the traditional liberal constituency which favored civil rights measures. Despite both the heated controversy over this issue and their own predominantly white racial composition, four out of five media leaders endorsed the use of strong affirmative action measures to ensure black representation in the workplace.

### Support Abortion

In their attitudes toward sex and sex roles, members of the media elite were virtually unanimous in opposing the constraints of both government and tradition. Large majorities opposed government regulation of sexual activities, upheld a pro-choice position on abortion, and rejected the notion that homosexuality was wrong. In fact, a majority would not characterize even adultery as wrong.

When asked whether the government should regulate sexual practices, only 4 percent agreed, and 84 percent strongly opposed state control over sexual activities. Ninety percent agreed that a woman had the right to decide for herself whether to have an abortion; 79 percent agreed

| TABLE 1B — MEDIA ELITE ATTITUDES | STRONGLY AGREE | AGREE | DISAGREE | STRONGLY DISAGREE |
|---|---|---|---|---|
| **Economics** | | | | |
| Big corporations should be publicly owned | 4% | 9% | 23% | 65% |
| People with more ability should earn more | 48 | 38 | 10 | 4 |
| Private enterprise is fair to workers | 17 | 53 | 20 | 10 |
| Less regulation of business is good for USA | 16 | 47 | 24 | 13 |
| Government should reduce income gap | 23 | 45 | 20 | 13 |
| Government should guarantee jobs | 13 | 35 | 33 | 19 |
| **Political Alienation** | | | | |
| Structure of society causes alienation | 12 | 37 | 32 | 20 |
| Institutions need overhaul | 10 | 18 | 31 | 42 |
| All political systems are repressive | 4 | 24 | 26 | 46 |
| **Social-Cultural** | | | | |
| Environmental problems are overstated | 1 | 18 | 27 | 54 |
| Strong affirmative action for blacks | 33 | 47 | 16 | 4 |
| Government should not regulate sex | 84 | 13 | 3 | 1 |
| Woman has right to decide on abortion | 79 | 11 | 5 | 5 |
| Homosexuality is wrong | 9 | 16 | 31 | 45 |
| Homosexuals shouldn't teach in public schools | 3 | 12 | 31 | 54 |
| Adultery is wrong | 15 | 32 | 34 | 20 |
| **Foreign Policy** | | | | |
| U.S. exploits Third World, causes poverty | 16 | 40 | 25 | 20 |
| U.S. use of resources immoral | 19 | 38 | 27 | 16 |
| West had helped Third World | 6 | 19 | 50 | 25 |
| Goal of foreign policy is to protect U.S. businesses | 12 | 39 | 28 | 22 |
| CIA should sometimes undermine hostile governments | 26 | 19 | 36 | 19 |

strongly with this pro-choice position. Three-quarters disagreed that homosexuality was wrong, and an even larger proportion, 85 percent, upheld the right of homosexuals to teach in public schools. (A mere 9 percent felt strongly that homosexuality was wrong.) Finally, 54 percent did not regard adultery as wrong, and only 15 percent strongly agreed that extramarital affairs were immoral. Thus, members of the media elite emerged as strong supporters of sexual freedom or permissiveness, and as natural opponents of groups like the Moral Majority, which seek to enlist the state in restricting sexual freedom.

In addition to these social and cultural issues, we inquired about international affairs, focusing on America's relations with Third World countries. Third World representatives to UNESCO have argued that the American press serves the interests of capitalism by "presenting developing countries in a bad light and suppressing their authentic voices," as a recent *New York Times* article put it. Such charges are supported by media critics like Herbert Gans, who claims that "conservative dictators...are apt to be treated more kindly [by the press] than socialist ones." We cannot address these questions of media coverage. But we can assess the sympathies of the elite press on several of the controversial issues raised by these critics. Among these are U.S. arms sales, CIA activity, and alleged American exploitation of developing countries.

### U.S. Exploits Third World

In most instances, majorities of the media elite voiced the same criticisms that are raised in the Third World. Fifty-six percent agreed that American economic exploitation had contributed to Third World poverty. About the same proportion, 57 percent, also found America's heavy use of natural resources to be "immoral." By a three-to-one margin, leading journalists soundly rejected the counterargument that Third World nations would be even worse off without the assistance they've received from Western nations. Indeed, precisely half agreed with the claim that the main goal of our foreign policy had been to protect American business interests.

Two issues dealing more directly with American foreign policy elicited a similar division of opinions. A majority of 55 percent would prohibit the CIA from ever undermining hostile governments to protect U.S. interests. The question of arms shipments produced an even split of opinion. Forty-eight percent would ban foreign arms sales altogether or restrict them to democratic countries. Forty-seven percent would supply arms to any "friendly" country, regardless of the regime. Only 4 percent would be willing to sell arms to all comers.

Thus, in several controversial areas of U.S.-Third World relations, the media elite was deeply divided, with slight majorities endorsing some key Third World criticisms of America. We noted earlier that many leading journalists criticized the American system from within, as "alienating" and in need of an overhaul. It appears that even larger numbers extended their criticisms to the international arena. About half charged America with economic exploitation and sought to limit CIA activity and arms sales as instruments of our foreign policy.

### A New Force

The pointed views of the national media elite are not mere wishes and opinions of those aspiring to power, but the voice of a new leadership group that has arrived as a major force in American society. Cosmopolitan in their origins, liberal in their outlooks, they are aware and protective of their collective influence. The rise of this elite has hardly gone unnoticed. Some hail them as the public's tribunes against the powerful -- indispensable champions of the underdog and the oppressed. Others decry them for allegiance to an adversary culture that is chiseling away at traditional values.

This study was directed by Rothman and Lichter, under the auspices of the Research Institute on International Change at Columbia University. The surveys of media and business leaders were supervised by Response Analysis, a survey research organization.

**CHAPTER ONE, STUDY 2**

# *"The Media Elite"*

## OVERVIEW

Study 1, which proved that Big Media reporters and correspondents were overwhelmingly liberal, did not deal with the entire media elite survey. In order to determine how journalists' ideological values impacted on their news judgments, S. Robert Lichter, Stanley Rothman and Linda Lichter spent the next few years collating and analyzing answers to some more complicated questions posed in the 1979 and 1980 interviews. They explained what they found in a 1986 book, *The Media Elite: America's New Power Brokers*, published by Adler & Adler.

The most telling discovery: Reporters believe liberals are more reliable than conservatives as sources of facts for stories.

The three social scientists asked where each respondent "would turn for reliable information on four topics" -- welfare reform, consumer issues, the environment and nuclear energy. In all these areas Robert Lichter and his colleagues discovered that Big Media reporters put their trust in liberals rather than conservatives.

## KEY FINDINGS

- On welfare reform "their choices are weighted heavily toward the liberal end. Three out of four journalists mention at least one liberal source. In sharp contrast, fewer than one in four cites a conservative source. In fact, avowedly liberal individuals, groups, and journals constitute by far the largest sources of information on which these journalists would rely." Among the liberal sources named: *Mother Jones* magazine, Jesse Jackson, and former Congresswomen Barbara Jordan and Bella Abzug.

- "When the media elite deal with consumer protection," Lichter noted, "their thoughts turn to Ralph Nader. Nearly two out of three mention Nader or one of his allied organizations, such as Congress Watch or Public Citizen."

• More than two out of three reporters preferred liberal activist groups for environmental information, including the Environmental Defense Fund, Friends of the Earth, Sierra Club and Natural Resources Defense Council. Less than a third as many cited business-related sources like the Edison Electric Institute, Business Roundtable or a business magazine. "One in four journalists cites groups or individuals not primarily associated with environmental issues," the survey determined. "These include Jane Fonda, Ralph Nader, and Tom Hayden, and such elected officials as Senators Edward Kennedy and Gary Hart."

• On nuclear power, Lichter found "no contest: anti-nuclear sources

| TABLE 1C | TYPES OF SOURCES CITED AS RELIABLE | |
|---|---|---|
| | | **MEDIA** |
| ***Welfare Reform*** | | |
| Liberals | | 75% |
| Federal Regulatory Agencies | | 51 |
| Federal Officials | | 38 |
| Conservatives | | 22 |
| State and Local Agencies | | 16 |
| ***Consumer Protection*** | | |
| Ralph Nader/Nader Groups | | 63 |
| Federal Regulatory Agencies | | 46 |
| Consumers Union | | 44 |
| Other Activist Groups | | 41 |
| State and Local Agencies | | 36 |
| Business Groups | | 22 |
| ***Pollution and Environment*** | | |
| Environmental Activists | | 69 |
| Activist Federal Agencies | | 68 |
| Business Groups | | 27 |
| Liberal Activists and Officials | | 24 |
| Other Federal Agencies | | 19 |
| ***Nuclear Energy*** | | |
| Anti-Nuclear | | 55 |
| Technical Magazines | | 40 |
| Federal Regualtory Agencies | | 39 |
| Other Government | | 37 |
| Pro-Nuclear | | 32 |

*Note: Excludes nonpartisan media sources and categories mentioned by fewer than 15 percent of all subjects.*

far outstrip their pro-nuclear opponents. A majority of those listing reliable sources mentioned an anti-nuclear group or individual. No more than 40 percent would turn to a scientific journal, a federal agency, or other government body. Even fewer, less than one in three, selected any pro-nuclear source." Some of those reporters found most reliable: Jane Fonda, Barry Commoner, Helen Caldicott and the Union of Concerned Scientists.

CHAPTER ONE, STUDY 3

## *"The Washington Reporters"*

### OVERVIEW

The same year Lichter released his survey, the Brookings Institution published a detailed profile of the Washington press corps, *The Washington Reporters*, by Stephen Hess. Hess based his book on extensive interviews conducted with, and questionnaires answered by, several hundred newspaper and wire service reporters based in Washington D.C., in 1977 and 1978. Right in line with Lichter's figures, Hess proved that the Washington newspaper bureaus from across the country are filled with liberals. Almost every reporter who considered the media biased found it biased to the left, but only 42 percent considered themselves liberal.

### KEY FINDINGS

- Hess asked: "Some reporters feel that there is a political bias in the Washington news corps. Do you agree?" The answer: "51 percent agreed and 49 percent disagreed. Those in agreement were then asked to describe the bias. Liberal said 96 percent, conservative said 1 percent."

- Requested to characterize their own political outlook, however, 42 percent called themselves liberal, 39 percent middle of the road, 19 percent conservative. [See Graph 1D]

- "Forty-six percent felt their views were in conformity with the politics of the press corps, 7 percent were more liberal, and 47 percent claimed they were more conservative."

- Hess concluded: "It is reminiscent of a famous Thomas Nast cartoon in which Boss Tweed and his henchmen are arranged in a circle, each pointing an accusing finger at his neighbor. The caption reads: 'Twas him.' Washington reporters seem to be similarly arrayed: the press corps is liberal, but not me. 'Tis him.'"

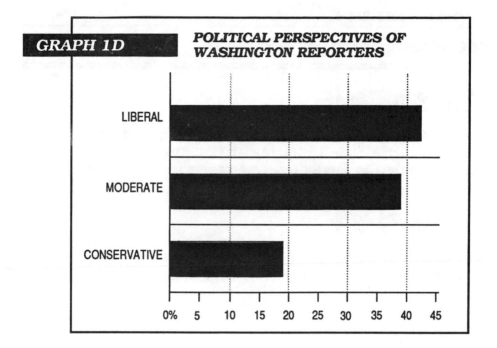

GRAPH 1D

POLITICAL PERSPECTIVES OF
WASHINGTON REPORTERS

LIBERAL

MODERATE

CONSERVATIVE

0%   5   10   15   20   25   30   35   40   45

**CHAPTER ONE, STUDY 4**

# *1980 Presidential Preference*

## OVERVIEW

Lichter's media elite poll left off with the 1976 presidential election. In 1982, California State University at Los Angeles scholars asked reporters from the fifty largest U.S. newspapers for whom they voted in 1980.

## KEY FINDING

- 51 percent cast a ballot for President Jimmy Carter, 24 percent for liberal third party candidate John Anderson, and 25 percent for winner Ronald Reagan.

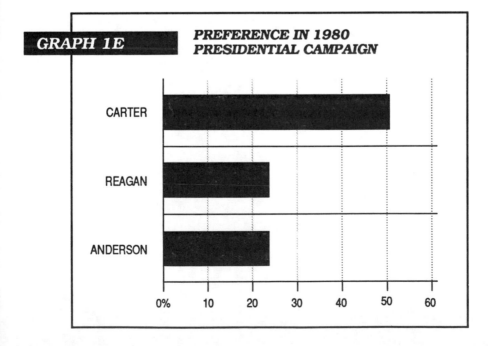

**GRAPH 1E**        **PREFERENCE IN 1980 PRESIDENTIAL CAMPAIGN**

**CHAPTER ONE, STUDY 5**

## *The Public, the Press, and the Liberal Agenda*

### OVERVIEW

In February 1985 the *Los Angeles Times* polled nearly three thousand members of the general public, separating out the responses of college-educated professionals. The *Times* then posed the same series of economic, social, and political questions to 2,703 news and editorial staffers at the 621 newspapers mentioned by the public. The survey sample was weighted by circulation -- so the larger the paper the greater the number of reporters and editors questioned. Slightly more than 22 percent worked for *The Washington Post, New York Times, Los Angeles Times* or *Chicago Tribune*. At 587 of the newspapers, the poll included the top editor.

### KEY FINDINGS

- Liberals outnumber conservatives in the newsroom by more than three-to-one: 55 percent considered themselves liberal, compared to just 17 percent who identified themselves as conservative.

- Newspaper journalists are far more liberal than others surveyed: less than a fourth of the public and only 38 percent of college-educated professionals described themselves as liberal.

- By a margin of two-to-one, reporters had a negative view of then President Ronald Reagan and voted, by the same margin, for Walter Mondale in 1984.

- The reporters and editors held extremely liberal views on foreign affairs: 84 percent supported a nuclear freeze; 80 percent were against increased defense spending; and 76 percent opposed CIA aid to the Nicaraguan Freedom Fighters, the Contras.

- On social issues the reporters and editors were also overwhelmingly liberal: 82 percent favored allowing women to have abortions; 81 percent backed affirmative action; and 78 percent wanted stricter gun control. [See Table 1F on next page]

| TABLE 1F | JOURNALISTS VS. PUBLIC AND PROFESSIONALS | JOURNALISTS | PUBLIC | COLLEGE EDUCATED PROFESSIONALS |
|---|---|---|---|---|
| Consider self/newspaper | Liberal | 55% | 23% | 38% |
| | Conservative | 17 | 29 | 30 |
| President Reagan | Favor | 30 | 56 | 57 |
| | Oppose | 60 | 27 | 33 |
| **Economic Issues** | | | | |
| Sympathize with | Business | 27 | 33 | 52 |
| | Labor | 31 | 32 | 27 |
| Government regulation of business | Favor | 49 | 22 | 26 |
| | Oppose | 41 | 50 | 57 |
| Government aid to those unable to support themselves | Favor | 95 | 83 | 81 |
| | Oppose | 3 | 11 | 12 |
| Government should reduce income inequality | Favor | 50 | 55 | 56 |
| | Oppose | 39 | 23 | 24 |
| **Foreign Affairs** | | | | |
| U.S. withdraw investments from South Africa | Favor | 62 | 31 | 48 |
| | Oppose | 29 | 27 | 27 |
| Verifiable nuclear freeze | Favor | 84 | 66 | 79 |
| | Oppose | 13 | 22 | 17 |
| CIA aid to Nicaraguan contras | Favor | 17 | 19 | 27 |
| | Oppose | 76 | 44 | 53 |
| Increase defense budget | Favor | 15 | 38 | 32 |
| | Oppose | 80 | 51 | 63 |
| **Social Issues** | | | | |
| Allowing women to have abortions | Favor | 82 | 49 | 68 |
| | Oppose | 14 | 44 | 28 |
| Prayer in public schools | Favor | 25 | 74 | 58 |
| | Oppose | 67 | 19 | 36 |
| Affirmative Action | Favor | 81 | 56 | 67 |
| | Oppose | 14 | 21 | 20 |
| Death penalty for murder | Favor | 47 | 75 | 67 |
| | Oppose | 47 | 17 | 26 |
| Hiring Homosexuals | Favor | 89 | 55 | 68 |
| | Oppose | 7 | 31 | 24 |
| Stricter handgun controls | Favor | 78 | 50 | 63 |
| | Oppose | 19 | 41 | 34 |

# "Journalists and Readers: Bridging the Credibility Gap"

## OVERVIEW

The Lichter, Hess and *Los Angeles Times* polls focused on influential national news outlets and Washington based reporters. But what about reporters outside the East Coast media elite? Are they as liberal, or less so?

The Associated Press Managing Editors Association (APME) commissioned a wide-ranging survey in 1985 on public attitudes toward the media and reporters' views about their profession. Although this APME study included *The Boston Globe* and the New York *Daily News*, most members of the media surveyed worked for small-town newspapers, such as the Milford *Statesman* (Connecticut), the *Oskaloosa Herald* (Iowa), and the *Mountain Statesman* (Grafton, West Virginia). The APME found reporters to be substantially more liberal than their readers.

In conducting the study for APME, MORI Research polled the public and then all the newsroom employees from those newspapers mentioned by respondents. "In all, 1,333 journalists from 51 newspapers answered the 153 questions in the survey," including reporters, news editors, feature reporters, editorial writers and even some photographers.

## KEY FINDINGS

- "Twice as many journalists (30 percent) as members of the public (15 percent) referred to themselves as 'liberal.' Only 10 percent of journalists said they were 'conservative,' compared with 26 percent of the population as a whole." [See Graph 1G]

- "In addition to their differences in political ideology, journalists also differed somewhat from the public in their political party affiliations. Fifteen percent of the journalists interviewed said they considered themselves Republicans, compared to 31 percent of the general population. And 42 percent of journalists said they usually thought of themselves as Democrats, compared to 37 percent of the general population." [See Graph 1H]

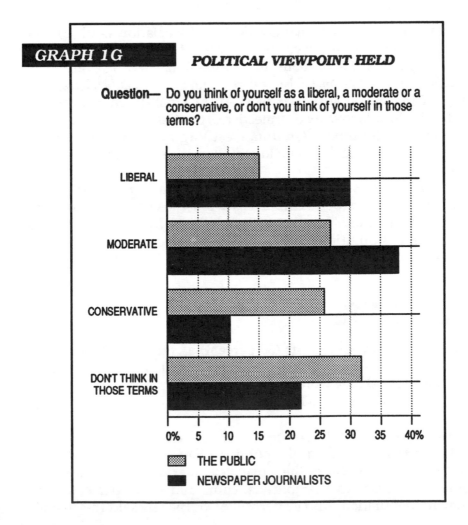

**GRAPH 1G**    *POLITICAL VIEWPOINT HELD*

**Question—** Do you think of yourself as a liberal, a moderate or a conservative, or don't you think of yourself in those terms?

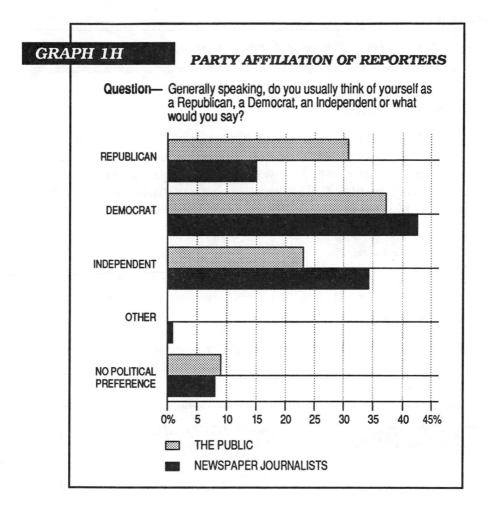

**GRAPH 1H**     *PARTY AFFILIATION OF REPORTERS*

**Question—** Generally speaking, do you usually think of yourself as a Republican, a Democrat, an Independent or what would you say?

REPUBLICAN

DEMOCRAT

INDEPENDENT

OTHER

NO POLITICAL PREFERENCE

0%  5  10  15  20  25  30  35  40  45%

THE PUBLIC

NEWSPAPER JOURNALISTS

**CHAPTER ONE, STUDY 7**

# "The Changing Face of the Newsroom"

## OVERVIEW

In 1989, the American Society of Newspaper Editors (ASNE) completed an extensive two-year survey of the attitudes and career goals of 1,200 reporters and editors at 72 newspapers. One question asked, "What is your political leaning?" The answer: Nearly three times as many newsroom employees consider themselves liberal as conservative.

## KEY FINDINGS

- 62 percent of newsroom employees identified themselves as "Democrat or liberal" or "independent, but lean to Democrat/liberal."

- 22 percent called themselves "Republican or conservative" or "independent, but lean to Republican/conservative." The rest answered "independent."

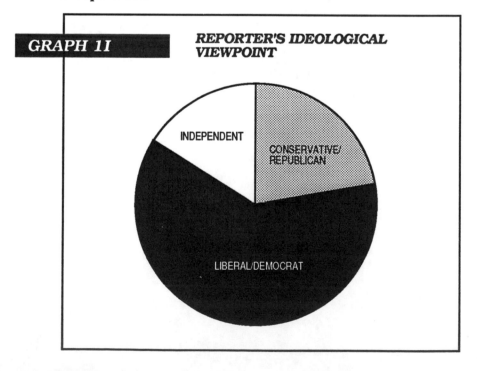

**GRAPH 1I**

**REPORTER'S IDEOLOGICAL VIEWPOINT**

INDEPENDENT

CONSERVATIVE/ REPUBLICAN

LIBERAL/DEMOCRAT

*CHAPTER ONE, STUDY 8*

# Survey of Business & Financial Reporters

## OVERVIEW

A 1988 poll confirmed that political reporters are not the only ones who bring liberal views to the job; business reporters are equally liberal. *The Journalist and Financial Reporting,* a New York-based newsletter, surveyed 151 business reporters from over thirty publications ranging from the *Los Angeles Times, Washington Post, USA Today, New York Times, Chicago Tribune, Boston Globe, Dallas Morning News* and *Philadelphia Inquirer* to *Money, Fortune, Business Week, Wall Street Journal, Investor's Daily, Venture, Inc.* and *Barron's.*

## KEY FINDINGS

- About 52 percent evaluated President Reagan's performance in office as "poor" or "below average." Only 16.5 percent gave him an "excellent" or "good," and the remaining 19 percent considered him "average." [See Graph 1J]

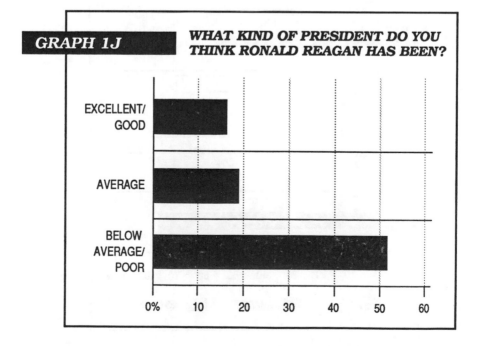

*GRAPH 1J*  **WHAT KIND OF PRESIDENT DO YOU THINK RONALD REAGAN HAS BEEN?**

- 54 percent of the business reporters identified themselves as Democrats, barely 10 percent as Republicans.

- Over 76 percent reported they opposed school prayer and 75 percent were against aid to the Contras, but an overwhelming 86 percent favored the "right to an abortion." [See Graph 1K]

- Asked who they wished to see become President, 27 percent named liberal New York Governor Mario Cuomo (D), trailed by 20 percent for Senator Bill Bradley (D-NJ) and 9 percent for Senator Paul Simon (D-Ill). Senator Bob Dole was the most popular Republican, garnering 8 percent.

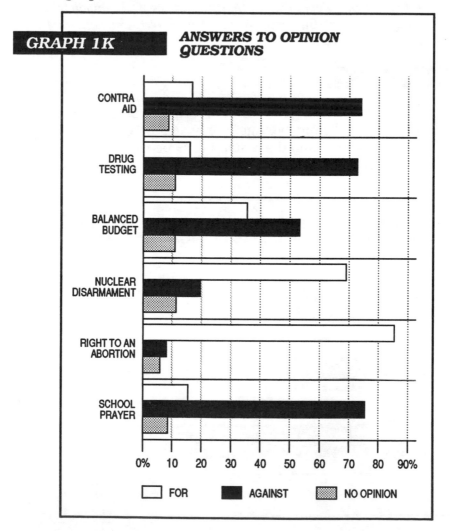

**GRAPH 1K** · **ANSWERS TO OPINION QUESTIONS**

CONTRA AID

DRUG TESTING

BALANCED BUDGET

NUCLEAR DISARMAMENT

RIGHT TO AN ABORTION

SCHOOL PRAYER

0%  10  20  30  40  50  60  70  80  90%

☐ FOR    ■ AGAINST    ▨ NO OPINION

- Conservative Pat Robertson topped the list -- at 44 percent -- of those the reporters would "least like to see as President," followed by 19 percent who must have become very upset: they named George Bush.

# "The Once and Future Journalists"

## OVERVIEW

A couple of years after completing their poll of 240 working reporters, Robert Lichter and Stanley Rothman, led by Linda Lichter, queried journalism school students to learn what beliefs future reporters would bring to the job. The interviews with Master's degree candidates at the prestigious Columbia University School of Journalism determined that aspiring reporters were even more liberal than those already in the profession.

## KEY FINDINGS

- 85 percent of the journalism students called themselves liberal.

- 90 percent of those who voted in 1972 went for George McGovern.

- A minuscule 4 percent voted for Ronald Reagan in 1980. Carter got 59 percent, third party candidate John Anderson the remaining 29 percent.

- 63 percent believed the government should guarantee jobs for everyone.

- Asked to evaluate a list of public figures, they gave the most positive ratings to Ralph Nader, followed by Gloria Steinem and Senator Ted Kennedy.

- Fidel Castro was rated higher than Reagan and the students viewed the Sandinistas more positively than Jerry Falwell, Jeane Kirkpatrick, Margaret Thatcher or President Reagan.

## STUDY EXCERPT

**The Once and Future Journalists** by Linda Lichter, S. Robert Lichter and Stanley Rothman. From the *Washington Journalism Review*, December 1982.

If today's media elite is one of the most liberal, anti-establishment groups in American society -- politically alienated from traditional values and institutions -- tomorrow's media elite is likely to be more so. That is what our survey of Columbia University School of Journalism students revealed. Our findings show that these aspiring journalists are more liberal in attitude, more cosmopolitan in background and more out of step with prevailing American beliefs than those already at the top of the profession.

In 1980, when we surveyed leading reporters and editors at *The New York Times, Washington Post, Wall Street Journal, Time, Newsweek* and *U.S. News & World Report* -- as well as the television networks and PBS -- we found that leading journalists lined up on the side of minorities, consumer groups and intellectuals and against both business and labor. They saw themselves as the natural opponents of both corporate chieftains and middle America. [See Study 1, this chapter]

How, we wondered, did the country's media elite come to be so different in attitude and background from mainstream Americans? Were they liberal and alienated because their profession made them that way,

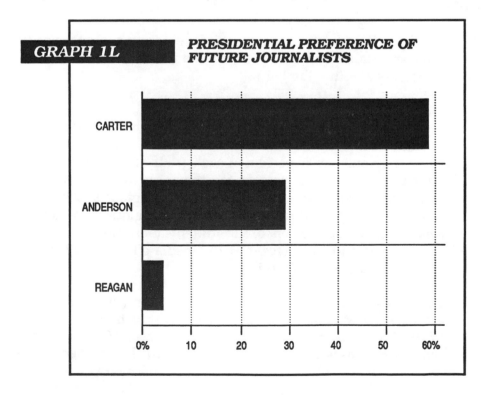

**GRAPH 1L** — **PRESIDENTIAL PREFERENCE OF FUTURE JOURNALISTS**

CARTER

ANDERSON

REAGAN

0%    10    20    30    40    50    60%

or did the press attract liberal and alienated people? To find out, last spring [1982] we interviewed a random sampling of Master's degree candidates at Columbia's School of Journalism. Twenty-eight of these aspiring journalists completed our hour-long interviews in which we questioned them about their backgrounds and attitudes, asking many of the same questions we had earlier put to their elders in the business. We also asked the students to evaluate public figures, political movements and the trustworthiness of newspapers, magazines and television broadcasts.

Although journalism is often thought to be an upwardly mobile profession, we found very few Horatio Algers among today's media stars -- and even fewer among aspiring journalists, 70 percent of whom have college-educated fathers (compared to 40 percent of the working journalists). In both groups, only one out of five had a father with a blue or white-collar job. Forty-five percent of the working journalists and an impressive 57 percent of the students rated their family income while they were growing up as "above average." Although today's successful journalists are the products of comfortable backgrounds, those likely to be tomorrow's leading journalists represent an even more privileged slice of society.

Like other privileged Americans, the media elite and a large majority of the journalism students hold the cosmopolitan, anti-establishment social views fashionable since the 1960s.

### Don't Go To Church
For one thing, both the media elite and the Columbia students are overwhelmingly non-religious. Although 83 percent of them were raised in a particular religion, over 80 percent of each group seldom or never attended church services, only 8 percent say they attended religious services regularly and nearly half claimed no current religious affiliation at all. Of the few in both groups who maintained a religious tie, about 25 percent were Protestant, 21 percent of the students identified themselves as Jewish, as compared to 14 percent of the media elite; fewer than 10 percent of either group were Catholic.

Politically, 54 percent of the working journalists and an overwhelming 85 percent of the students described themselves as liberals; only 19 percent of those now in the profession and 11 percent of the students called themselves conservatives. Their voting records matched these self-descriptions. In 1972, when 61 percent of the American electorate voted for Richard Nixon, 81 percent of the media elite and over 90 percent of the journalism students chose George McGovern. (Because of their youth, only 41 percent of the students cast a vote that year.)

In the election of 1976, when 50 percent of American voters cast their ballots for Jimmy Carter, more than 75 percent of the students and working journalists voted for him. In 1980, 4 percent of the students voted for Ronald Reagan, but 52 percent of the American voters did so; 59 percent of the students voted for President Carter, 29 percent for third party candidate John Anderson.

### Hostile to Private Enterprise

On specific social and political questions, the journalism students tended to be at least as liberal as established journalists and more hostile toward business and private enterprise, more alienated from the political system than today's media elite [See Table 1M]. A quarter of the students believed the private enterprise system was "fair" to workers compared to 70 percent of their elders in the profession. Almost 66 percent of the established journalists believed less regulation of business would be good for the country, but only 34 percent of the students held that view. The aspiring journalists were three times more likely than those already at work in the profession to advocate public ownership of corporations; almost 40 percent of the students subscribed to this notion.

In both groups, dissatisfaction with the economic order was accompanied by pronounced political alienation. Forty-nine percent of the media elite and 71 percent of the students believed the very structure of American society caused alienation. Twice as many students as media leaders believed our social institutions needed a complete overhauling.

The groups were about equal in their support of environmental protection, women's rights and homosexual rights. At least 90 percent of both groups supported a woman's right to have an abortion and rejected government regulation of sexual practices. At least 75 percent of both groups did not believe that homosexuality was wrong; moreover, 85 percent of the media elite and 93 percent of the students upheld a homosexual's right to teach in public schools.

Unexpectedly, the students condemned adultery more strongly than their elders: 75 percent of them saw adultery as wrong compared with only 47 percent of the established journalists. Also unexpected was the students' comparative lack of enthusiasm for affirmative action. Eighty percent of the media leaders, but only 67 percent of the students, believed in strong affirmative action for blacks. Possibly today's students feel directly competitive with minorities for the few media jobs at the bottom of the career ladder, while the media elite has no reason to feel threatened.

| TABLE 1M | ATTITUDES OF FUTURE JOURNALISTS |
|---|---|

**Economics**

| | |
|---|---|
| Big corporations should be publicly owned | 39% |
| People with more ability should earn more | 77 |
| Private enterprise is fair to workers | 32 |
| Less regulation of business is good for USA | 39 |
| Government should reduce income gap | 82 |
| Government should guarantee jobs | 63 |

**Political Alienation**

| | |
|---|---|
| Structure of society causes alienation | 71 |
| Institutions need overhaul | 50 |
| All political systems are repressive | 36 |

**Social-Cultural**

| | |
|---|---|
| Environmental problems are overstated | 14 |
| Strong affirmative action for blacks | 67 |
| Government should not regulate sex | 93 |
| Woman has right to decide on abortion | 96 |
| Homosexuality is wrong | 18 |
| Homosexuals shouldn't teach in public schools | 7 |
| Adultery is wrong | 78 |

**Foreign Policy**

| | |
|---|---|
| U.S. exploits Third World, causes poverty | 75 |
| U.S. use of resources immoral | 74 |
| Goal of foreign policy is to protect U.S. businesses | 89 |
| CIA should sometimes undermine hostile governments | 33 |

Both groups echoed Third World criticism of capitalism, although that criticism was stronger among the students. Seventy-five percent of the students believed the United States exploited Third World countries and was responsible for their poverty, while only 56 percent of the working journalists held this view. Eighty percent of the media elite and a resounding 89 percent of the students believed the protection of American business was a main goal of our foreign policy.

We first asked both groups to rate seven American leadership groups in terms of their influence in the nation's life and then asked them to rate the amount of influence those groups *should* have. The established and aspiring journalists agreed on how power is now distributed in American society, and both groups would make drastic changes -- stripping business and labor of their perceived influence and boosting the status of blacks, feminists and intellectuals.

### Adore Ralph Nader the Most, Ronald Reagan the Least

When we asked the students to rate prominent American and world leaders, they gave their strongest endorsement to such liberals as Ralph Nader, Gloria Steinem and Edward Kennedy and put Ronald Reagan and the Moral Majority at the bottom of their approval scale. Overall, the students found more to condemn than to praise in American as well as world leaders. They gave an average "strong approval" rating to only 13 percent of them.

Since the journalism students are prime candidates to become tomorrow's media elite, we asked them to rate the reliability of a dozen media institutions, including newspapers, television and opinion journals of the left and right. The results, which seemed to reflect a mix of the students' liberal sentiments with their professional standards, contained some surprises.

The students rated *The New York Times*, *The Washington Post* and public television, all pillars of the journalistic establishment, as highly reliable. But they rated the *New York Review of Books*, a journal of the intellectual left, as equally trustworthy. They saw little difference among *Time*, *Newsweek* and *U.S. News*. And they rated *The New Republic* and *The Nation*, two long-time representatives of liberal and left opinion respectively, as no less trustworthy than *Time*. They reserved their lowest rating and trust for the *National Review* and *Commentary*, two conservative magazines.

The aspiring journalists are different from those already in place and successful in the profession in one respect: they are more diverse racially and sexually. While a majority of both groups is white and male, 45 percent of the students are female, more than twice the proportion of women among the established journalists. The student group contains four times as many minority members -- 21 percent compared to only 5 percent of those already at the top.

Our 1980 survey confirmed the popular impression that today's national news leadership is one of the most liberal and cosmopolitan groups in American society. Our 1982 survey of Columbia School of Journalism graduate students indicates that potential media leaders outstrip their elders on both counts.

Although we cannot predict how their views may change as they mature and become professionals, it is clear that they will come to journalism with firmly established liberal attitudes and views that place them at considerable odds with Middle American values.

Reprinted with permission. Copyright © 1982 by *Washington Journalism Review.*

# 2 Who Becomes a Reporter?

What kind of people become reporters? This chapter looks at two issues: First, are the more liberal areas of the country overrepresented in media ranks? Second, since many political operatives (campaign managers, aides to elected political officials) look to the media for career advancement -- improved job security and better pay -- will veteran liberal politicians find it easier than conservatives to obtain a media job?

The studies presented here show that reporters are far more likely to come from liberal families in the Northeast than from conservative families in the Midwest and South, and that openings are frequently filled by liberals from the world of politics, but rarely by conservatives.

---

**CHAPTER TWO, STUDY 1**

## "Media and Business Elites"

### OVERVIEW

In 1979, Professors S. Robert Lichter and Stanley Rothman set out to determine not only reporters' political views, but also the socio-economic makeup and background of the "media elite." In the following excerpt from their study (described more fully in Chapter One, Study 1), the two professors discuss what they learned from interviews with 240 journalists with "the most powerful media outlets," including the television networks and three news magazines.

### KEY FINDINGS

• 93 percent of the journalists interviewed have college degrees.

- 40 percent come from three states: New York, Pennsylvania and New Jersey.

- 86 percent "seldom" or "never" attend religious services.

## STUDY EXCERPT

**Media and Business Elites** by S. Robert Lichter and Stanley Rothman. From *Public Opinion,* October/November 1981.

The social and personal backgrounds of the media elite are summarized in Table 2A. In some respects, the journalists we interviewed appear typical of leadership groups throughout society. The media elite is composed mainly of white males in their thirties and forties. Only one in twenty is nonwhite; one in five is female. They are highly educated, well-paid professionals. Ninety-three percent have college degrees, and a majority (55 percent) attended graduate school as well. These figures reveal them as one of the best educated groups in America. They are also one of the better-paid groups, despite journalism's reputation as a low-paying profession. In 1978, 78 percent earned at least $30,000, and one-in-three had salaries that exceeded $50,000. Moreover, nearly half (46 percent) reported family incomes above $50,000.

Geographically, they are drawn primarily from northern industrial states, especially from the Northeast corridor. Two-fifths come from

| TABLE 2A | BACKGROUNDS OF THE MEDIA ELITE |
|---|---|
| White | 95% |
| Male | 79 |
| From Northeast or North Central states | 68 |
| From metropolitan area | 42 |
| Father graduated college | 40 |
| Father occupation "professional" | 40 |
| College graduate | 93 |
| Postgraduate study | 55 |
| Income $30,000+ | 78 |
| Family income $50,000+ | 46 |
| Religion "none" | 50 |

three states: New York, New Jersey, and Pennsylvania. Another 10 percent hail from New England, and almost one-in-five was raised in the big industrial states just to the west -- Illinois, Indiana, Michigan and Ohio. Thus, over two-thirds of the media elite come from these three clusters of states. By contrast, only 3 percent are drawn from the entire Pacific coast, including California, the nation's most populous state.

Journalism is a profession associated with rapid upward mobility, yet we found few Horatio Alger stories in the newsroom. On the contrary, many among the media elite enjoyed socially privileged upbringings. Most were raised in upper-middle-class homes. Almost half their fathers were college graduates, and one-in-four held a graduate degree. Two-in-five are the children of professionals -- doctors, lawyers, teachers, and so on. In fact, one-in-twelve is following in his father's footsteps as a second generation journalist. Another 40 percent described their fathers as businessmen. That leaves only one-in-five whose father was employed in a low status blue or white collar job.

In sum, substantial numbers of the media elite grew up at some distance from the social and cultural traditions of small town "middle America." Instead, they were drawn from big cities in the Northeast and North Central states. Their parents tended to be well off, highly educated members of the upper middle class, especially the educated professions.

All these characteristics might be expected to predispose people toward the social liberalism of the cosmopolitan outsider. And indeed, much of the media elite upholds the cosmopolitan or anti-bourgeois social perspective that Everett Ladd has termed the "new liberalism."

A predominant characteristic of the media elite is its secular outlook. Exactly 50 percent eschewed any religious affiliation. Another 14 percent were Jewish, and almost one-in-four (23 percent) was raised in a Jewish household. Only one-in-five identified himself as Protestant, and one-in-eight as Catholic. Very few are regular churchgoers. Only 8 percent went to church or synagogue weekly, and 86 percent seldom or never attended religious services.

This study was directed by Rothman and Lichter, under the auspices of the Research Institute on International Change at Columbia University. The surveys of media and business leaders were supervised by Response Analysis, a survey research organization.

CHAPTER TWO, STUDY 2

# The Revolving Door

## OVERVIEW

Preparing for his notorious interview with then Vice-President George Bush early in the 1988 presidential campaign, *CBS Evening News* anchorman Dan Rather was coached by a consultant recently hired by the network: Tom Donilon. What qualifications did Donilon bring to his new role as presidential campaign coverage adviser? A long list of jobs with liberal Democrats, including Senior Adviser to Senator Joseph Biden's short-lived presidential campaign, Deputy Manager of the Mondale-Ferraro 1984 campaign, and chief delegate counter for the 1980 Carter-Mondale campaign.

Donilon reported to CBS News Political Editor Dotty Lynch. She served as deputy pollster for George McGovern in 1972, worked for Ted Kennedy in 1980, and served as chief pollster for Gary Hart in 1984. She also worked with Donilon on the Mondale-Ferraro effort.

Correspondent Ike Pappas was released by CBS in 1987. In 1988 the Democratic National Committee hired him to produce puff pieces on their Atlanta convention for satellite distribution. About the same time CBS named David Burke, then Executive Vice President of ABC News, as President of its news division. In the late 1960's Burke was Chief of Staff to Senator Edward Kennedy. Just after the conventions, the Dukakis-Bentsen campaign apparatus hired Donilon to help coach the two Democrats on debate techniques.

How typical is the situation at CBS News? Very, according to an ongoing Media Research Center (MRC) study of the "Revolving Door," a term coined to describe the movement of people from political to media jobs, and vice versa.

Since the viewpoints of most in the media coincide with those of dedicated, active liberals, it's no wonder liberal political workers slide easily into the media profession. Conservatives cannot match that compatibility, which might just explain why so few are able to swing through the "Revolving Door."

As of early 1990 the MRC had identified 235 reporters, editors, producers and news division executives who had passed through the "Revolving Door" at least once. Far from representing a cross-section of the American political spectrum, virtually all belonged on the liberal side.

## KEY FINDINGS

- 178 current or former Big Media reporters, editors, producers, and executives were connected at one time to liberal political groups, but only 57 had ties to Republicans or conservatives.

- Top executives for ABC, CBS and NBC News gained political experience by serving on the staff of liberal Democratic officials.

- *Time, Newsweek,* and *U.S. News & World Report* all employ reporters and/or editors who previously worked for liberal politicians.

## STUDY EXCERPT

Following are brief biographies of the most recognizable and visible Revolving Door examples. The names are divided into two categories: "Liberals or Democrats" and "Conservatives or Republicans." The complete list appears in Appendix A, starting on page 285.

### Liberals and Democrats:

**Kenneth Banta** Senior Correspondent, *Time* magazine London bureau, 1989-; Eastern Europe bureau chief, Vienna, 1985-89

- Issues adviser, Gary Hart for President, 1984

- Reporter, *Time,* 1981-1984

**Rebecca Bell** Press Secretary, Senator John Glenn (D-OH), 1989-

- Director of affiliate news services for NBC News, 1986-89

- Paris Bureau Chief, NBC News, 1977-85

**Douglas Bennet** President and Chief Executive Officer, National Public Radio, 1983-

- Director, Agency for International Development (AID), 1979-1981
- Assistant Secretary of State for congressional relations, 1977-79
- Administrative Assistant to Senator Abraham Ribicoff (D-CT), 1973-74
- Administrative Assistant to Senator Tom Eagleton (D-MO), 1969-1973
- Assistant to to Vice President Hubert Humphrey, 1967-69

**Ken Bode** Chief Political Correspondent, NBC News, 1979-1989

- Aide to Morris Udall's presidential campaign, 1976
- Politics Editor, *The New Republic*, 1975-79
- Author, McGovern Commission Democratic delegate reform rules, 1972

- Contributing White House correspondent, CNN Special Investigation Unit, 1990-
- Director, Center for Contemporary Media at DePauw University, June 1989-

**David Burke** President, CBS News, 1988-

- Chief of Staff to New York Governor Hugh Carey (D), 1975-77
- Chief of Staff, Senator Ted Kennedy, 1965-1971

- Assistant to Secretary of Commerce Luther Hodges; Assistant to Secretary of Labor Willard Wirtz, 1961-65
- Executive Secretary, President's Advisory Committee on Labor Management Policy, 1965

- Executive Vice President, ABC News, 1986-1988
- Vice President for planning and Assistant to the President of ABC News, 1977-1986

**Kathryn Bushkin**   Director of Editorial Administration, *U.S. News & World Report*, 1985-; Vice President for Corporate Affairs, 1984-85

- Press Secretary, Gary Hart presidential campaign, 1983-84

**Margaret Carlson**   Senior Writer, *Time* magazine, 1988

- Special Assistant to the Chairman of Consumer Product Safety Commission, 1977-81

- Washington correspondent, *Esquire*, 1985-87

**Wally Chalmers**   Director of Broadcast Research, CBS News, 1984-86; CBS News Political Editor, 1984

- Executive Director and Chief of Staff, Democratic National Committee, 1986-88
- Executive Director of Nuclear Freeze Foundation and Fund for a Democratic Majority, early 1980s
- Kennedy for President, Midwest and Southern coordinator, 1980
- Assistant Secretary, Dept. of Health, Educations and Welfare, Carter Administration
- Udall for President, Northeast coordinator, 1976

**Tom Donilon**   Dukakis and Bentsen debate coach, September-November 1988

• Consultant to CBS News for campaign coverage, January-August 1988

• Senior adviser, Joe Biden for President Committee, 1987
• Deputy Manager, Mondale-Ferraro campaign, 1984
• Chief of Staff, Mondale campaign plane, 1984
• Chief Delegate Counter, Carter-Mondale, 1980

**Hedley Donovan**  Editor-in-Chief, Time Inc., 1964-1979

• Senior Adviser to President Jimmy Carter, 1979-1981

**Anne Edwards**  Senior Editor, National Public Radio, 1987-

• Mondale-Ferraro campaign scheduler, 1984
• Director, White House Television Office, Carter Administration, 1977-1980

• Assignment Editor, CBS News Washington bureau, 1980-84

**Bob Ferrante**  Executive Producer of morning news, National Public Radio, 1989-

• Director of Communications, Democratic National Committee, 1986- 1988

• Senior Producer, CBS Election News unit, 1984-85
• Executive Producer, *CBS Morning News*, 1983-84
• Executive Producer, CBS News *Nightwatch*, 1982-83

**Jeff Gralnick**  Vice President of ABC News for special events/political coverage

• Press Secretary, Senator George McGovern, 1971

• Executive Producer, 1988 campaign coverage
• Executive Producer, *Jennings-Koppel Report*, 1987

- VP and Executive Producer, specials, 1985-
- Executive Producer of ABC's 1984 campaign coverage
- Executive Producer, political broadcasts, 1983-85
- Executive Producer, ABC's *World News Tonight*, 1979-83

**James Greenfield** Assistant Managing Editor, *New York Times*, 1977-; and Editor, *New York Times Magazine*, 1987-

- Assistant Secretary of State, Johnson Administration, 1964-66
- Deputy Assistant Secretary of State for Public Affairs, Kennedy Administration

**Jeff Greenfield** Media reporter, ABC News *Nightline*; political correspondent, ABC News, 1983-

- Speechwriter, Senator Robert Kennedy, 1967-68

- Media critic, CBS News *Sunday Morning*, 1979-1983

**Bettina Gregory** ABC News Washington correspondent

- Campaign Manager for husband John Flannery, Democratic opponent to U.S. Rep. Frank Wolf (R-VA), 1984

**Rick Inderfurth** ABC News Moscow correspondent, 1989-

- Deputy Staff Director for political and security affairs, Democratic controlled Senate Foreign Relations Committee, 1979-80
- Special Assistant to the National Security Council Director, Carter White House, 1977-79
- Legislative Assistant in mid-'70s for Senators George McGovern and Gary Hart

- National Security Affairs correspondent, ABC News, 1984-89
- Pentagon correspondent, ABC News, 1981-84

**Mickey Kaus** Senior Writer, *Newsweek*, 1987-88

- Speechwriter for Senator Ernest Hollings (D-SC), 1983-1984

- Senior Editor, *The New Republic*, 1989-


**Deborah Leff** Senior Producer, ABC's *World News Tonight*, 1989-

- Director of Public Affairs, Federal Trade Commission, 1979-80
- Trial Attorney, U.S. Department of Justice, 1977-79

- Senior Producer of ABC's *Nightline*, New York bureau, 1989
- Senior Producer of ABC's *Nightline*, London bureau, 1988-1989


**Dotty Lynch** CBS News Political Editor, 1985-

- Chief pollster, Gary Hart for President, 1984
- Pollster, Mondale-Ferraro campaign, 1984
- Polling Director, Democratic National Committee, 1981-82
- Polling Director, Ted Kennedy for President, 1980
- Deputy Pollster for the 1972 McGovern campaign


**Patricia O'Brien** National affairs and congressional reporter, Knight-Ridder Washington bureau, 1984-87

- Press Secretary to Michael Dukakis for President campaign, April-November 1987


**Jane Pauley** Correspondent and anchor, NBC News, New York, 1990-

- Administrative Assistant, Indiana Democratic State Central Committee, 1972

- Co-host, NBC's *Today*, 1976-1989
- Anchor, *NBC Nightly News* on Sundays, 1980-82

**Harrison (Lee) Rainie**  Assistant Managing Editor, *U.S. News & World Report*, 1988-

- Chief-of-Staff to Senator Patrick Moynihan, (D-NY), 1987
- Associate Editor for political coverage, *U.S. News & World Report*, 1987-88
- Reporter, New York *Daily News*, Washington bureau , 1979-87

**Tim Russert**  NBC News Vice President and Washington Bureau Chief, 1989-; NBC News Vice President, 1984-88

- Counselor and media strategist for New York Governor Mario Cuomo, 1983-84
- Chief-of-Staff to U.S. Senator Patrick Moynihan, until 1983

**Robert Shapiro**  Vice President, Progressive Policy Institute, 1989-

- Associate Editor, *U.S. News & World Report*, 1985-88

- Deputy Director for Issues, Dukakis for President Committee, 1988
- Legislative Director for Senator Patrick Moynihan, 1981-85
- Fellow, Institute for Policy Studies, 1972-73

**Walter Shapiro**  Senior Writer, *Time* magazine, (covered the 1988 campaign), 1987-

- Speechwriter, President Carter, 1979
- Press Secretary for Labor Secretary Ray Marshall, Carter Administration, 1977-78

- General Editor, national affairs, *Newsweek*, 1983-87
- Staff writer, *Washington Post Magazine*, 1980-83

**Douglas Waller**  *Newsweek* foreign affairs reporter, Washington bureau, 1988-

- Legislative Assistant to Senator William Proxmire (D-WI), 1985-88
- Legislative Director, U.S. Representative Ed Markey (D-MA), 1983-85

## Conservatives/Republicans

***Cissy Baker*** Managing Editor, Cable News Network, 1984-

- Republican candidate for U.S. House seat from Tennessee, 1982

- Washington correspondent, CNN, 1983-84
- Assignment Editor, CNN Washington bureau, 1980-81

***David Beckwith*** Press Secretary to Vice President Dan Quayle, January 1989-

- Correspondent, *Time* , 1971-78, 1980-88
- Reporter, *Legal Times*, 1978-80

***Richard Burt*** Chief strategic arms negotiator in Geneva, February 1989-

- National Security Affairs Reporter, *New York Times*, 1977-1981

- Ambassador to the Federal Republic of Germany, 1985-1989
- Assistant Secretary of State for European and Canadian Affairs, 1982-85
- Director, Bureau of Politico-Military Affairs, 1981-82

***Jack Fuller*** Editor, *Chicago Tribune*, 1989-

- Special Assistant to Attorney General Edward Levi, 1975-76

- Executive Editor, *Chicago Tribune,* 1987-89
- Editor of the editorial page, *Chicago Tribune,* 1981-87
- Editorial writer, *Chicago Tribune,* 1978-81
- Washington correspondent, *Chicago Tribune,* 1977-78

**Ron Nessen**  Vice President for News, Mutual Broadcasting System

- Press Secretary to President Gerald Ford

**Peggy Noonan**  Speechwriter for George Bush, 1988-1989

- Writer, Dan Rather radio commentary, 1981-1984
- Writer/Editor CBS Radio News network, 1977-1981
- Newswriter, WEEI Radio Boston, 1974-1977

- Speechwriter for President Ronald Reagan, 1984-87

**Dorrance Smith**  Executive Producer, *Nightline,* 1989-; Executive Producer, *This Week with David Brinkley,* 1981-1989

- Staff Assistant, Advance Office, Ford White House

- Producer, ABC News Washington bureau, 1977-1981

**Chase Untermeyer**  Personnel Director, Bush Administration 1988-

- Reporter, *Houston Chronicle,* 1972-74

- Executive Assistant to Vice President Bush, 1981-83
- Texas legislator, 1977-81
- Intern in the office of U.S. Representative Bush, 1966

# 3 Reporters & Politics: Cheerleaders for the Left?

Polls show that on a wide range of topics reporters hold views that match the liberal Democratic position. Unstated professional rules of conduct prohibit members of the media from publicly expressing their positions on political issues for fear of damaging their credibility. But do reporters and media company corporate executives always keep their political ideas private?

The following studies, by looking at what reporters say when they let their guard down, what type of political magazines journalists write for, and what kind of political groups the foundations controlled by media corporations support, show that the answer is no.

## CHAPTER THREE, STUDY 1

### Notable Quotes from Members of the Media

#### OVERVIEW

Reporters will occasionally divulge their personal opinions on issues such as the Nicaraguan Freedom Fighters or a presidential candidate. Usually these emerge in magazine interviews or during a talk show appearance. Sometimes, however, it occurs during a news story when a reporter endorses a particular position.

The Media Research Center has been collecting these quotes for the past few years. The political opinions listed over the next pages include those of several network anchors, correspondents, producers and news magazine reporters. They provide further evidence that liberals permeate the media.

## Political Tilt

**Walter Cronkite,** former CBS News anchorman

"I think most newspapermen by definition have to be liberal; if they're not liberal, by my definition of it, then they can hardly be good newspapermen." -- as quoted in *The Establishment vs. The People* by Richard Viguerie.

"I know liberalism isn't dead in this country. It simply has, temporarily we hope, lost its voice....

"We know that unilateral action in Grenada and Tripoli was wrong. We know that *Star Wars* means uncontrollable escalation of the arms race. We know that the real threat to democracy is the half of the nation in poverty. We know that no one should tell a woman she has to bear an unwanted child....

"Gawd Almighty, we've got to shout these truths in which we believe from the housetops. Like that scene in the movie *Network,* we've got to throw open our windows and shout these truths to the streets and the heavens. And I bet we'll find more windows are thrown open to join the chorus than we'd ever dreamed possible." -- speech at People for the American Way banquet, quoted in *Newsweek*, December 5, 1988.

**Reuven Frank,** former NBC News President

"I'm a life-long Democrat." -- at a People for the American Way sponsored forum broadcast by C-SPAN, November 1989.

**Mickey Kaus,** *Newsweek* Senior Writer

"I can only speak for myself, but I was a longhaired Ivy League left-

ist in the late '60s and I'm still basically proud of what I did then."
-- *Newsweek*, "Confessions of an Ex-Radical," September 5, 1988.


**Geraldo Rivera,** talk show host and former ABC News reporter

"Remember that I'm coming from a radical background...I was politically far out." -- as quoted in *The Establishment vs. The People* by Richard Viguerie.


**Diane Sawyer,** ABC's *Prime Time Live* co-anchor

"Once I got a card at *60 Minutes* that said, 'You are a brazen right-wing hussy,' she recalls, 'I was able to write back and say, I'm not right-wing." -- *The Washington Post*, August 2, 1989.


**Nancy Traver,** *Time* Washington reporter

"I always get a lot of criticism, even among my colleagues, when I reveal that I'm actually a registered member of the Democratic Party. Many journalists tell me 'Oh, you should be an independent.' I say that it's a personal thing. I want to vote in primaries. I want to be involved in the political process. I want to cast my ballot and that's why I'm registered to the Democratic Party." -- C-SPAN, March 23, 1990.


**Mike Wallace,** CBS *60 Minutes* correspondent

"I read *Mother Jones* carefully and look forward to every issue. After all, stories that started out in *Mother Jones* have wound up on *60 Minutes*." -- as quoted in a subscription letter for the far-left magazine *Mother Jones*.

# Political Heroes

**David Brinkley**, host, ABC's *This Week with David Brinkley*; former Anchor, *NBC Nightly News*

"If I had to pick the best Presidents in my lifetime, I would of course pick Roosevelt and Kennedy, and I would also pick Harry Truman." -- *Washington Post Magazine*, April 10, 1987.

**Marc Fisher**, *Washington Post* reporter

"Ralph Nader is a legend, perhaps the only universally recognized symbol of pure honesty and clean energy left in a culture that, after being shot through with greed, cynicism and weariness, is oddly proud of its hardened self. Two decades after he slew General Motors, Nader, the young dynamo who could not be bought, is a reminder of what we once hoped to be." -- *Washington Post Magazine*, July 23, 1989.

**Bryant Gumbel**, *NBC Today* show co-host

"'I like him [Governor Mario Cuomo] because he's part jockstrap and part street kid. That's me on both counts....His wonderful speaking ability is obvious. He's also fair. I can identify with his approach to things....He could certainly win my vote.'" -- *Playboy* interview, December 1986.

**Ted Koppel**, *Nightline* anchor

"A testament to courage: the courage of some unabashed trade unionists and civil rights workers, Leftists and yes, American Communists, who fought for principles that we now take for granted." -- endorsement of Carl Bernstein's book *Loyalties*.

# Taxes and Spending

**Lesley Stahl**, CBS News White House correspondent

"I think that when you have the kind of problems that are being created for the future, that you just simply have to raise taxes. Period. And that the big tax cuts, coupled with the increase in the military spending, was an unhealthy thing for the country." -- Howard Cosell's *Speaking of Everything*, April 10, 1988.

"We have this drug problem, we have an education problem in the country. All we keep doing is cutting the domestic budget because taxes aren't being asked for. When does it become necessary to start investing in our future by fixing these problems, and when you do decide it becomes necessary, won't it become necessary to raise taxes? And just isn't that a bald truth?" -- question to OMB Director Richard Darman, *Face the Nation*, July 23, 1989.

**John Chancellor**, *NBC Nightly News* commentator and former anchor

"The squeeze is on and a modest tax increase would help a lot, but the candidates rule it out. Bush's no new taxes position seems to mean that taxes would go up only if there were an economic crisis. That drastically limits the flexibility any government should have. Is it smart to wait for a crisis? Bush has accused Dukakis of being for unilateral disarmament, yet Bush has disarmed himself by promising no new taxes. Taxes are one of the most important economic weapons a government has." -- *NBC Nightly News*, November 2, 1988.

**Michael Duffy** and **Richard Hornik**, *Time* reporters

"The borrow-and-spend policies that Ronald Reagan presided over have bequeathed to his chosen successor a down-sized presidency devoid of the resources to address long domestic problems. The Bush campaign strategists -- with the candidate's active complicity -- burdened the new President with an obdurate stance on taxes." -- *Time*, February 20, 1989.

**Mortimer Zuckerman**, *U.S. News & World Report* Editor-in-Chief

"We cannot simply sidestep what is happening by resorting to the old ideologies or to new slogans. Who wants to read Bush's lips when to do so in the face of a gigantic budget deficit means the slow decline of the America we know and believe in?" -- *U.S. News & World Report*, February 6, 1989.

**Timothy Noah**, *Newsweek* reporter

"To be sure, I'm alarmed by the widening gulf between the rich and poor in our society. But George Bush's 'kinder and gentler' rhetoric doesn't include any practical solutions to the problem, such as a stiffer tax on the rich, or an expensive federal jobs program. In fact, Bush's inaugural speech explicitly downplayed the use of public money to end society's problems." -- *The New Republic*, February 13, 1989.

**Bill Moyers**, former CBS News commentator; frequent PBS contributor

"Behind the smiles, behind the one-liners, the pretty pictures, the manipulation of emotions, the government rots. Its costs soar, its failures mount, from the folly of Star Wars to the scandals of HUD. But on the bridge of the ship of state, no one is on watch and below the deck, no one can see the iceberg. But everybody feels good." -- *Bill Moyers: The Public Mind*, November 15, 1989.

**Stanley Cloud**, *Time* Washington Bureau Chief

"I think that if we had a balanced budget amendment through the Reagan years, we would have had a depression...One of the functions, at least in the modern economy, of the federal government, is to act as a pump primer. Reagan's Administrations did it inadvertently, as it were, other administrations have done it intentionally. But I think the deficit, the monstrous deficit must be dealt with, but one still has to concede it was largely responsible for driving the economic recovery out of the '81-'82 recession." -- C-SPAN, January 12, 1990.

**Dale Russakoff,** *Washington Post* reporter

"Without a surplus to mask the deficit, the White House and Congress would have to confront it more honestly -- raise taxes or gouge the Pentagon." -- *Washington Post*, January 18, 1990.

**Jim Wooten,** ABC News reporter

"Ah yes. The dreaded federal deficit, created, for the most part, by the most massive peacetime military buildup in America's history." -- *Nightline*, January 29, 1990.

**Bryant Gumbel,** NBC *Today* show co-host

"[Except] for capital gains, it is certain the President won't mention the T-word, and yet taxes are very much at the heart of what all out potential solutions are. How long can both sides pretend that a hike's not needed?" -- *Today*, before President Bush's State of the Union address, January 31, 1990.

**Roger Rosenblatt,** former editor *U.S. News & World Report*

"Federal help is indispensable. The antigovernment line trumpeted during the Reagan years and continued, though in muted tones, in the Bush Administration is based on the flimsiest evidence, and reports of the failures of federal programs have been exaggerated." -- *Life*, February 1990.

# Social Issues

## Equal Rights Ammendment

**Liz Carpenter**, Cox Newspapers reporter

"The most dramatic way for Bush to come out from under Reagan's shadow would be to declare himself for ERA. He used to be for it but changed his position after the Republicans discarded support for the ERA in their platform. That was the beginning of the gender gap." -- *USA Today*, August 17, 1988.

**Linda Ellerbee**, former NBC and ABC correspondent

"It's 1986, and I say the fact it was defeated in this country was and is proof we need it." -- ABC's *Our World*, December 11, 1986.

## Abortion

**Tom Brokaw**, *NBC Nightly News* anchor

"I think it comes down to the question of whether a woman has a right to control her own body." -- *Mother Jones*, April 1983.

**Richard Harwood**, *Washington Post* Ombudsman

"The antiabortion forces, for example, believe that the *Post*, institutional, is 'pro-choice.' Of course it is. Any reader of the paper's editorials and home-grown columnists is aware of that. Moreover, while the shadings are more subtle, close textual analysis probably would reveal that our news coverage has favored the 'pro-choice' side." -- *Washington Post*, March 18, 1990.

# Foreign Affairs

**Karen DeYoung,** *Washington Post* Assistant Managing Editor for national news and former Foreign Editor and Central America reporter

"Most journalists now, most Western journalists at least, are very eager to seek out guerrilla groups, leftist groups, because you assume they must be the good guys." -- during a 1980 class taught by DeYoung at the Institute for Policy Studies Washington School, as reported by Cliff Kincaid in the *AIM Report*.

**Kenneth Walker,** former ABC White House reporter

"He [Nelson Mandela] knows that Yasser [Arafat] is a freedom fighter just like he is." -- Fox's *Off The Record*, March 3, 1990.

## Nicaraguan Freedom Fighters

**Sam Donaldson,** ABC News correspondent

"I think the House was right to turn down aid the Contras." -- *This Week with David Brinkley*, February 7, 1987.

**Robert Bazell,** NBC News science reporter

"When I was asked to write my first piece for *The New Republic* three years ago, I was honored and proud to have some of my work appear in a journal with such a distinguished liberal tradition. When I read your editorial 'The Case for the Contras' (March 24), I was angry and ashamed that my piece on the space shuttle had appeared in the magazine." -- Letter to *The New Republic*, May 5, 1986.

**Lucy Spiegel,** CBS News producer/reporter

"Personally, I think the Contras are worthless." -- Quoted by David Brock, *American Spectator*, January 1987.

**Mort Rosenblum**, Associated Press Paris reporter and former *International Herald Tribune* Editor

"If we could warm up to the former Evil Empire, why were we obsessed with one of its distant clients? Suppose our Contras won. Would that be progress, installing a bickering junta of former Somocistas?" -- from his book, *Back Home: A Foreign Correspondent Rediscovers America*.

**Bill Moyers**, former CBS News commentator; frequent PBS contributor

"And in Nicaragua, the Contras used weapons from the 'enterprise' against civilians. It's a terrorist war they're fighting. Old men, women and children are caught in the middle or killed deliberately as the Contras use violence against peasants to pressure their government. Thousands have died. Even when the hearings were taking place in Washington this summer, a Contra raid in Nicaragua killed three children and a pregnant woman. As the casualties mounted, the secret government in Washington knew that the Contra leaders were not such noble freedom fighters after all." -- *The Secret Government, the Constitution in Crisis*, hosted by Bill Moyers on PBS, September 14, 1988.

**John Chancellor**, NBC News commentator

"The Duke of Wellington, one of England's greatest soldiers, once said, 'There is no such thing as a little war for a great nation.'...The Johnson administration became obsessed with Vietnam, the Kremlin became obsessed with Afghanistan and the Reagan Administration became obsessed with Nicaragua. That led to bad troubles for the Reagan Administration. Big countries have to pick their fights very carefully. Victory has to be certain in a fight with a small enemy; if not, things can get out of hand. The Duke of Wellington knew that. It's a pity the White House didn't remember what he said when it got involved with Nicaragua." -- *NBC Nightly News* commentary, January 15, 1986.

**John Dancy**, NBC reporter

"But Ortega, an irritant to Carter, became an obsession to Reagan, who saw him as an instrument of Moscow. The Contra rebels were the blunt instrument in Ronald Reagan's attack on Daniel Ortega. Reagan's dogged support for the Contras forever marked and ultimately scarred his foreign policy....Many of the Contras were former members of the Nicaraguan National Guard, Somoza's enforcers. They were brutal, often inept...It has been one of the longest and most traumatic chapters in U.S. history in Latin America, and tonight it seems to be ending, and ending in a way Ronald Reagan never could have imagined." -- *NBC Nightly News*, February 26, 1990.

## El Salvador

**J.F.O. McAllister**, *Time* Washington correspondent

"A grisly fantasy of a different sort may soon be conjured up out of the frustration by ultra-rightists in the Salvadoran army and government who are considering a campaign of terror to suppress the insurgents...Already the government is betraying distressingly fascist leanings...The future for El Salvador looks to be a free-for-all between a buoyant and rearmed F.M.L.N. and generals willing to make the country a boneyard." -- *Time*, December 11, 1989.

## Oliver North

**Martin Schram**, former *Washington Post* reporter

"Whether it's in the White House, or it's in Central Park, the American people don't want to tolerate wilding, and that's what those guys did. They mugged the U.S. Constitution...Ollie North...should serve time." -- CNN's *Capital Gang*, May 6, 1989.

**Lewis Lapham**, *Harper's* magazine Editor

"Oliver North presented himself as the immortal boy in the heroic green uniform of Peter Pan. Although wishing to be seen as a humble patriot, the colonel's testimony showed him to be a treacherous and lying agent of the national security state, willing to do anything asked of him by a President to whom he granted the powers of an Oriental despot." -- Lapham narrating his PBS series *America's Century*, November 28, 1989.

## Strategic Defense Initiative

**John Chancellor**, NBC *Nightly News* commentator and former anchor

"The administration says Star Wars is needed as an insurance policy against Soviet cheating. But even if the Star Wars shield works, there's doubt about that, it's more that ten years in the future. What was being discussed here was a practical and concrete plan to end the threat of intercontinental nuclear war. The American negotiators said that, but it all fell apart because of Mr. Reagan's insistence on a theory -- the Star Wars shield, a theory that many scientists say is impractical and irresponsible. What I'll remember most about Reykjavik are the faces of some of the American negotiators last night, men who had come so close to a dream of peace, only to see it slip away." -- *NBC Nightly News*, October 13, 1986.

**Ted Koppel**, ABC *Nightline* anchor

"I think that what is being proposed for expenditures on Star Wars, for example, is absolute nonsense." -- Appearance on *Donahue*, October 30, 1987.

## Fidel Castro

**Kathleen Sullivan**, former CBS *This Morning* co-host

"Now half of the Cuban population is under the age of 25, mostly Spanish speaking, and all have benefited from Castro's Cuba, where their health and their education are priorities." -- *CBS This Morning*, December 9, 1988.

**Peter Jennings**, ABC *World News Tonight* anchor

"Medical care was once for the privileged few. Today it is available to every Cuban and it is free. Some of Cuba's health care is world class. In heart disease, for example, in brain surgery. Health and education are the revolution's great success stories." -- *World News Tonight*, April 3, 1989.

## Soviet Union and Eastern Europe

### *Ted Turner*, founder of CNN

"I absolutely trust them [Soviet leaders] with my life. They're not even an enemy anymore." -- *Washington Post*, April 13, 1989.

"Gorbachev has probably moved more quickly than any person in the history of the world. Moving faster than Jesus Christ did. America is always lagging six months behind...I think we can get by easily with a $75 billion military budget. Those bombers and all of this stuff is an absolute waste of money and a joke." -- *Time*, January 22, 1990.

### *Carl Bernstein*, *Time* New York correspondent

"They love their country. The German Democratic Republic, not the Federal Republic of the West. They believe in socialism. Not the socialism of their disgraced and discredited leaders but the socialism they have been taught as an ideal for 40 years. Now the attainment of that socialism may be possible, they said. The tyrants are gone....We in the U.S. are tempted to see the triumph of democracy in Eastern Europe wholly through an American prism: as a triumph of American values as opposed to human values." -- *Time*, January 22, 1990.

### *Strobe Talbott*, *Time* Editor-at-Large

"Gorbachev is helping the West by showing that the Soviet threat isn't what it used to be -- and what's more, that it never was." -- *Time*, January 1, 1990.

**Andy Rooney,** *60 Minutes* commentator

"Communism got to be a terrible word here in the United States, but our attitude toward it may have been unfair. Communism got in with a bad crowd when it was young and never had a fair chance...

"The Communist ideas of creating a society in which everyone does his best for the good of everyone is appealing and fundamentally a more uplifting idea than capitalism. Communism's only real weakness seems to be that it doesn't work." -- *New York Times* op-ed article, June 26, 1989.

# Presidential Preference

## Jesse Jackson

**Jane Pauley**, *Today* co-host

"I'm a Jesse fan." -- *USA Today*, July 21, 1988.

**Eleanor Clift**, *Newsweek* Washington correspondent

"Jackson is speaking to blue-collar voters for Wallace, who voted for Reagan. Jackson is right on South Africa, Jackson is right on Central America." -- *The McLaughlin Group*, weekend of April 9, 1988.

**Judy Muller**, CBS Radio reporter

"When Geraldine Ferraro became the Democratic candidate for Vice President, I stood on the convention floor and fought back tears. Forget objectivity; the moment transcended politics. As I followed the Jesse Jackson campaign in Philadelphia yesterday, I fell on the same phenomenon: a transcendent pride in this person's breakthrough. You could see it on the faces of people on Locust Street...you could hear it in the voice of the gospel singer at a Jackson rally." -- CBS Radio, "Correspondent's Notebook," April 26, 1988.

**Walter Cronkite**, former *CBS Evening News* anchor

"Jesse Jackson succeeded in conducting a brilliant presidential campaign in which he enlisted white support as well as black support...and conducted a mainstream campaign." -- Democratic National Convention, July 20, 1988.

**Eric Sevareid**, former CBS News correspondent

"He [Jackson] has become here, a kind of new, he's acquired a new status. He's almost like Hubert Humphrey was, a sort of conscience of the country." -- Democratic Convention, July 20, 1988.

## Michael Dukakis

**Walter Shapiro**, *Time* Senior Writer

"Dukakis offers more of a risk and potentially more of a reward. His selection would mark a return to more communal values, as the nation gave liberalism another chance to adapt to a changed environment and redeem its faith in activist government." -- *Time*, November 7, 1988.

**Chris Black**, *Boston Globe* reporter

"'I have a favorable view of him [Michael Dukakis],' political reporter Chris Black says, 'My outlook and ideology can't be divorced from my copy, but as a reporter I try to be dispassionate.' She says she occasionally drops an 'adjective or phrase' so her stories won't appear too favorable to Mr. Dukakis. Ms. Black expects the governor will win in November. 'I would love to come to Washington,' she says." -- *Wall Street Journal* article, quoted in *Washington Journalism Review*, July/August 1988.

**Scott Lehigh**, *Boston Globe* reporter

"I'd much rather have Dukakis than Bush as President today." -- *Bostonia* magazine, July/August 1989.

**Richard Harwood**, *Washington Post* Ombudsman

"The huge newsroom staff, thought (by me) to be viscerally Democratic and L------ in its sympathies, lurks in the wings as a sort of silent, nonvoting regiment of Jiminy Crickets, peering, in a metaphorical sense, over the shoulders of the editorial custodians of the newspaper's 'soul.' They would, if given a vote, go like a shot, I suspect, for Dukakis." -- Referring to *Washington Post* staff, October 30, 1988.

**Robert Scheer**, *Los Angeles Times* reporter

"Dukakis is a centrist." -- *The McLaughlin Group*, weekend of June 11, 1988.

## George Bush

**Garry Wills**, *Time* writer

"Bush won by default, and by fouls. His 'mandate' is to ignore the threats to our economy, sustain the Reagan heritage of let's pretend, and serve as figurehead for what America has become, a frightened empire hiding its problems from itself." -- *Time*, November 21, 1988.

**Eleanor Clift**, *Newsweek* reporter

"This is about racism, and it's not particularly about Boston. We were all had in this country because we all buy the racial stereotypes, and George Bush gave the green light with the Willie Horton campaign." -- *McLaughlin Group*, January 14, 1990.

**Dick Thompson**, *Time* Washington correspondent

"Several signals, including Bush's slow response to the Alaska oil spill and his refusal even to consider an increase in the gasoline tax have raised concern that he is not the kind of forceful, decisive leader the country needs to deal with the growing environmental crisis." -- *Time*, May 22, 1989.

## *Time* magazine:

"Though heir to an Administration that had been myopic about the sensitivities of minorities, Darwinian about the plight of the poor and shockingly permissive about the ethics of its members, Bush tactfully made clear his own sterner standards...Bush put his hand to his chest, managing to convey the patrician's distaste for the grimy standards he had lived with, though uncomplainingly, since 1981." -- *Time* book, *The Winning of the White House 1988*.

## President Carter

**Lesley Stahl**, CBS News White House correspondent

"I covered President Carter as well as Reagan. And President Carter, on the issues, on the women's issues, was right. He was for equal rights and got all the issues right." -- Appearance on *Donahue*, August 1986.

**Margaret Carlson**, *Time* Senior Writer

"Perhaps the Democrat who best personifies this republic of virtue is former President Jimmy Carter. His reputation burnished by the elevated tone of his retirement, Carter would actually bring to the task energy, integrity and his legendary distaste for congressional business as usual. He could even boast a made-to-order campaign slogan: 'After the Wright stuff, why not the best?'" -- *Time*, June 5, 1989.

**Sam Donaldson**, former ABC News White House correspondent

"Historians, however, will concentrate on the record, dispassionately, and history, I am sure, will treat Carter better than the voters did in 1980. His record, particularly on foreign affairs, is quite good...Carter completed the SALT II arms control treaty with the Soviets...Contrary to Reagan's opinion, I think it was a step forward in imposing limits on the arms race." -- from his book, *Hold On, Mr. President*.

What do media stars think of Ronald Reagan? Not much. Chapter Eight, Study 4 contains a list of such quotes.

**CHAPTER THREE, STUDY 2**

# "Reporters Write Left, Not Right"

## OVERVIEW

Reporters, producers, and editors for major media outlets often come up with ideas for articles that their superiors reject. On other occasions they merely want to write about a subject outside their normal beat. Either way, reporters frequently find an outlet for their writing in political opinion magazines.

Discovering where these articles appear is another useful way of learning with which ideological view the members of the media are more comfortable. A liberal would want his or her story to appear in a liberal, rather than in a conservative magazine, and vice versa. More to the point, ideological magazines only run pieces that conform to, or at least do not contradict, their political perspective. To determine whether reporters' pieces appeared more often in conservative or liberal magazines, Media Research Center analysts looked at three-and-a-half years of magazine articles, from January 1986 to the end of June 1989.

## KEY FINDINGS

- News reporters for major newspapers and magazines overwhelmingly preferred contributing to liberal opinion journals, writing 15 times as many articles for liberal magazines as for conservative opinion journals.

- Of the 315 articles written by reporters in liberal publications, 73 appeared in the three best-known far-left magazines: *Mother Jones*, *The Progressive* and *The Nation*. The most frequently read conservative journals, *National Review*, *American Spectator*, and *Human Events*, carried only 14 pieces.

- All eight liberal magazines surveyed ran stories by reporters, but three conservative magazines had no articles at all by non-opinion journalists.

## STUDY EXCERPT

**Reporters Write Left, Not Right** by the Media Research Center. From *Media-Watch*, September 1989.

Faced with the mid-1989 resignation of Michael Kinsley as Editor of *The New Republic*, Publisher Martin Peretz considered replacing him with *Newsweek*'s Washington Bureau Chief, Evan Thomas. He could have been thinking of returning a favor: a few years before, *Newsweek* needed a Washington Bureau Chief and hired Morton Kondracke from *The New Republic*. When *Mother Jones* needed an Editor in 1987, it hired Douglas Foster, who developed stories for *60 Minutes* under the aegis of the left-wing Center for Investigative Reporting. *The Progressive* has former CBS reporter and current National Public Radio (NPR) commentator Daniel Schorr sitting on its editorial advisory board. When *The New Republic* was looking for a regular columnist on "Science and Society," it settled on NBC's Robert Bazell.

With this kind of networking in effect between the mainstream media and liberal opinion magazines, does it follow that more freelance articles by major journalists get published in liberal rather than conservative opinion magazines?

To ascertain the freelance record, *MediaWatch* analysts looked at three-and-a-half years of magazine articles, from January 1986 to the end of June 1989. On the liberal side, we examined *The New Republic, The Nation, The Progressive, Ms., Mother Jones, Dissent, Foreign Policy*, and *The Washington Monthly*. On the conservative side, we looked for articles in *National Review, The American Spectator, Commentary, Chronicles, Policy Review, The National Interest, The Public Interest*, and *Human Events*. We counted only "objective" journalists -- reporters, editors, producers, and news executives committed to the traditional journalistic expectations of accuracy and balance.

The *MediaWatch* study determined that news reporters overwhelmingly prefer contributing to liberal opinion journals, writing 315 articles in 42 months, compared to 22 in conservative ones. In other words, reporters wrote 14 times as many articles for liberal magazines as they did for conservative ones.

The subjects of study were from the major television/radio networks

(ABC, CBS, CNN, NBC, PBS and National Public Radio); news magazines (*Time, Newsweek, and U.S. News & World Report*); major papers (*The Washington Post, New York Times, Wall Street Journal*, and the *Los Angeles Times*); and any other major paper in which two or more articles by its reporters appeared (the Baltimore *Sun, Boston Globe, Chicago Sun-Times* and *Tribune, Miami Herald, New York Post*, and *Newsday*).

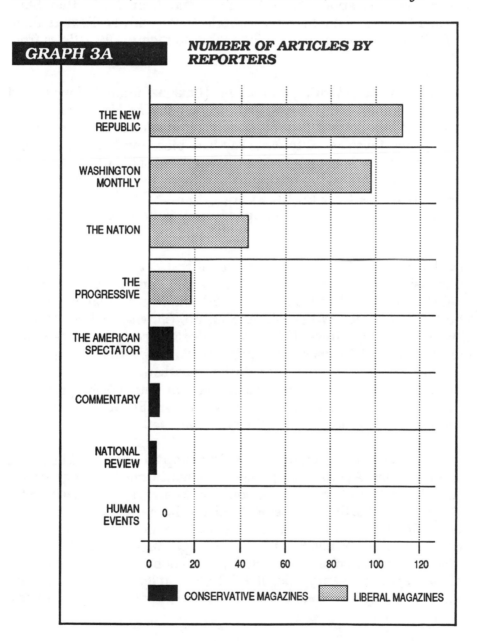

GRAPH 3A

NUMBER OF ARTICLES BY REPORTERS

CONSERVATIVE MAGAZINES          LIBERAL MAGAZINES

The favorite freelancing outlet for reporters is *The New Republic*, which carried 112 articles by major reporters, producers, or executives during the study period. *Newsweek* writers led the pack with 32 articles, paced by Washington reporter Timothy Noah's 13 contributions. All three networks were represented, with articles by CBS News Executive Political Editor Martin Plissner and producer Richard Cohen, ABC News White House correspondent Brit Hume, and from NBC, then-State Department Correspondent Anne Garrels (now with NPR) and then-Chief Political Correspondent Ken Bode, not to mention 19 articles from Bazell.

Bazell hasn't been writing for the liberal magazine solely for fun and profit, but because of his liberal politics. When *The New Republic* endorsed aid to the Contras in 1986, Bazell wrote a letter to the editor in protest: "When I was asked to write my first piece for *The New Republic* three years ago, I was honored and proud to have some of my work appear in a journal with such a distinguished liberal tradition. When I read your editorial, 'The Case for the Contras' (March 24), I was angry and ashamed that my piece on the space shuttle had appeared in the magazine."

*The Washington Monthly*, edited by neoliberal Charles Peters, is also a popular haven for reporter freelancing, with 98 articles by "objective" journalists. The board of Contributing Editors is a regular roll call of reporters: *Time* Senior Writer Walter Shapiro, *Christian Science Monitor* staff writer Jonathan Rowe, *U.S. News & World Report* Associate Editor Arthur Levine and Chicago correspondent Paul Glastris, and a whole contingent from *Newsweek*: Senior Writer Jonathan Alter, Contributing Editors Gregg Easterbrook and Joseph Nocera, and Washington Correspondents Timothy Noah and Steven Waldman. Between them, these reporters wrote 82 articles for the liberal magazine.

But the freelancing temptation didn't stop at safe establishment liberal magazines. Another 73 articles appeared in the three biggest far-left periodicals. CNN Senior Correspondent Stuart Loory has written for *The Progressive*. Shortly after being fired by the network in 1988, CBS Producer Richard Cohen wrote one of the 11 articles in *Mother Jones*. Contributors to *The Nation* included a CNN producer (Linda Hunt), an ABC News production associate (Richard Greenberg), a *MacNeil/Lehrer NewsHour* reporter (Nancy Nichols), NPR's Foreign Editor (John Dinges), and *Newsday*'s National Security Correspondent (Roy Gutman).

Four current *Washington Post* reporters (Marc Fisher, Douglas Farah, Walt Harrington, and Steven Mufson) have been published in *Mother Jones*.

*Dissent*, which describes itself as "a critical magazine for the concerned, inquisitive reader who views the world from the democratic left, the democratic socialist position," published eight articles by reporters, four from *Washington Post* political correspondent Thomas B. Edsall and two pieces by Charles Lane, *Newsweek* El Salvador Bureau Chief. *Ms.* ran 16 stories.

Conservative opinion magazines, on the other hand, rarely contain articles from reporters or executives. Of the 22 articles that appeared from 1986 through mid-1989, *The American Spectator* led with 11, with three articles each from ABC's Brit Hume, ABC Radio reporter Robert Kaplan, and John Podhoretz, a contributing editor at *U.S. News & World Report* (now a *Washington Times* Assistant Managing Editor). *Time* Senior Editor George Russell wrote five articles or book reviews for *Commentary*. *National Review* ran only three articles, from a *Los Angeles Times* news editor (Robert Knight), a former *Time* military correspondent (David Halevy), and a former President of CBS News (Fred Friendly). Two articles appeared in *The Public Interest* and one in *The National Interest*. In three-and-a-half years, not one news reporter for a major media outlet wrote anything for *Human Events*, *Chronicles* or *Policy Review*.

Journalists should certainly be allowed to escape the constraints of objective news reporting and write for the opinion magazines they enjoy. But this overwhelming preference for liberal journals, this "freelance gap," offers quite a telling insight into the personal biases that color the news.

## CHAPTER THREE, STUDY 3

# *"Media Money Moves Left"*

### OVERVIEW

Most people assume that corporations support conservative policies for their own economic interest. If that were true, it would be safe to assume that the corporations that control media outlets further conservative policies. A look at media company donation patterns by the Media Research Center showed just how wrong that assumption really is. Major newspapers, magazines, and television networks give to many charities, educational groups and organizations with a political agenda. This study found that money for these political cause groups went predominantly and substantially to liberal political operations through a number of philanthropic arrangements, from private and company foundations to informal and unpublicized corporate contribution programs.

### KEY FINDINGS

- Of nearly four million dollars contributed to political organizations, the foundations for ten of the biggest media empires allocated 90 percent to liberal organizations and only 10 percent to conservative ones.

- The New York Times Company Foundation gave over 96 percent of the money allotted for political purposes to liberal organizations, just under 4 percent to conservative ones.

- The Times Mirror Foundation and Capital Cities Foundation donated over 93 percent of its political money to liberal groups.

- The foundation of Gannett, publisher of *USA Today*, allocated 98 percent of its political donations to liberal groups, including Prostitutes and Other Women for Equal Rights (POWER).

- The Knight Foundation and the Boston Globe Foundation did not give any money to conservative organizations.

• No pro-life womens group received any contributions, but virtually every major media company gave to the National Organization for Women Legal Defense and Educational Fund.

## STUDY EXCERPT

**Media Money Moves Left** by the Media Research Center. From *Media-Watch*, May 1989 and March 1990.

To discover the media's trends in political philanthropy, *MediaWatch* examined annual reports and publicly available foundation records at the Foundation Center in Washington, D.C. The records show a recurring attachment to liberal groups, including many which often serve as authoritative news sources. This symbiotic relationship -- media funds source, media quotes source -- raises serious questions about media impartiality. The National Organization for Women Legal Defense and Education Fund (N.O.W. L.D.E.F.), for example, enjoys the financial support of many major media companies. Its 1986 annual report listed these contributors: Capital Cities/ABC Inc., CBS Inc., Columbia/Embassy Television, ESPN Inc., Fox Television, Gannett Company Inc., Hearst Corporation, Lorimar Productions, NBC, the New York Times Company, *USA Weekend*, and the Washington Post Company.

**TIMES MIRROR FOUNDATION:** The Times Mirror Company owns the *Los Angeles Times*, *Newsday*, and the Baltimore *Sun*. Every year

---

### TABLE 3B — *TIMES MIRROR FOUNDATION* (1982-86)

**Liberal: $608,500 (93.5%)**

| | | | |
|---|---|---|---|
| $ 1,000 | ACLU Foundation | $ 90,000 | National Audubon Society |
| $55,500 | Brookings Institution | $ 6,000 | National Urban League |
| $ 2,500 | Center for National Policy | $ 50,000 | Planned Parenthood |
| $ 5,000 | Committee for a Responsible Federal Budget | $115,000 | Urban Institute |
| | | $ 1,500 | United Nations Association |
| $10,000 | NAACP | $105,000 | Urban League—Los Angeles |
| $10,000 | NAACP Legal Defense and Education Fund | $157,000 | World Wildlife Fund |

**Conservative: $32,500 (6.5%)**
American Enterprise Institute

from 1982 to 1986, Times Mirror gave $10,000 to Planned Parenthood. While it contributed $32,500 to the moderate-conservative American Enterprise Institute, it supplied Brookings and the Urban Institute with at least $170,000, not to mention a few thousand for the Democrat-connected Center for National Policy headed by Edmund Muskie. [See Table 3B]

**NEW YORK TIMES COMPANY FOUNDATION:** The *New York Times'* foundation gave to the largest number of liberal groups. Annual reports from 1982 to 1986 reveal such grants as $5,000 to the far-left magazine *The Nation* for a publishing internship. The *Times* has been a consistent supporter of environmental groups, from the National

---

**TABLE 3C**        **NEW YORK TIMES COMPANY FOUNDATION** (1982-86)

**Liberal: $436,000 (96.5%)**

| | |
|---|---|
| $ 10,000 American Friends Service Committee | $ 5,000 National Commission on U.S.-China Relations |
| $ 19,000 Aspen Institute for Humanistic Studies | $ 20,000 National Public Radio |
| $ 29,000 Brookings Institution | $ 20,000 National Urban League |
| $ 10,000 Children's Defense Fund | $ 6,000 National Wildlife Federation |
| $ 9,000 Conservation Foundation | $ 5,000 The Nation Institute |
| $ 20,000 Council on Foreign Relations | $ 11,500 Natural Resources Defense Council |
| $ 25,000 Environmental Action Coalition | $ 19,000 NOW Legal Defense and Education Fund |
| $ 21,000 Environmental Defense Fund | $ 24,500 Planned Parenthood |
| $ 15,000 Environmental Law Institute | $ 12,000 Population Resource Center |
| $ 15,000 Feminist Press, Inc. | $ 10,000 Sierra Club |
| $ 28,000 Foreign Policy Association | $ 5,000 Urban Institute |
| $ 3,000 Government Accountability Project | $ 24,000 Wilderness Society |
| $ 3,000 King Center for Nonviolent Social Change | $ 5,000 World Resources Institute |
| $ 45,000 NAACP | $ 4,000 World Wildlife Fund |
| $ 5,000 NAACP Legal Defense and Education Fund | |
| $ 8,000 National Audubon Society | |

**Conservative: $16,000 (3.5%)**

$ 6,000 American Enterprise Institute
$ 10,000 Media Institute

Wildlife Federation (creator of "stimulating educational packages" for schools like "Welcome to the USSR"), to the World Resources Institute (which opposes "cramming nuclear power down the throats of an unwilling public and unwilling investors"). Foundation President Fred Hechinger told *MediaWatch* that "our decision to make grants is guided entirely by indications of the usefulness and effectiveness of the applicants and not by ideological considerations." [See Table 3C]

**PHILIP L. GRAHAM FUND:** This foundation of the *Washington Post-Newsweek* empire gives mostly to local charities, but in its 1983-1987 annual reports, its grants to political groups were substantial. It gave $20,000 to the Lawyers Committee for Civil Rights Under Law in 1987, the same year the group fought to reject Robert Bork's nomination to the Supreme Court. Its annual report called that "the most heartening event for the civil rights community last year." [See Table 3D]

**GENERAL ELECTRIC FOUNDATION:** NBC's parent company foundation is the least one-sided, contributing more than a fourth of its money to conservative groups. The list below comes from its 1986 annual report. In response to a request by *MediaWatch* for further information, GE Foundation President Paul Ostergard responded by pointing out that in 1988 GE gave $15,000 to both the conservative Heritage Foundation and Hudson Institute. [See Table 3E]

**CAPITAL CITIES FOUNDATION:** Capital Cities owns ABC and a chain of newspapers that includes the *Kansas City Star* and *Times.* Among

---

**TABLE 3D**

**PHILIP L. GRAHAM FUND** (1982-87)

**Liberal: $170,000 (94.4%)**

$ 15,000  Central American Refugee Center
$ 25,000  Council on Foreign Relations
$ 75,000  Kennan Institute for Advanced Russian Studies
$ 20,000  Lawyers Committee for Civil Rights Under Law
$  5,000  NAACP
$ 30,000  Women's Legal Defense Fund

**Conservative: $10,000 (5.6%)**
American Enterprise Institute

1986 recipients: the Gloria Steinem-founded Women's Action Alliance and the NOW Legal Defense and Education Fund which works to educate "media decision-makers about the complex equality issues that comprise the women's rights agenda," including "reproductive freedom" and "affirmative action." [Table 3F]

**GANNETT FOUNDATION:** The company foundation of the publishers of *USA Today* and more than 85 other daily newspapers (including the *Des Moines Register, Detroit News,* and *Louisville Courier-Journal*), the Gannett Foundation followed a predictable path in the years 1982-89, donating heavily to minority activists who lobbied for liberal policies like affirmative action and increased welfare spending. [See Table 3G] Do the readers of Gannett's family newspapers know their subscription dollars supported the Canadian group Prostitutes and Other Women for Equal Rights?

**KNIGHT FOUNDATION:** Endowed in 1950 by profits from the Knight-Ridder chain (which currently includes the *Miami Herald, Seattle Times,* and *Philadelphia Inquirer*), the Knight Foundation declined to fund conservative groups from 1982-89. [See Table 3H] In a letter to *Media-*

| TABLE 3E | GENERAL ELECTRIC FOUNDATION (1986) | |
|---|---|---|

**Liberal: $321,000 (72.4%)**

| | | | |
|---|---|---|---|
| $40,000 | Brookings Institution | $10,000 | National Urban Coalition |
| $10,000 | Center for National Policy | $50,000 | National Urban League |
| $25,000 | Conservation Foundation | $30,000 | Urban Institute |
| $25,000 | Council on Foreign Relations | | |
| $20,000 | Environmental Law Institute | **Conservative: $122,500 (27.6%)** | |
| $10,000 | Foreign Policy Association | $10,000 | American Council for Capital Formation |
| $34,000 | Institute for International Economics | $ 5,000 | American Council on Science and Health |
| $ 5,000 | Joint Center for Political Studies | $80,000 | American Enterprise Institute |
| $35,000 | NAACP | $10,000 | Institute for Contemporary Studies |
| $ 2,000 | NAACP Legal Defense and Education Fund | $ 7,500 | Institute for Research on the Economics of Taxation |
| $25,000 | National Audubon Society | $10,000 | Manhattan Institute |

*Watch,* Foundation President Creed C. Black insisted the foundation "is wholly separate from and independent of Knight-Ridder, Inc." Technically yes, but Knight-Ridder Chairman Alvah Chapman and CEO James K. Batten both serve on its board of trustees, and the foundation tries to make grants only in cities where Knight-Ridder newspapers are published. Black also said "we make no grants in support of any candidates or partisan organizations." Again, for tax purposes, he is technically correct; but tax-exempt lobbies like the Urban League and Planned Parenthood were heavy hitters in the fight against the Supreme Court nomination of Judge Robert Bork.

**HEARST FOUNDATIONS:** Also endowed by the personal profits of newspaper chain chieftains, the Hearst Foundation and the William Randolph Hearst Foundation grant lists strike more of a balance. [See Table 3I] Although Hearst has sold some of its major newspapers, its diversified holdings (*Cosmopolitan,* King Features Syndicate, Boston ABC affiliate WCVB-TV) insure substantial influence. Like the other foundations, the Hearst Foundations took a liking to minority advocacy groups active in the fight against Bork, but they also funded conservative think tanks like the Hoover Institution, and corrected some of their funding of the judicial left by supporting newly formed conservative legal foundations in the years 1982-89.

**BOSTON GLOBE FOUNDATION:** While it's heavily involved in local charitable and arts programs, when the *Globe*'s foundation gave to political groups from 1982-88, it gave decisively to the Left. [See Table 3J]

---

**TABLE 3F**          **CAPITAL CITIES FOUNDATION** (1986)

*Liberal: $43,500 (97.8%)*

| | |
|---|---|
| $15,000 | NAACP |
| $ 1,500 | National Council of Negro Women |
| $ 3,500 | National Urban Coalition |
| $15,000 | National Urban League |
| $ 5,000 | NOW Legal Defense Fund |
| $ 2,500 | United Nations Association |
| $ 1,000 | Women's Action Alliance |

*Conservative: $1,000 (2.2%)*

Manhattan Institute

## TABLE 3G    GANNETT FOUNDATION (1982-89)

**Liberal: $903,718 (98.0%)**

| | |
|---|---|
| $ 6,000 | Center for Law and Social Policy |
| $ 7,300 | Central American Refugee Center |
| $ 5,000 | Delaware Lesbian and Gay Health Advocates |
| $ 6,000 | International Institute for Environment and Development |
| $ 15,000 | King Center for Non-violent Social Change |
| $ 25,600 | LULAC |
| $ 5,000 | Mexican American Legal Defense and Education Fund |
| $200,000 | National AIDS Network |
| $ 16,000 | National Council of LaRaza |
| $ 5,000 | National Council of Negro Women |
| $ 7,500 | National Puerto Rican Foundation |
| $ 15,000 | National Women's Political Caucus |
| $ 45,000 | NAACP |
| $ 10,500 | NAACP Legal Defense and Education Fund |
| $325,000 | Planned Parenthood |
| $ 6,000 | Project on Military Procurement |
| $ 7,618 | Prostitutes and Other Women for Equal Rights |
| $ 12,500 | Puerto Rican Legal Defense and Education Fund |
| $ 5,000 | Southwest Voter Registration and Education Project |
| $117,200 | Urban League |
| $ 55,000 | Urban Institute |
| $ 5,000 | Wilderness Society |
| $ 1,500 | Women's Equity Action League |

**Conservative: $18,500 (2.0%)**

| | |
|---|---|
| $ 8,500 | Manhattan Institute |
| $ 5,000 | Media Institute |
| $ 5,000 | Rockford Institute |

## TABLE 3H    KNIGHT FOUNDATION (1982-89)

**Liberal: $394,000 (100%)**

| | |
|---|---|
| $ 50,000 | Center for Environmental Education |
| $ 10,000 | Izaak Walton League |
| $ 5,000 | NAACP |
| $ 65,000 | Planned Parenthood |
| $ 15,000 | Urban Coalition |
| $249,000 | Urban League |

**Conservative: None**

Globe grant recipients included the Natural Resources Defense Council (NRDC), the group behind the Alar apple scare, and the Grey Panthers, the senior citizen champions of left-wing causes. For grants targeted toward "public policy/advocacy," the Globe gave to the Children's Defense Fund (CDF), which advocated the diversion of defense spending to social programs long before talk of a "peace dividend." Its 1988 *Children's Defense Budget* reported that on CDF positions, Ted Kennedy scored a 90.

**CHICAGO TRIBUNE FOUNDATION:** Although it's involved in community affairs like the Globe Foundation, the Tribune Foundation also contributed to liberal groups like the Brookings Institution, which has received at least $149,500 from media foundations. In looking at its 1985 and 1986 giving, they also funded the National Committee for Responsive Philanthropy, which has fought successfully to increase funding of the Left through the federal government and corporate giving programs. [See Table 3K]

| TABLE 3I | *HEARST FOUNDATIONS* (1982-89) | |
|---|---|---|
| **_Liberal: $541,400 (72.6%)_** | $15,000 | Women's Action Alliance |
| $10,000 Audubon Society | $25,000 | Women's Legal Defense Fund |
| $10,000 Brookings Institute | | |
| $ 5,000 Child Care Action Now | | |
| $15,000 Children's Defense Fund | **_Conservative: $205,000 (27.4%)_** | |
| $10,000 Coalition for the Homeless | | |
| $15,000 Educators for Social Responsibility | $10,000 | American Enterprise Institute |
| $15,000 Foreign Policy Association | $70,000 | Hoover Institute |
| $20,000 Mexican American Legal Defense and Education Fund | $40,000 | Institute for Contemporary Studies |
| $15,000 National Council of LaRaza | $10,000 | Institute for Educational Affairs |
| $75,000 National Puerto Rican Coalition | $ 5,000 | National Legal Center for the Public Interest |
| $70,000 NAACP | | |
| $91,400 NAACP Legal Defense and Education Fund | $20,000 | Mid-American Legal Foundation |
| $85,000 National Urban Coalition | $ 5,000 | Pacific Institute for Public Policy Research |
| $25,000 Native American Rights Fund | | |
| $40,000 Urban League | $45,000 | Pacific Legal Foundation |

**TABLE 3J**          **BOSTON GLOBE FOUNDATION** (1982-88)

*Liberal: $110,350 (100%)*

| | |
|---|---|
| $ 3,000 | American Friends Service Committee |
| $ 3,000 | Children's Defense Fund |
| $ 1,500 | Grey Panthers |
| $ 3,000 | Lawyers Committee for Civil Rights Under Law |
| $15,000 | Massachusetts Audubon Society |
| $27,500 | NAACP |
| $17,500 | NAACP Legal Defense and Education Fund |
| $10,000 | National Public Radio |
| $ 1,500 | Natural Resources Defense Council |
| $26,000 | Oxfam America |
| $   350 | Physicians for Social Responsibility |
| $ 2,000 | Women's Equity Action League |

*Conservative: None*

**TABLE 3K**          **CHICAGO TRIBUNE FOUNDATION** (1985-86)

*Liberal: $29,125 (93.6%)*

| | |
|---|---|
| $ 5,000 | Brookings Institution |
| $ 4,500 | Council on Foreign Relations |
| $ 3,000 | National Committee for Responsive Philanthropy |
| $ 3,125 | Northeast-Midwest Institute |
| $13,500 | Urban League |

*Conservative: $2,000 (6.4%)*

| | |
|---|---|
| $ 2,000 | Media Institute |

**CHAPTER THREE, STUDY 4**

## "Reporting Follows Media Money"

### OVERVIEW

The previous study (Chapter 3, Study 3) documented the pattern of financial support for liberal groups by the media's philanthropic foundations. Taking the research a step further, the Media Research Center set out to determine whether there was any correlation between the amount given to a particular group and the amount of coverage that group received.

### KEY FINDINGS

- In the two public policy areas most supported by the media foundations in 1987 and 1988, newspapers whose foundations donated money to a group also gave that group more coverage.

- The Environmental Defense Fund (EDF), for example, which received a donation from the New York Times Company Foundation, was mentioned 123 times in *The New York Times*, far more coverage than the EDF received from non-contributing media companies.

### STUDY EXCERPT

**Reporting Follows Media Money** by the Media Research Center. From *MediaWatch*, June 1989.

*MediaWatch* used the Nexis ® news data retrieval system to survey all news stories on selected political grantees from 1987 and 1988 in the *New York Times, Los Angeles Times*, and *Washington Post*. The foundations connected to them are, respectively, the New York Times Company Foundation, the Times Mirror Foundation, and the Philip L. Graham Fund.

*MediaWatch* selected two issue areas that received the most support from media foundations: environmental groups and judicial groups opposed to the nomination of Robert Bork to the Supreme Court. The study found that newspapers whose foundations donate money to a group also give that group more coverage.

**Environmental Groups:** A good example of the differences in coverage emerged in stories on the environment. The Environmental Defense Fund (EDF), a recipient of $21,000 from the New York Times Company Foundation, had 123 mentions in *The New York Times*. By comparison, non-contributing media companies covered EDF much less than: 70 mentions in the *Los Angeles Times*, and 46 in *The Washington Post*. The National Audubon Society, given $8,000 by the New York Times Company Foundation and $90,000 by Times Mirror, was a subject of 72 stories in *The New York Times* and 69 stories in the *Los Angeles Times*. The Philip L. Graham Fund gave no money, and *The Washington Post* mentioned it in only 27 stories. The World Wildlife Fund-Conservation Foundation, which took in $157,000 from Times Mirror and $13,000 from *The New York Times*, appeared in the *Los Angeles Times* on 66 occasions and

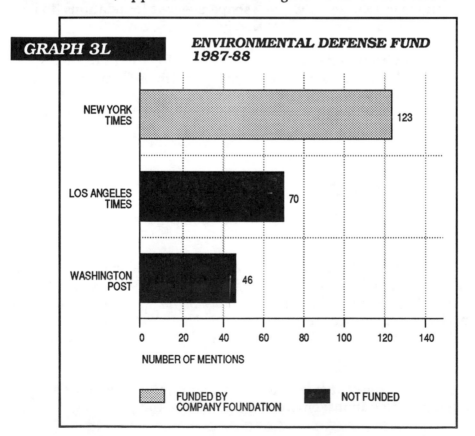

GRAPH 3L          ENVIRONMENTAL DEFENSE FUND
                  1987-88

NUMBER OF MENTIONS

FUNDED BY COMPANY FOUNDATION          NOT FUNDED

*The New York Times* on 61 occasions. The Graham Fund did not contribute, and the *Post* included them in only 27 articles.

**Bork Opponents:** A second area of marked difference in coverage was among judicial interest groups who opposed the nomination of Judge Robert Bork to the Supreme Court. The Lawyers Committee for Civil Rights Under Law, one of the most active anti-Bork lobbies, took in $20,000 from the Philip L. Graham Fund in 1987 and $4,000 from the New York Times Company Foundation over four years. Times Mirror did not provide any financial support. In 1987 and 1988, The Lawyers Committee was a subject in 50 *Washington Post* stories, 14 in *The New York Times*, but only 7 in the *Los Angeles Times*.

The Women's Legal Defense Fund (WLDF) was granted $30,000 by the Philip L. Graham Fund, and was mentioned in 25 stories in *The Washington Post*. Compare that to 16 mentions in *The New York Times*, and five in the *Los Angeles Times*, which refrained from giving. The Graham Fund has given to WLDF's domestic violence project in Washington and not ostensibly for their liberal judicial agenda, but when the D.C. police department decided to make arrests in domestic violence cases, the Post placed the story on the front page and referred to WLDF four times, using their statistics.

The Children's Defense Fund (CDF) received $2,000 from the Washington Post Company and $10,000 from the New York Times Company Foundation. CDF tallied 86 mentions in *The Washington Post* and 51 in *The New York Times*. The *Los Angeles Times*, which did not give, was last with 41.

The Feminist Press has received $15,000 from the New York Times Company Foundation, but nothing from Times Mirror or the Philip L. Graham Fund. In 1987 and 1988, the *Times* mentioned the Feminist Press in 15 book features, compared to two each in *The Washington Post* and *Los Angeles Times*. The *Post's* "Book World" gave two brief mentions to Feminist Press books in its "New In Paperbacks" section. The *Los Angeles Times* reviewed one book and mentioned another in passing. But *The New York Times* gave them an entire feature story, two mentions in their "New and Noteworthy" section, and nine full-fledged reviews of 12 Feminist Press books.

It's hard to imagine any direct orders from corporate management to reporters demanding more coverage for grant recipients, but the pattern that emerges reveals very interesting, if perhaps coincidental, correlations. A media company which feels that a group is impressive enough to deserve funding seems to feel it is impressive enough to deserve its publicity.

# 4 The Media & Labeling: A Double Standard?

Do the media apply ideological labels in a fair and balanced manner? Do reporters, for example, attach descriptive tags to conservative organizations, elected officials, and policy experts more often than to liberal ones? The answer is important because if reporters were without bias, they would be just as likely to label a liberal "liberal" as a conservative "conservative." Thus, the media's use of labels gives the reader or listener an insight into the political slant of a newsmaker, just as the absence of a label gives the perception of objectivity and reliability.

The studies collected for this chapter demonstrate that Big Media reporters think conservatives hold extreme views which should be identified as such. Liberals, on the other hand, are seen as belonging in the mainstream, and therefore do not require a label.

*CHAPTER FOUR, STUDY 1*

## Senator Ted Kennedy versus Senator Jesse Helms

### OVERVIEW

The National Conservative Foundation (NCF), using the Nexis ® news retrieval system, obtained every mention of Senator Jesse Helms (R-NC), a conservative, and Senator Edward Kennedy (D-MA), a liberal, that appeared during 1984 and 1985 in four print publications: *The Washington Post, New York Times, Newsweek* and *Time.* For a study published in the July, 1986 *Newswatch,* analysts tabulated all labels reporters attached to the two Senators. Labels attributed to someone else were not counted.

## KEY FINDINGS

- "Overall," NCF found "the four publications placed an ideological label on Helms in 34 percent of the news stories mentioning him," and on Kennedy 3.4 percent of the time.

- *Washington Post* news stories gave labels to Kennedy in just 4.1 percent of 650 articles. Helms, though, was labeled in 22 percent of 476 stories, more than five times as often. To label Helms "conservative" is accurate NCF argued; but the *Post* labeled Helms "arch-conservative" and "saber-rattling far right," terms that portrayed him as outside the American liberal to conservative political spectrum. "In contrast, the *Post* never attached 'arch-liberal' or any similar tag to Kennedy."

- "The same pattern held for *The New York Times*, which labeled Kennedy in only 2.3 percent of the articles, but Helms in 21.3 percent, nine times as often." In an even more creative flourish, the *Times* tagged Helms the "doyen of the New Right." The *Times* had no such provocative term for Kennedy.

- *Time* magazine labeled Helms nearly half the time (47 percent), but tagged Kennedy in barely one of twenty stories.

| TABLE 4A | IDEOLOGICAL LABELING | |
|---|---|---|
| | **HELMS** | **KENNEDY** |
| The Washington Post | 105/476=22% | 27/650=4.1% |
| The New York Times | 86/104=21% | 13/558=2.3% |
| Newsweek | 19/43=44% | 4/71=5.6% |
| Time | 17/36=47% | 2/58=3.5% |
| **Total** | **227/659=34%** | **46/1337=3.4%** |

**CHAPTER FOUR, STUDY 2**

## *"Looking for the Liberal Label"*

### OVERVIEW

American newspaper readers are bombarded daily with the opinions of "experts" from a variety of Washington-based organizations who comment on the latest news in their area of specialty. Since few have the time to sift through pounds of material to determine the political nature of these groups, readers have to rely on the descriptions and labels applied by reporters.

To learn whether reporters for some major newspapers and magazines accurately identify the political viewpoints of the "experts" they quote, the Media Research Center reviewed every 1987 and 1988 news story mentioning three prominent groups on the right and three others on the left. The study included *The Washington Post, New York Times, Los Angeles Times, Newsweek, Time,* and *U.S. News & World Report.* The results show an astonishing contrast in treatment.

### KEY FINDINGS

- Conservative groups were labeled an average of 58 percent of the time while liberals were identified a mere 2 percent of the time.

- Reporters labeled the conservative Heritage Foundation more than 35 times as often as the liberal Brookings Institution.

- The conservative Concerned Women for America got tagged almost twenty times more frequently than the liberal National Organization for Women.

- Judicial expert Ralph Neas, the liberal head of the Leadership Conference on Civil Rights, attracted less than one tenth of the labels attached to the conservative Patrick McGuigan of the Free Congress Foundation.

*Looking for the Liberal Label* by the Media Research Center. From *Media-Watch*, March 1989.

### Think Tanks: Brookings and Heritage

Perhaps the national media's favorite source of expert opinion, the Brookings Institution was labeled just 10 times in 737 news stories (1.4 percent). [See Graph 4B] Five of those labels came from 152 *Los Angeles Times* stories. *The Washington Post* applied a label merely 3 times in 200 stories (1.5 percent). In 270 of 271 mentions (99.6 percent), *The New York Times* failed to label Brookings. *Time* magazine applied a label once in 39 stories, while *U.S. News* (45) and *Newsweek* (30) never did.

By dramatic contrast, the Heritage Foundation was accurately described as "conservative" or by a similar term in 217 of 370 stories (58.6 percent). The *Los Angeles Times* attached a conservative label most often,

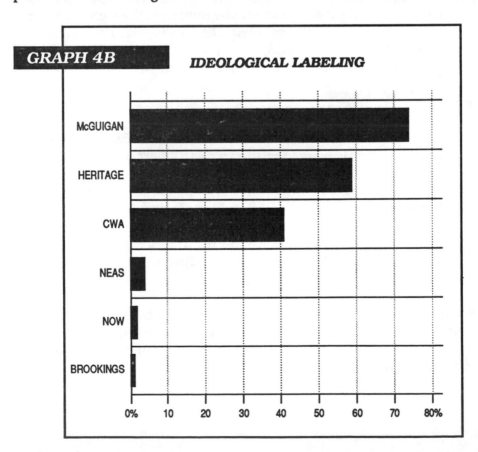

GRAPH 4B — IDEOLOGICAL LABELING

71 times in 79 stories (89.9 percent). *Time* was second with 13 labels in 19 stories (68.4 percent), followed by *The New York Times* (74 out of 126, or 58.7 percent), *U.S. News* (7 out of 14, or 50 percent), and the *Post* (51 out of 129, for 39.5 percent). *Newsweek* refrained from issuing a label in three mentions of the think tank, but did see fit to describe Heritage as an "ideological guerrilla outfit" which could advance "politically outlandish proposals." *Time* writers Richard Hornik and Michael Duffy best demonstrated the double standard in a December 5, 1988, story: "Neither Bush nor the nation will risk serious damage if he ignores the recommendations of groups ranging from the archconservative Heritage Foundation to the Brookings Institution."

### Women's Groups: National Organization for Women (NOW) and Concerned Women for America (CWA)
The liberal NOW also escaped categorization, labeled a mere 10 times in 421 stories (2.4 percent). The *Los Angeles Times* issued six labels in 166 stories, five "liberal" and one "mainstream." In 124 stories, *The New York Times* never once placed a liberal label on NOW. Out of 100 stories in the *Post*, two included the term "liberal." Among magazines, *Time* used no labels in 10 stories, while *Newsweek* and *U.S. News*, in 9 and 8 respectively, applied "liberal" once each.

On the other hand, the conservative CWA got labeled 25 times in 61 news accounts (41 percent). The *Los Angeles Times* issued the lion's share of labels, describing CWA as "conservative" five times, "right-wing" on four occasions, and "New Right" once. Of six labels in 16 *New York Times* stories, three were "conservative," two were "strongly conservative," and one was "New Right." In 17 *Post* stories, all eight labels were "conservative." Though NOW claims 160,000 members and CWA about 600,000, it's worth noting that reporters mentioned the liberal group nearly seven times more often.

### Judicial Experts: Patrick McGuigan and Ralph Neas
The battle over Robert Bork's nomination by President Reagan to fill a Supreme Court slot made McGuigan and Neas often-quoted sources, but reporters were far from balanced in adding ideological tags to each. Less than 4 percent of pieces referring to Neas, head of the Leadership Conference on Civil Rights (LCCR), described him as "liberal." McGuigan of the Free Congress Foundation, however, was identified as conservative nearly 75 percent of the time.

The New York Times in 39 stories and the Post in 50 reports never called Neas "liberal." In fact, both papers referred to him as "Republican" on one occasion. The Los Angeles Times identified Neas as "liberal" just once in 23 stories. U.S. News called Neas "liberal" once in five stories, Time labeled the LCCR "liberal" once in four stories, and Newsweek avoided any labels whatever in four pieces.

Yet, in 74 percent of 42 stories mentioning McGuigan, either he or the Free Congress Foundation were labeled conservative, 15 times more frequently than Neas or LCCR. The Los Angeles Times added a "conservative" label in all six mentions. U.S. News did the same, four times in four stories. The Post, which never saw a need to label Neas, labeled McGuigan 15 times in 19 stories. Newsweek's only mention of McGuigan referred to him as part of the "religious right."

This imbalance demonstrates that reporters are unwilling to issue ideological labels in an objective manner. If reporters call conservative groups "conservative," then it's only logical that they label liberal groups "liberal." Until they do, reporters will continue to distort the public's perception of sources quoted in "news" stories.

# "Networks Choose Pro-Choice"

## OVERVIEW

Since they believe life begins at conception, abortion foes consider themselves "pro-life" and describe their opponents as "pro-abortion." In contrast, Planned Parenthood's Faye Wattleton argues that the issue "is about who makes the choice." This, she says, explains why those favoring legal abortion want to be called "pro-choice," while labeling their antagonists "anti-abortion."

To reach the public, both sides of the abortion debate rely on the news media. Which side do the media favor? To find out, the Media Research Center reviewed all stories that discussed abortion aired on ABC's *World News Tonight*, the *CBS Evening News*, *CNN PrimeNews*, and *NBC Nightly News*. The study covered the last four months of 1988, a time when the presidential campaign and the Supreme Court's decision to hear a major abortion case prompted extensive media coverage of the issue.

The study proved the networks have stacked the decks against those who want to overturn the *Roe vs. Wade* decision. How? By consistently using the terms promoted by those favoring abortion: "pro-choice" and "anti-abortion."

By doing so, the media have implicitly agreed that the issue is one of "choice," not one of "life." The "anti-abortion" label is, according to Susan Smith of the National Right to Life Committee, "narrow and negative," and by employing it reporters similarly limit the entire "anti-abortion" cause.

## KEY FINDINGS

- The media adhered to the "pro-choice" forces' preferred label 97 percent of the time, whereas the "pro-life" forces received theirs only 21 percent of the time.

- With 87 mentions, the "anti-abortion" tag was used most often by reporters or anchors, with another five references to "abortion foes." The terms "pro-life" or "right to life" were applied on 24 times, less than one-third as often.

## STUDY EXCERPT

**Networks Choose Pro-Choice** by the Media Research Center. From *MediaWatch*, January 1989.

"Pro-choice groups said today that their battle is not over," *NBC Nightly News* anchor Tom Brokaw announced on November 10, 1988. Reporter Andrea Mitchell proceeded to detail the actions of "anti-abortion activists" and "abortion opponents" in election day referenda on public abortion funding. "Pro-choice activists," she said, were "very worried about Bush and Quayle." NBC's story, and its use of labels to describe the two sides in the abortion debate, typified network news coverage of the issue.

How did they label abortion supporters? The networks were far more sympathetic. Only once were those groups described as "pro-abortion." Instead, they were called by the term they prefer, "pro-choice," 19 times. Thirteen other times, they were given euphemistic labels such as "abortion rights advocates," "family planning advocates" or "birth control advocates." In other words, the "pro-choice" forces were designated by their preferred labels 97 percent of the time. The "pro-life" forces were afforded their desired label only 21 percent of the time. [See Graph 4C]

Some networks were less objective than others. For instance, NBC used the "anti-abortion" label 17 times, while using the "pro-life" label just once. When it came to abortion proponents, though, NBC reporters dubbed them "pro-choice" three times, "abortion rights" once, and "family planning advocates" twice. No one at NBC used the term "pro-abortion." CBS used "pro-life" labels most often -- 38 percent of the time -- but still gave a great advantage to abortion supporters, using positive, euphemistic terms to describe them 92 percent of the time.

Most abortion labels arose in three areas:

1. **Judicial Decisions**: On November 11, CBS' Rita Braver informed viewers that  a court ruling against federal abortion funding would please "anti-abortion" activists. Anchor Dan Rather characterized *Roe vs.*

*Wade* as the Supreme Court's 15-year-old ruling on "abortion rights." In a December 20 report by NBC's Jim Miklaszewski, Jack Fowler of the Ad Hoc Committee in Defense of Life was captioned as an "anti-abortion activist." But in Andrea Mitchell's November 10 report, pro-abortion spokeswoman Dottie Lamm was labeled simply as "wife of former Governor" Richard Lamm.

**2. Abortion Demonstrators:** When pro-lifers taunted Democratic presidential candidate Michael Dukakis on September 6, the networks presented the protestors as "anti-abortion activists." CNN's Tom Mintier called the demonstrators "pro-life," but only after a lead-in by anchor Bernard Shaw labeled them "anti-abortion" three times. That same night, NBC's Chris Wallace outlined the candidates' positions on abortion. Bush, he said, "opposes abortion," while Dukakis is "pro-choice."

The efforts of Operation Rescue protesters did not go unnoticed by

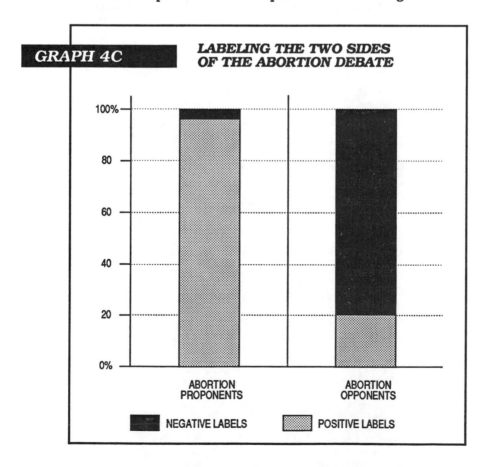

GRAPH 4C

**LABELING THE TWO SIDES OF THE ABORTION DEBATE**

NEGATIVE LABELS    POSITIVE LABELS

the networks, but again the labeling favored abortion advocates. On October 4, NBC's Kenley Jones followed anchor Tom Brokaw's introduction about the arrest of "anti-abortion protesters" by remarking that "abortion rights advocates" believed the demonstrators had little effect. CBS' James Hattori gave perhaps the most even-handed report on October 29, referring to the two sides as "pro-life" and "pro-choice."

**3. Medical Developments:** ABC's George Strait remarked without irony on September 23 that an abortifacient pill, opposed by "anti-abortion groups," could be "a lifesaver" in the Third World. On September 15, CBS' Susan Spencer characterized the debate over fetal research as a battle between "science" and the "anti-abortion movement."

A controversial social issue such as abortion demands even-handed treatment. The networks have proven themselves incapable of this task. By their biased use of labels to characterize the two sides of the issue, reporters have unfairly colored the national debate on abortion.

**CHAPTER FOUR, STUDY 4**

# No Labels for Liberal Environmentalists

## OVERVIEW

Few causes inspire more passionate reporting than the environment. Reporters who normally naysay charges of media bias concede -- even boast -- of their advocacy on the issue. During a September, 1989 global warming conference, Charles Alexander declared: "As the science editor at *Time*, I would freely admit that on this issue we have crossed the boundary from news reporting to advocacy." For many journalists, it's a can't-miss opportunity to demonstrate their conscience: after all, who's against saving the planet?

The popular impression left by media coverage is that environmental groups are simply working to improve the environment. But what about their proposed solutions? The environmental groups behind events like Earth Day propose a "national energy policy" including more taxes and government regulations, the same liberal  policies that were tried in the 1970s and led to economic stagnation and worsened the energy crisis. By refusing to describe these advocates as liberal, the media are refusing to concede that there is more than one side to the debate.

## KEY FINDINGS

- Out of 2,903 stories on ten liberal environmental groups in the *Los Angeles Times*, *The New York Times*, and *The Washington Post* in 1987, 1988, and 1989, only 29 labels were used by reporters, or in less than one percent of the stories.

- The radical group Earth First!, renowned for advocating tactics like "tree spiking," which has injured several loggers, received 22 of the labels. Only two other organizations, Greenpeace and the Natural Resources Defense Council received any ideological labels.

- Even the individual gurus who inspired Earth Day and the left-wing environmental movement, including Jeremy Rifkin, Barry Commoner, Lester Brown and Paul Ehrlich, were only labeled once in 211 stories. Free-market environmental theorist Julian Simon was never consulted for a newspaper story during the study period.

• Newspaper reporters also committed bias by omission: four free-market environmental groups, including the Competitive Enterprise Institute and the American Council on Science and Health, were only mentioned in 60 stories, compared to 2,903 for the ten liberal groups.

## STUDY EXCERPT

**Tags Not Planted on Green Groups** by the Media Research Center. From *MediaWatch*, April 1990.

Coverage of the environment provides a dramatic example of how the media's mindset prevents a balanced discussion of both sides of an issue. Reporting on left-wing environmental groups promotes their save-the-planet intentions as non-controversial, indeed beyond dispute. Reporters ignore their underlying liberal anti-industrial agenda: the same combination of crippling regulations, prohibitive taxes, and government boondoggles that stunted the economy and killed job opportunities in the late 1970s.

The media's pattern of environmental bias is vividly illustrated by a three-year study of ideological labeling of environmental groups. *Media-Watch* analysts used the Nexis ® news data retrieval system to review every story on ten environmental groups in the *Los Angeles Times, The New York Times,* and *The Washington Post* in 1987, 1988 and 1989. Out of 2,903 news stories, we found 29 ideological labels, or less than one percent. Of those, 22 were applied to Earth First!, five were given to Greenpeace, and the other two went to the Natural Resources Defense Council. The rest were label-free.

Not only did newspaper reporters fail to identify their liberal tilt, but they usually failed to refer to them as partisan political activists in Washington. Reporters used the words "activist," "advocacy," "lobbying," "militant" or variations thereof, only 155 times (5.3 percent). The newspaper reporters also committed bias by omission -- four of the most active conservative environmental groups were mentioned only 60 times (an average of 15 mentions apiece). By contrast, the ten liberal groups merited about 290 stories each. That's almost 20 times more attention than the conservative groups received.

Among the liberal groups receiving special treatment:

**Wildlife Groups.** Cloaked in a nonpartisan public image, the "defenders of wildlife" are uncompromising liberals who have blocked a number of Reagan and Bush Administration appointments. A memo from the editor of *Audubon Society* magazine revealed in *The Washington Post* last May 31 described the environment as "being royally [expletive] by our Environmental President (gag!). Maybe with a two-pronged attack (from sportsmen and conservation groups) we can shorten Manny Luhan's [sic] tenure at Interior." Still, the National Audubon Society suffered no harsher reference to activism than "arch-advocates of bird conservation," and no ideological labels in 457 stories.

The World Wildlife Fund, whose officers included Bush EPA Administrator William Reilly, was referred to as "mainstream" three times in 260 stories, even though they gave a medal to doomsday ecologist Paul Ehrlich. The Wilderness Society, counseled by Earth Day founder Gaylord Nelson and once home to Earth First! founder Dave Foreman, also went unlabeled.

**Self-Described Activist Groups.** The Environmental Defense Fund (EDF) received no liberal labels in 355 stories and only 20 references to activism, 16 of them in *The New York Times. The Washington Post* referred to EDF's activism only three times and the *Los Angeles Times* just once, using a *Post* account that described them as "strong clean-air advocates." Environmental Action, a group that grew directly out of Earth Day 1970 and pre-dated Earth First! "ecotage" by teaching conscientious types how to sprinkle nails on freeway interchanges in the 1970s, received no labels and only six references to activism in 51 stories.

The League of Conservation Voters (LCV) is often described as "the political arm of the environmental movement," but the print media refused to identify their political slant. The LCV has endorsed Michael Dukakis for President, New Jersey Gov. James Florio, Sen. Frank Lautenberg, Sen. Joseph Lieberman, California gubernatorial candidate Leo McCarthy (all Democrats), to name just a few. They gave President Bush a "D" report card in 1988. In 111 stories, the League was never given a liberal label. But they were described twice as "nonpartisan."

**Direct Action Groups.** Greenpeace, famous for disrupting Trident missile tests, had five political labels in 426 stories. Four were "radical" and one was "liberal-leaning." Despite Greenpeace's militant tactics, reporters used activist references only 41 times, or less than 10 percent of the time. Earth First!, the self-proclaimed "ecological saboteurs" who are renowned for "tree-spiking," which has severely injured several loggers, received the harshest treatment of the lot. In 83 news stories (70 in the *Los Angeles Times*), Earth First! got labeled 22 times, (roughly 25 percent). *The New York Times* called them "radical" once, but also referred to them as "conventional." The *Los Angeles Times* employed "radical" or variants like "sometimes radical" 20 times.

**Consumer Environmentalists.** The Natural Resources Defense Council (NRDC), the anti-pesticide activists responsible for last year's apple panic, was the most mentioned environmental group of those studied. Yet in 691 stories, they were labeled only two times. One of those came in Andrew Rosenthal's May 25, 1989 *New York Times* article headlined "When Left of Center Finds Itself in Mainstream." The *Los Angeles Times* once called the NRDC "generally liberal," but it also described them as "a group dedicated to saving the planet from pollutants."

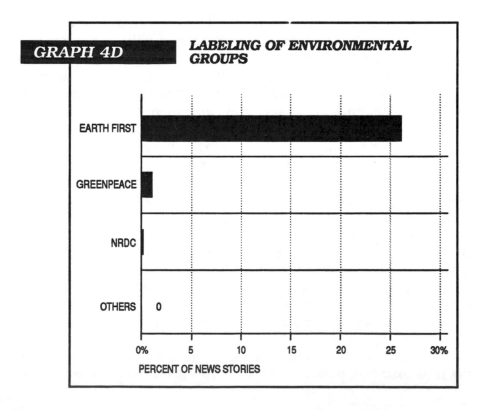

**GRAPH 4D**  *LABELING OF ENVIRONMENTAL GROUPS*

The Center for Science in the Public Interest (CSPI), a Ralph Nader spinoff also active in promoting regulation of the food supply, never received a liberal label. Nor were their Naderite origins disclosed in 254 stories. They did have the highest number of activist references (64), but most were positive-sounding, such as "consumer advocacy" and "health advocacy."

On the other hand, the American Council on Science and Health, a prominent opponent of NRDC and CSPI headed by Elizabeth Whelan, got much more suspicious treatment. In 23 stories, reporters called them conservative only once, but referred to them with adjectives like "industry-supported" or listed their corporate donors seven times. Not one story in 2,903 mentioned the industry funding of the liberal environmental groups.

**Earth Day Evangelists.** Even the individual gurus who inspired Earth Day avoided the liberal label, getting tagged only once in 211 stories. It came in one of 123 stories mentioning Jeremy Rifkin's Foundation on Economic Trends. Rifkin's anti-technology group was also described twice as nonpartisan. Barry Commoner, the 1980 standard-bearer of the far-left Citizens Party, received no ideological labels in 39 stories, but was referred to as "one of the nation's foremost environmental consciences" by the *Los Angeles Times*.

Lester Brown and the Worldwatch Institute appeared unlabeled in 34 stories, but the *Los Angeles Times* did call Worldwatch "respected" and "widely quoted," and referred to Brown as "one of the world's most influential thinkers." Paul Ehrlich, NBC's favorite doomsayer, went unlabeled in 15 print accounts. But Julian Simon, author of the free-market standard *The Ultimate Resource*, was not once consulted for news stories in the three papers.

**Free-Market Environmentalists.** Those urging the use of market incentives to encourage changes in company policies were mostly ignored. The Competitive Enterprise Institute, headed by former EPA official Fred Smith, was mentioned only eleven times, and not once on an environmental issue. The Reason Foundation, a California-based free-market think tank, was mentioned 12 times in the *Los Angeles Times*. Of its three mentions between the news sections of *The New York Times* and *The Washington Post*, two were in obituaries. The Political Economy Resource Center, an up-and-coming free-market environmental research foundation based in Bozeman, Montana, merited only one mention. *The New York Times* labeled it a "tiny, hard-core, market-incentives think tank."

As environmental issues become more prominent on the American political scene, the public would be better served if reporters spent some time investigating the liberal, anti-business agenda of most environmental groups, and provided more than token attention to organizations that suggest market-based solutions.

# 5 The Media & Superpower Relations: Reporters or Advocates?

In his book *Reluctant Farewell*, former *Newsweek* Moscow Bureau Chief Andrew Nagorski described the appalling quality of American news reporting from the Soviet Union. Ninety percent of all Associated Press wire service filings were simply rewritten from TASS and other Soviet news agency reports; the other news outlets relied on the Soviet government almost as much. Why? For one reason, half the correspondents based in Moscow lacked even a rudimentary knowledge of Russian; thus, as Nagorski found, they were totally dependent for their stories on Soviet government sources, Soviet "journalists," or largely isolated Western diplomats.

Michael Binyon, who reported for the London *Times* in Moscow, wrote in his book *Life in Russia* that he largely used official sources "because it is far wiser and more tactful to let the Russians make their own criticisms of their society than to judge them and pontificate as an outsider with different assumptions and outlook." It was this kind of reasoning, Nagorski concluded, that kept reporters from delving into Soviet society: "Many correspondents, who would not accept such a rationalization for continually echoing a government-controlled press elsewhere, shared Binyon's view that this was perfectly acceptable in Moscow."

Some reporters, moreover, viewed alternative news sources with downright scorn. Take dissidents, for example. *U.S. News & World Report*'s Nick Daniloff told the *Washington Journalism Review* in June 1985: "I don't consort with dissidents. The magazine considers them a passing phenomenon of little interest. In a political sense they don't have an influence -- and they are perishing." *The New York Times'* Serge

Schmemann agreed: "Ah, yes, dissidents. This is always a problem, both in whether to see them and whether to run their story. In some ways it's a humanitarian dilemma. How do I tell them, 'You are of no interest'? Do I meet with them? 'Your wife is on a hunger strike' -- how do I tell them to go to hell?"

Did the cozy relationship between U.S. reporters and the Soviet government affect coverage of U.S.-Soviet relations when the two nations were so often in conflict in the early to mid-1980s? Indeed. As the following studies show, during the major U.S.-Soviet engagements, the Soviet Union was promoted as a credible world leader meriting the same moral respect as the democratic West.

---

**CHAPTER FIVE, STUDY 1**

# *"Moscow Meets Main Street"*

## OVERVIEW

"The Soviets exploit the openness of our system to promote their global agenda," warned the U.S. Advisory Commission on Public Diplomacy (USACPD) in 1986. Its report, "Soviet Advocacy and the U.S. Media," explained how the Soviets use the American television networks "to promote the perception of equivalence between the USSR and the United States." In the past, the Soviets always stonewalled the Western media. But, USACPD reported, their "new corps" of spokesmen skillfully "massage" reporters during television appearances.

*Moscow Meets Main Street*, a Media Institute monograph by Ted J. Smith III, a Virginia Commonwealth University Associate Professor of Mass Communications, confirmed the advisory report's contention. According to Smith, the American networks have increasingly considered official Soviet spokesmen credible sources of information. Thus, the number of Soviet spokesmen and government officials on the American airwaves has proliferated in the 1980s. Smith analyzed all Soviet Union stories that appeared on the three major network evening newscasts in 1981, 1983 and 1985.

## KEY FINDINGS

- The number of stories using at least one Soviet source increased throughout the years. In 1981, there were 291 stories. By 1985, the Soviets had gained unprecedented access to American homes, as the number of stories with at least one Soviet source hit 477. [See Graph 5A]

- The total number of Soviet sources cited in a given year rose from 328 in 1981 to 604 in 1985.

- The number of stories featuring at least one Soviet on-camera speaker, the vast majority of which were Soviet government officials or "journalists," rose 407 percent -- from 42 stories in 1981 to 213 in 1985. [See Graph 5B]

- The total number of Soviet on-camera spokesmen in a given year rose from 50 in 1981 to 325 in 1985, a 550 percent jump. Thus, by 1985, Soviet propagandists were appearing on American television news almost daily. [See Graph 5C]

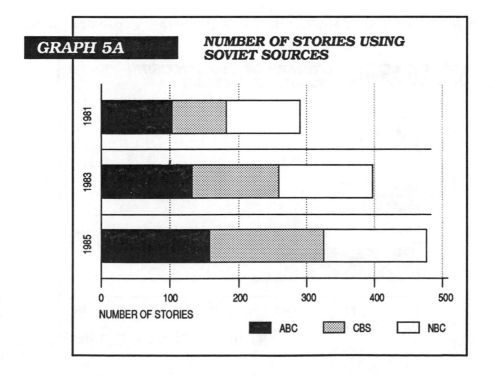

**GRAPH 5A**

**NUMBER OF STORIES USING SOVIET SOURCES**

- A great number of Soviet appearances occurred when civilian airliner KAL-007 was shot down over Soviet airspace. Between September 1, 1983, and September 30, 1986, the three networks broadcast 152 stories, seven and one-quarter hours of airtime, covering the incident. Another 45 stories had brief mentions. Of the 152 stories, 96 (63 percent) included some form of criticism of the Soviet Union. However, 59 stories (39 percent) included criticism of the United States. Why? Because, Smith explained, an inordinate amount of time was given the Soviet position. Fifty-nine stories used at least one Soviet source; 22 of them had Soviets appear on camera. In total, Soviet sources were cited 119 times and 37 spokesmen appeared on camera.

- How did Soviet appearances affect what the news shows reported? In the three years studied, the Soviet viewpoint -- that the plane was on a spy mission -- was reported in 47 stories. The U.S. viewpoint -- that the Soviets knew or suspected that the plane was a civilian airliner and shot it down -- received only 25 mentions. Smith concluded that the official Soviet position was represented all too well, despite the fact that it was widely held that the Soviets had committed an atrocity.

- Smith accused the networks of "a deliberate expansion of the

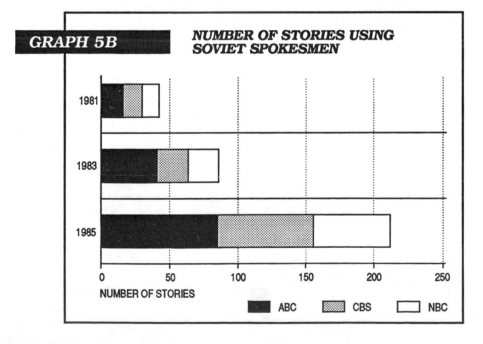

**GRAPH 5B**   **NUMBER OF STORIES USING SOVIET SPOKESMEN**

NUMBER OF STORIES

ABC   CBS   NBC

American political dialogue, in which hostile propaganda of foreign regimes is placed on equal footing with the statements of American political leaders." What explains this increased willingness to put Soviets on the air? Smith suggested the blame lay with the "intellectualization" of the media elite and their "culturally neutral" outlook on reporting of world affairs.

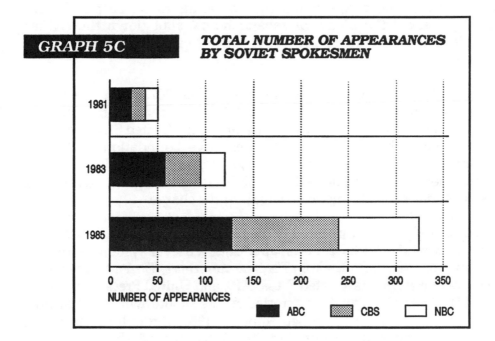

GRAPH 5C

**TOTAL NUMBER OF APPEARANCES BY SOVIET SPOKESMEN**

## CHAPTER FIVE, STUDY 2

# The Media and the KAL Spy Charges

## OVERVIEW

When Soviet fighter planes shot down Korean Airline's (KAL) flight 007 on September 1, 1983, the world was outraged. KAL had strayed off course into Soviet airspace and the Soviet air force, despite having visually tracked the plane for several hours, shot down the civilian aircraft. The massacre of 269 people met swift condemnation from around the world.

First, the Soviets denied shooting down KAL-007. Then, as evidence mounted to the contrary, to save face the Soviets charged that the passenger aircraft was on a secret spy mission for the United States. According to a study by the National Conservative Foundation (NCF), the outlandish Soviet charges were given great credibility in the American press. In fact, the study showed that the Soviet spy story was given more credence than official American denials of the charge.

For a study which appeared in the September, 1986 *Newswatch*, NCF analysts used the Nexis ® newspaper data retrieval system to identify non-opinion, news articles from *The New York Times*, *The Washington Post*, *Time*, *Newsweek*, the Associated Press (AP), and United Press International (UPI). Researchers analyzed stories on the shootdown of the airliner over the Sea of Japan (from September 1, 1983, through the spring of 1986) that mentioned the word "spy" or "intelligence." The stories were placed into one of four categories: "Spy," "Accusation," "Rebuttal," and "Mistake."

## KEY FINDINGS

- 42.9 percent of the stories (96 of the 224 stories in the study) were "Spy" stories. These dealt with the theory that the airliner was on an intelligence gathering mission for the U.S. None of these stories included any denial of the charges from American officials or experts. [See Graph 5D]

- 28.6 percent (64 of 224) were categorized as "Accusation." These stories reported Soviet accusations that the plane was on a spy mission with only brief rebuttals to the charge from American officials.

- Just 21.4 percent (48 of 224) fit the "Rebuttal" category. These articles only reported American and South Korean denials of intelligence gathering through the civilian aircraft.

- 4.7 percent (10 stories) mentioned a more likely scenario: the Soviet air force might have honestly mistaken the Boeing 747 for a military reconnaissance aircraft.

- Thus, the news outlets offered more than three times as many stories pushing the Soviet theory (Spy and Accusation stories combined = 160) as opposing it (Rebuttal = 48).

- The Best and the Worst. AP played up the spy charges the most: 50 percent of its stories fit the "Spy" category, 29.6 percent the "Accusation" one. UPI did much the same, 49.1 percent and 28 percent, respectively. While lending substantial credibility to the Soviets,

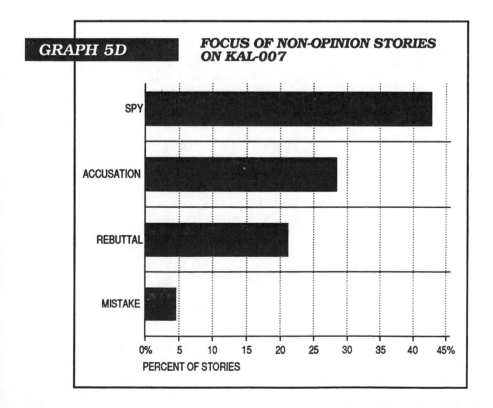

**GRAPH 5D**

**FOCUS OF NON-OPINION STORIES ON KAL-007**

SPY

ACCUSATION

REBUTTAL

MISTAKE

0%  5  10  15  20  25  30  35  40  45%

PERCENT OF STORIES

*Time* and *Newsweek* spread the charges the least often. Their combined "Spy" and "Accusation" percentages were 41.6 percent and 55.5 percent respectively.

- The study concluded: "Far-left journals like *The Nation* played up unfounded theories of an evil CIA connection. Sadly, the supposedly mainstream press gave that agenda priority over the U.S. side. A look back at the coverage makes it clear that no matter how evil the accusation, there will always be those, even in major American news organs, eager to blame America first in order to excuse the Soviets for committing their inexcusable actions."

**CHAPTER FIVE, STUDY 3**

# Repeating The Soviet Agenda At Geneva

## OVERVIEW

Soviet leader Mikhail Gorbachev agreed to attend the November, 1985 Geneva summit because he hoped to block any further development of the U.S. Strategic Defense Initiative (SDI). The Soviets wanted to remain ahead in strategic arms by calling for "peace" and an "arms agreement." Gorbachev was also interested in promoting himself as a credible world leader and the Soviet Union as morally equal to the West.

But President Ronald Reagan had strikingly different priorities. He went to Geneva not only committed to SDI but also to take the Soviets to task on what he saw as egregious human rights abuses, aggression abroad, and arms pacts violations. Only after raising these issues, did the U.S. President then want to discuss arms control.

Both parties declared a total press blackout for the summit, yet, according to a National Conservative Foundation (NCF) study published in the November 1986 *Newswatch*, the American contingent of reporters had no shortage of stories, nor of opinions to be voiced. On every major issue, from arms control to human rights, the study concluded that the American news media -- the third party at Geneva -- promoted the Soviet agenda over the American one.

NCF researchers studied all ABC's *World News Tonight, CBS Evening News, and NBC Nightly News* reports from November 1 to November 22, 1985. The study included 187 stories in 51 broadcasts. The networks devoted 387 minutes to the Geneva summit over the 22-day period. Researchers broke coverage down into five categories: human rights, defense and SDI, detente, attacks on the U.S. administration, and comparisons of American and Soviet society.

The majority of the stories appeared in the few days during and surrounding the November 19-21 summit. Yet coverage was quite extensive in the weeks prior to the meeting, including a CBS series by Bruce Morton titled "Over There" and an ABC series titled "ABC's Strategic Guide to the Summit."

- Reagan's attempts to expose Soviet human rights violations were largely ignored by the three networks' reporters. NCF analysts found just 19 stories on the subject, most of which referred to the "Soviet propaganda stunt" of allowing ten Soviets to rejoin their spouses in the U.S. Only four stories (21 percent of the human rights coverage) were critical; just one ninety second story, aired on CBS, covered abuses in detail. [See Graph 5E]

- When Soviet rights violations did come up, the media often offered excuses for the Soviets. The networks even aired six-minutes worth of reports (23 percent of human rights coverage) praising Soviet "bold moves" in the area of human rights. The NCF study quoted Tom Brokaw on November 16 gushing: "I wouldn't be surprised if the Soviets will do something more in this area. They are very eager to put the best face, of course, on the Soviet Union under Mikhail Gorbachev."

- In line with Gorbachev's agenda, SDI received the greatest media

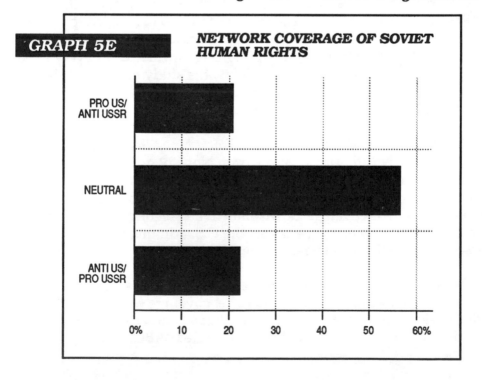

**GRAPH 5E**    **NETWORK COVERAGE OF SOVIET HUMAN RIGHTS**

PRO US/ ANTI USSR

NEUTRAL

ANTI US/ PRO USSR

0%    10    20    30    40    50    60%

scrutiny. Only 11 percent of all SDI coverage was pro-SDI, while 3.5 times more coverage (38 percent) was given to the anti-SDI, Soviet side. The NCF study cited Dan Rather's November 18 comment as a typical example: "The President's dream of a system to destroy missiles in space is the most troublesome issue facing the super-powers. And in a world stalked by the shadow of nuclear nightmare, the one issue that has provoked the most debate." [See Graph 5F]

- Five stories focused on the strategic weapons buildup: none dealt with Soviet capabilities, but "all dwelled on American might."

- The networks harkened back nostalgically to the age of detente, devoting 14 minutes of coverage to the topic. All of it focused on positive aspects; negative implications were never mentioned. On November 20, NBC's Jim Bitterman yearned for the return of the Apollo-Soyuz missions: "There's been much recent nostalgia about the good old days of detente, for those brief intervals since the war when Moscow and Washington cooperated on the earth and off."

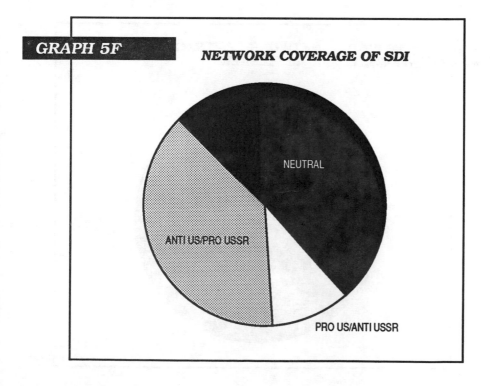

**GRAPH 5F**

**NETWORK COVERAGE OF SDI**

NEUTRAL

ANTI US/PRO USSR

PRO US/ANTI USSR

- The networks found many ways to present the Soviet Union as a country standing in good faith throughout the world. Seventy-nine percent of the 85 minutes in the "Moral Equivalence" category promoted the view that the Soviet Union was morally equal to the West in all areas: lifestyle, political system, and leaders. For example, CBS' Bruce Morton declared in a pre-summit "Over There" report: "All of these services are part of an explicit bargain the Soviet workers have made with their government. They are less free than workers in the West, but more secure." [See Graph 5G]

- Twenty-eight minutes of the moral equivalence coverage were spent positively portraying Gorbachev. For example, on November 14, ABC's Richard Threlkeld described the Soviet leader "as cosmopolitan as Peter the Great," as "a great communicator," and "more polished than Nikita Khrushchev, but just as much the populist reformer."

- The networks mentioned the nature of the Soviet government, the repression in everyday life, or the Soviet economic failures just 21 percent (5 of 31 stories) of the time.

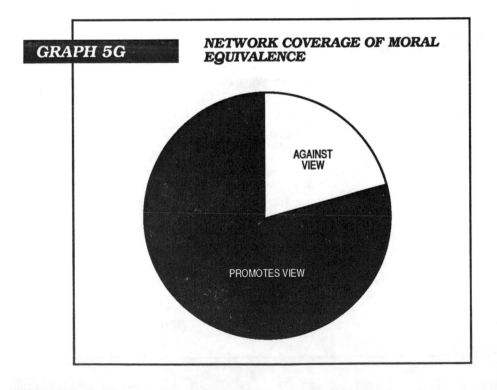

**GRAPH 5G**

**NETWORK COVERAGE OF MORAL EQUIVALENCE**

AGAINST VIEW

PROMOTES VIEW

**CHAPTER FIVE, STUDY 4**

# Summit 1987 -- Gorbymania With A Twist

## OVERVIEW

A Media Research Center (MRC) study of the December 1987 Reagan-Gorbachev summit confirmed that TV viewers received the Soviet line on detente, glasnost, Afghanistan, and the moral equivalence of the two superpowers. In most respects, stories on these subjects mirrored those surrounding the Geneva summit three years earlier [See Chapter Five, Study 3].

But the study documented an astonishing twist as well: when it came to the Strategic Defense Initiative (SDI) and Soviet human rights violations, ABC, CBS, and NBC dumped the pro-Soviet line taken in Geneva in favor of the American position.

The Media Research Center analyzed the 47 evening newscasts that appeared on ABC's *World News Tonight,* *CBS Evening News,* and *NBC Nightly News* from November 23, two weeks before Gorbachev's arrival in Washington, to December 10, the night of his departure. All the ideas expressed (reporters' and network commentators' statements as well as comments from political leaders and experts) were placed into one of nine "issue" categories: Intermediate Nuclear Forces (INF), Moral Equivalence, Glasnost, Strategic Arms Reduction Talks (START), Human Rights, SDI, Afghanistan, Detente, and Other Regional Conflicts. The nine categories totaled 285 minutes or 74.9 percent of summit airtime. A tenth category, "non-issue/fluff," contained stories or parts of stories that were non-political in nature (i.e. summit schedule, Washington hotels and police preparations, the Raisa Gorbachev/Nancy Reagan meetings, summary montages, etc.). This category amounted to 95 minutes and 51 seconds (25.1 percent of the summit coverage).

## KEY FINDINGS

- Of all summit coverage, 37.1 percent concerned arms issues: INF, START, SDI, or past treaty violations. Another 25.5 percent of the coverage concerned detente, glasnost, or the moral equivalence of the superpowers. Only 12.1 percent focused on human rights in the Soviet Union or regional conflicts around the world. [See Graph 5H]

- Of overall network coverage of INF, 39.4 percent promoted the treaty while 24.8 percent opposed it.

- 59 percent of the "moral equivalence" network coverage portrayed the Soviet leader or regime as morally equal to the U.S. in world affairs.

- Of network airtime on glasnost and perestroika, 56.4 percent portrayed the policies as genuine. Just 12 percent of all network coverage viewed glasnost as ungenuine.

- Of network time on detente, 75 percent encouraged the policy.

- In a turnround from the Geneva and Reykjavik summits, nearly 75 percent of human rights coverage mentioned Soviet infractions and Jewish emigration restrictions.

- In another change, the study found summit news reports firmly supportive of SDI. Nearly 40 percent of the time promoted SDI. Only 15.1 percent was anti-SDI.

- The networks offered equal airtime to the Soviet and U.S. positions on Afghanistan. Other Soviet aggression abroad received almost no coverage.

## STUDY EXCERPT

**Gorbymania With a Twist** by the Media Research Center. From *Media-Watch*, January 1988.

*INF (93:36 minutes; 24.6 percent of entire summit coverage) and START (27:20; 7.2 percent).* Overall, 39.4 percent of INF coverage promoted the treaty, while 24.8 percent opposed the agreement. MRC media analysts considered the remaining 35.9 percent to be informational. A diverse selection of people was featured promoting the treaty, including substantial time given to Reagan and Gorbachev. Those featured opposing the treaty were usually Republican presidential candidates. CBS anchor Dan Rather was one of the few newsmen who exhibited a healthy bit of skepticism toward the agreement, noting on November 30: "Both sides are trying to accentuate the positive, but negotiators from both sides know that the enormous Russian army may well benefit plenty."

Despite decades of Soviet cheating on previous accords, only 4.5 minutes of the INF coverage (1.2% of total summit news) concerned past Soviet treaty violations. Incredibly, 51 percent of this treaty time excused past treaty infringements and believed they should have no bearing on signing the INF treaty. ABC's Sam Donaldson complained on December 2: "The White House deliberately threw a damper on things by sending Congress a report on Soviet violations of past treaties, a report which could have been delayed." Only 14 percent of the coverage viewed past violations as consequential to INF. Coverage promoting a START agreement (9 minutes, 30 seconds) overshadowed airtime allotted critics opposing a strategic agreement by more than five-to-one.

*Are the Powers Morally Equal? (46:46 minutes; 12.3 percent).* Yes, according to the networks, since over 59 percent portrayed the Soviet leader or his regime as morally equal to the U.S. in world affairs. Only 21.6 percent portrayed Gorbachev and his system as less credible or moral than Reagan and the U.S. As part of their campaign to promote moral equality, the media spent an exorbitant amount of time praising the sincerity of Gorbachev. On November 27, NBC's Sandy Gilmour delivered this glowing portrait: "Unlike his stone-faced predecessors, Mikhail Gorbachev is congenial, confident, charismatic -- a gifted politician, tough infighter, a superb salesman, who wants to change his country's dark and gloomy image....Gorbachev seems to be genuinely liked here." ABC's Walter Rodgers offered the most fervent endorsement of moral equivalence. In a December 9 story, he summed up Gorbachev's view: "Gorbachev revealed another basic difference he has with President Reagan and many Americans on human rights." Rodgers then put on Gorbachev who said that the United States has no moral right to pressure the Soviets on the issue. Apparently Rodgers agreed since he offered no criticism of Gorbachev's assertion.

*The Validity of Glasnost and Perestroika (33:14 minutes; 8.7 percent).* The study confirmed that most in the media had little doubt that Gorbachev was sincere in his campaign to "reform" Soviet social and economic life. Of airtime devoted to *glasnost* and *perestroika*, researchers identified 56.4 percent as promoting the policies as genuine. NBC was clearly the most enthusiastic, promoting glasnost as legitimate 80 per-

cent of the time. CBS was far more skeptical, promoting the policy only
15.3 percent of the time. NBC's Gilmour pushed Gorbachev's programs,

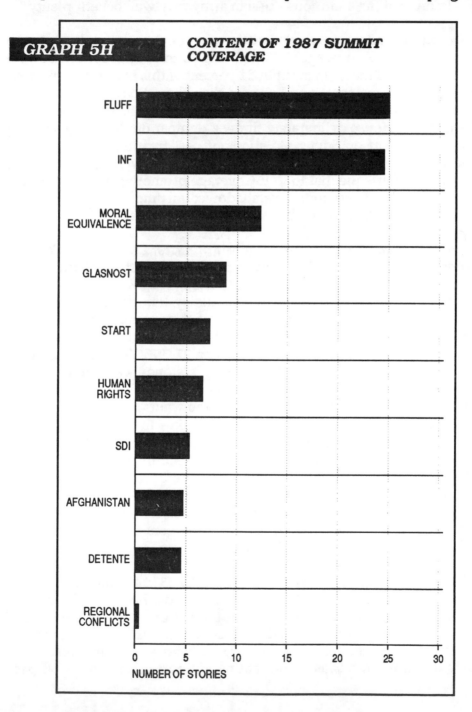

**GRAPH 5H**

**CONTENT OF 1987 SUMMIT COVERAGE**

NUMBER OF STORIES

calling *perestroika* "the most radical economic and social reforms in Soviet history." Gilmour's November 27 report continued: "All that and more openness are the drastic changes sought by this life-long communist....Gorbachev may be the right man at the right time." Only 12 percent of the views aired by the networks characterized glasnost as superficial or false. [See Graph 5I]

*Calls for Detente (17:24 minutes; 4.6 percent).* When it came to future relations with the Soviet Union, 13 minutes or 75 percent of the time was devoted to offering the views of people encouraging a new detente framework similar to the 1970s. Only 14.7 percent saw a return to detente as a threat to U.S. national security. Promotion of detente ranged from a high of 93 percent for ABC to a low of 49 percent for CBS, with NBC at 89 percent.

*Human Rights (26:50 minutes; 7.0 percent).* Almost 75 percent of airtime devoted to human rights called to mind Soviet evils, such as restrictions on Jewish emigration. Only 21 percent could be described as excusing Soviet behavior, such as characterizing the situation as improv-

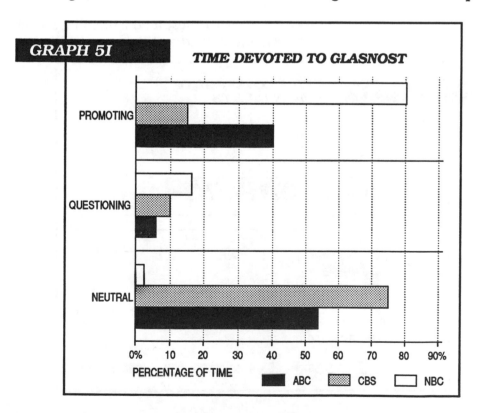

GRAPH 5I          TIME DEVOTED TO GLASNOST

PERCENTAGE OF TIME          ABC          CBS          NBC

ing. In contrast, coverage during the Geneva summit was evenly split on the issue [See Chapter Five, Study 3]. ABC's Rodgers was one of the few willing to give the Soviets credit. On the occasion of the reunification of some Soviet families, Rodgers stated on November 25: "For these Soviets, Mr. Gorbachev's policy of *glasnost* translates into a home-coming." But Wyatt Andrews of CBS saw through the charade of pre-summit releases, explaining on December 3: "By now, this is all a predictable pre-summit process. Joyful reunions one day, little rejections the next. And no fundamental change on the Soviet side that would make international travel and both of these emotional scenes unnecessary." [See Graph 5J]

*SDI: A Media Turnaround (20:37 minutes; 5.4 percent).* In another reversal from the Reykjavik and Geneva summits, 39.7 percent of SDI news coverage promoted deployment, research, or funding. Only 15.1 percent of coverage was anti-SDI. At the 1985 Geneva summit, 10.7 percent of the coverage was pro-SDI, while 38.4 percent was anti-SDI [See Chapter Five, Study 3]. The major difference between the two summits: Gorbachev decided not to make SDI an issue this time. [See Graph 5K]

*Afghanistan (17:53 minutes; 4.7 percent).* Despite the ongoing Soviet occupation of Afghanistan, the American media still gave an amazing

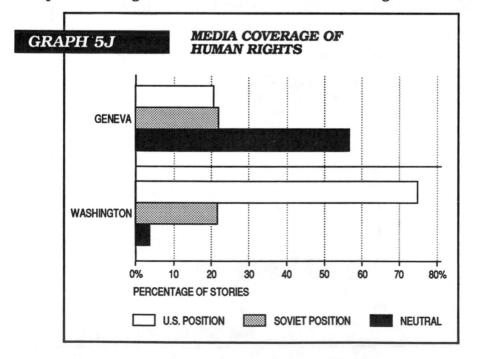

GRAPH 5J    **MEDIA COVERAGE OF HUMAN RIGHTS**

PERCENTAGE OF STORIES

U.S. POSITION    SOVIET POSITION    NEUTRAL

level of credibility to the Soviet propaganda line. 40 percent of Afghanistan coverage on ABC, CBS and NBC endorsed the Soviet position that the Red Army must remain until a "political" solution is reached. Not once did the networks portray the Soviets as the aggressors or recount their 1979 invasion. The Free World's position that there is no excuse for continued occupation received the same amount of news time. [See Graph 5L]

ABC News failed to air any reports from the front lines of the war while NBC aired just one and CBS three. When asked why the situation in Afghanistan was not deemed important enough for at least one feature story, ABC press representative Karen Reynolds dismissed the concern: "It was just an editorial judgment."

Even the few lengthy stories, by CBS' Mark Phillips and NBC's Peter Kent, avoided the most fundamental issues. Instead of asking why the Soviets have made no effort to scale down their occupation and pull out, both correspondents preferred to paint the Soviets as more victim than villain. As Kent reported on December 9: "The Soviets seem to be hunkering down, in effect, until they can work a deal to extract themselves from their own Vietnam." Phillips assessed the situation from the Soviet angle. On December 3 he reported: "A Soviet withdrawal, [the Af-

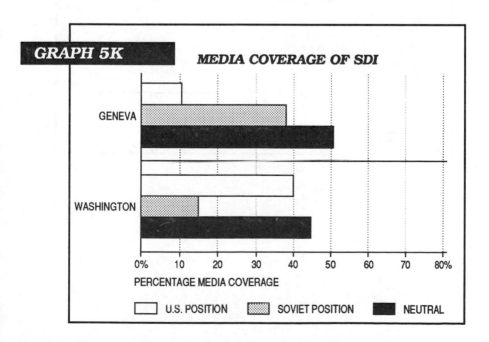

GRAPH 5K   MEDIA COVERAGE OF SDI

PERCENTAGE MEDIA COVERAGE

□ U.S. POSITION     ▨ SOVIET POSITION     ■ NEUTRAL

ghan President] now says, can take place in a 12-month period once the Mujahideen stop fighting and the United States stops supporting them."

*Other Regional Conflicts (1:51 minutes; 0.5 percent).* Except for vague, passing references to Nicaragua, Cambodia and Angola, totalling a piddling 0.5 percent of all coverage, the networks ignored Soviet aggression in other parts of the world.

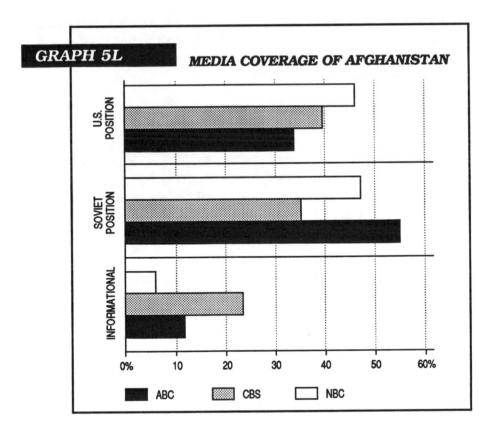

# 6 The Media & Regional Conflicts: Blame America First?

As Chapter 5 showed, "Moral Equivalence" -- treating U.S. and Soviet positions as morally equal -- has become the underlying tenet of the American media's coverage of U.S.-Soviet relations. At times, reporters even tilt away from Western values, covering Soviet views and positions far more frequently (and favorably) than American ones. If "Moral Equivalence" describes U.S.-Soviet coverage, its deadlier corollary "Blame America First" is an apt phrase to describe the reporting on the world's regional "hot spots."

The human rights abuses, foreign aggression, and despotic nature of any regime would seem newsworthy, but such topics are generally reported by the American media only if the offenders are American allies. "Victims of Communism" is all too often a taboo subject as reporters soft-pedal the totalitarian nature of pro-Soviet Marxist regimes. Meanwhile, American efforts to liberate countries from Marxism during the 1980s were regularly condemned by the media.

**CHAPTER SIX, STUDY 1**

## "TV Networks and Human Rights"

### OVERVIEW

In general, the media are much more inclined to document the human rights abuses of America's allies than those of Soviet allies. That's the conclusion reached by the National Conservative Foundation (NCF) when it reviewed all July 1986 ABC, CBS, and NBC evening newscasts. The NCF's August, 1986 *Newswatch* study found that Chilean and South African human rights violations dominated network news coverage while those of Soviet client states received scant attention.

## KEY FINDINGS

- A total of 198 minutes and 42 seconds of human rights coverage appeared on the three major network evening newscasts during July 1986. 188 minutes and 45 seconds, or 95 percent of the time, covered the abuses of U.S. allies. The three networks devoted less than ten minutes to communist atrocities. [See Graph 6A]

- On average, a single nightly newscast that month included two minutes on human rights abuses in pro-American countries. On average, a bare 6.5 *seconds* per broadcast covered abuses in pro-Soviet countries.

- South Africa received 173 minutes of coverage, seven times more than all other countries combined.

- Network executives often claim they need pictures to make a good story and excuse their lack of attention to communist abuses by citing the difficulty in penetrating war-torn areas or closed societies. (They often used that excuse in the case of Afghanistan.) Yet despite the restrictions put on foreign journalists in South Africa in 1985, the networks kept the South Africa story alive. For the violent scenes they could no longer record, reporters substituted interviews and analyses from prominent anti-apartheid activists both in the United States and South Africa -- 15 reports in all.

- Chile received the next greatest amount of coverage. Nine stories devoted to Chilean abuses were broadcast by the three networks in July 1986.

- In the month studied, the only Soviet allies mentioned as abusing human rights were Nicaragua and Afghanistan. The networks featured 15 stories on Nicaragua, but only four mentioned violations by the Sandinista government. Of the five stories on Afghanistan, just three mentioned human rights. No network time was spent on abuses in Cuba, Cambodia, Vietnam, North Korea, or Laos.

- Dissident Solidarity leader Zbigniew Bujak was imprisoned by the Polish communist government on May 31, 1986. But not one story appeared in July about Poland or Bujak's continued political persecution. At the time, Yelena Bonner and Andrei Sakharov were still exiles in Soviet Siberia. Not one story mentioned their plight in Gorky or any other Soviet abuses.

- The NCF study concluded: "While the media argue that disdain for apartheid is newsworthy because it simply reflects the current political agenda, they chose to ignore other high-ranking national leaders who highlight another agenda -- human rights abuses in

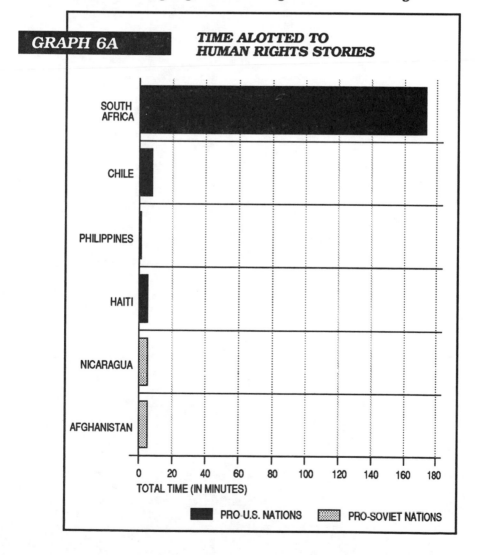

GRAPH 6A

**TIME ALOTTED TO HUMAN RIGHTS STORIES**

pro-Soviet nations. To ignore the equally or more evil repression and genocide in communist nations is a double standard."

**CHAPTER SIX, STUDY 2**

# Selective Eye on Central America

## OVERVIEW

During 1984, charges of human rights violations were leveled against both the Nicaraguan Marxist regime and the democratically-elected government of El Salvador. Building on its earlier human rights study (Chapter 6, Study 1), the National Conservative Foundation (NCF) set out to compare U.S. media coverage of Nicaraguan and Salvadoran atrocities in that year. Not surprisingly, its earlier premise -- that the media are prone to cover human rights violations of U.S. allies far more frequently than those of its enemies -- held true. Marxist Sandinista atrocities were largely ignored in 1984, while prominent and scathing coverage was focused on Jose Napoleon Duarte's Christian Democratic Salvadoran government.

For its January, 1987 *Newswatch* study NCF again used the Nexis ® newspaper data retrieval system to analyze all 1984 stories in *The New York Times*, *The Washington Post*, *Time*, and *Newsweek* that dealt with atrocities in the two nations. To locate the stories, researchers used code words, such as "killing," "murder," and "torture." To focus the study exclusively on government actions against civilian non-combatants (for example, soldiers murdering or torturing peasants), researchers set aside all stories that did not blame the governments for atrocities and violations as well as those that dealt with battle-related casualties. Any stories that blamed the Marxist FMLN guerrillas in El Salvador or the Contras in Nicaragua for atrocities were also left out of the study.

## KEY FINDINGS

- The four publications ran approximately five times more news stories on Salvadoran government atrocities than on those committed by the Nicaraguan government. Of the 260 articles on human rights, 216 or 83 percent documented Salvadoran abuses. Only 44 stories or 17 percent dealt with Nicaraguan government infractions. [See Graph 6B]

- The vast majority of the 216 stories on El Salvador concerned the deaths of two labor organizers and four nuns killed by government security personnel. While properly documenting those atrocities, the media outlets neglected the equally well-documented murder of thousands of Miskito Indians in Nicaragua by the Sandinistas. A mere seven stories appeared on that subject the entire year. There was certainly definitive evidence to back up the Miskito massacre story. As *Time* noted on August 20, an Organization of American States report reviewed "a shower of accumulated charges against the Sandinistas. The accusations have ranged from illegal killings, disappearances, and torture to indiscriminate air attacks on Miskito settlements."

- *Newsweek* was the most one-sided, reporting on Sandinista atrocities on just one occasion the entire year. Yet it found time to write 14 stories about Duarte government violations. The least un-balanced, *Time* wrote about Salvadoran infractions 13 times compared to Nicaragua six times.

- *The New York Times* ran 118 stories on Salvadoran government murders or torture, but just 21 on Nicaragua, a 5.5-to-1 ratio. The *Post*

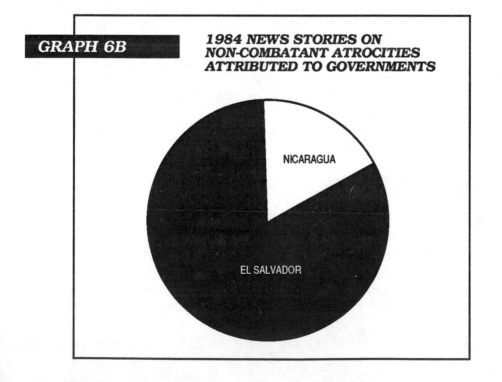

**GRAPH 6B**

**1984 NEWS STORIES ON NON-COMBATANT ATROCITIES ATTRIBUTED TO GOVERNMENTS**

NICARAGUA

EL SALVADOR

ran 71 stories on Salvador and 16 on Nicaragua, a greater than 4-to-1 ratio.

- The study concluded that the biased reporting had an adverse effect on American national security and foreign policy: "While El Salvador has democratically elected leaders dedicated to halting abuses, Nicaragua commits them as a matter of official policy. By concentrating almost solely on El Salvadoran 'death squads' and military excesses, while deliberately ignoring far more prevalent murders by the Sandinistas, the media relayed a distorted view of the relative merits of aid to the Duarte government and the Contras."

# Contra-Diction, Media Style

## OVERVIEW

Contra aid battles raged on Capitol Hill in the 1980s. A Media Research Center (MRC) study in 1988 showed that congressional opponents of aid had loyal allies in the U.S. media. The MRC looked at how ABC's *World News Tonight, CBS Evening News, CNN PrimeNews,* and *NBC Nightly News* covered six official Sandinista statements promising compliance with peace accords or reform versus coverage of ten instances when the communist regime violated agreements or rejected reform. The MRC's conclusion: selective reporting was rampant between September 1988 and May 1989: Sandinista violations and contempt for the peace process were routinely ignored while promises were liberally covered.

## KEY FINDINGS

- The six instances studied in which the Sandinistas pledged compliance or reform were each covered by at least three of the four networks. Actions betraying those pledges were ignored or barely mentioned.

- ABC, CBS, NBC and CNN viewers saw more than five times as many stories (22) on Sandinista reforms and compliance than stories (4) mentioning Sandinista indiscretions or violations. [See Graph 6C]

- All 13 feature-length stories by reporters in the field from September 1987 to May 1988 on Nicaragua dealt with alleged moves by the Sandinistas to comply with peace accords.

## STUDY EXCERPT

**Contra-Diction, Media Style** by the Media Research Center. From *MediaWatch,* May 1988.

The Contras "should be thankful that we're not offering them the guillotine or the firing squad, which is what they deserve," Nicaraguan dictator Daniel Ortega proclaimed in his 1988 May Day speech. The city of Managua, Ortega sneered, would have to be "disinfected" after the Contra negotiators left. But virtually every major media outlet, including all four TV networks, ignored Ortega's mockery of the Central American "peace process."

In late March, however, when the Sandinistas were touting the Sapoa accord promises of free speech, amnesty for the Contras, and the release of political prisoners, ABC's *World News Tonight*, *CBS Evening News*, *CNN PrimeNews*, and *NBC Nightly News* all covered the story.

Other examples. When the opposition newspaper *La Prensa* was finally reopened in 1987, anchor Sam Donaldson led the September 19 *World News Sunday* with the announcement. In April 1988, when the Marxist government withheld newsprint from *La Prensa*, forcing it to close again, the TV newscasts remained silent. On September 22 ABC, CBS, and NBC carried a story that Radio Catolica could resume broadcasting. However, when Radio Catolica was censored a month later the networks ignored the story.

On December 13, 1987 Ortega vowed to "never give up power." Tom Brokaw overlooked that in announcing on December 14 that the Sandini-

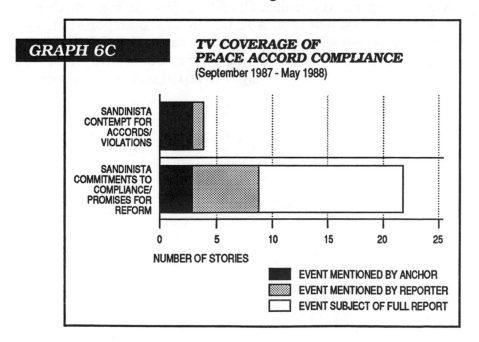

GRAPH 6C

**TV COVERAGE OF PEACE ACCORD COMPLIANCE**
(September 1987 - May 1988)

SANDINISTA CONTEMPT FOR ACCORDS/ VIOLATIONS

SANDINISTA COMMITMENTS TO COMPLIANCE/ PROMISES FOR REFORM

0    5    10    15    20    25

NUMBER OF STORIES

■ EVENT MENTIONED BY ANCHOR
▨ EVENT MENTIONED BY REPORTER
☐ EVENT SUBJECT OF FULL REPORT

stas had plans for a Christmas cease-fire if the Contras would also agree. CNN's Lou Waters chose to report Ortega's charge that the U.S. is "not interested in peace." In January the networks all reported that the Sandinistas lifted the state of emergency, which again supposedly ended all radio censorship. But on May 1, *The Miami Herald*'s Sam Dillon reported that Interior Minister Tomas Borge "punched on the forehead and chin" anti-government radio operator Jose Castillo. The networks once again failed to pick up on the contradiction.

The monitoring commission led by Costa Rican President Oscar Arias released a report on January 4 detailing Sandinista non-compliance with promised reforms. On February 21, *The Washington Times* carried a front-page story quoting Ortega's vow to "crush the Contras." Television news ignored both stories. The Sandinistas pledged to free 10,000 political prisoners; 985 were let go on November 22 and 100 more were released on March 27. The networks faithfully covered the events. But in early March, when Sandinista mobs attacked a peaceful march by mothers protesting the military draft, no network even mentioned it. In another obvious display of oppression, hoodlums threw rocks and violently disrupted a meeting of opposition leaders on January 23. Only NBC's Ed Rabel found time to make a brief reference to this incident.

Even an apparent exception to this trend reinforced the MRC findings. When Ortega asked Cardinal Obando y Bravo to mediate Contra-Sandinista talks, CNN, NBC, and ABC ran on-location reports to tell the November 6 story. But when Ortega fired the cardinal on March 3, CBS, CNN, and NBC anchormen gave it only brief mention. ABC, which had sent reporter John Quinones to Managua to report on Obando's appointment, spiked the story completely.

CHAPTER SIX, STUDY 4

## "Reporting the War on FMLN Terms"

### OVERVIEW

When the Marxist FMLN guerrillas of El Salvador went on an urban offensive in November 1989 to oust the democratically elected government of Alfredo Cristiani, many reporters turned a blind eye to the rebels' killings, assassination campaigns, and even their communist nature. That's the conclusion of a December 1989 study by the Media Research Center (MRC). Once again, as the National Conservative Foundation found in "Selective Eye on Central America" (Chapter Six, Study 2), the American media chose to discredit the Salvadoran government. Ignoring the communist terror, the news outlets highlighted government links to "right-wing" death squads and terror, while rarely informing their audience that President Cristiani was the Salvadoran people's chosen leader.

To study the media's El Salvador coverage, MRC analysts reviewed all news stories from November 11, when the offensive began, to November 30 in three newspapers (*The Washington Post, New York Times,* and *Los Angeles Times*), and on the ABC, CBS, CNN and NBC evening news shows. Analysts also reviewed the issues of *Time, Newsweek,* and *U.S. News & World Report* dated November 27, December 4 and 11, 1989.

### KEY FINDINGS

- Most reporters portrayed alleged right-wing assassinations as more important than FMLN killings. Newscasts and newspapers were dominated by the murders of six Jesuits by "right-wing" elements. Only one story contrasted the Jesuit killings with the continuing campaign of assassinations of government officials by the FMLN.

- The news outlets described the right as "extreme" but never the left. In the twenty days of coverage, not one reporter identified the FMLN as "communist," but simply as "leftist" (123 times) or "Marxist-led" (20 times). But reporters continually used terms such as "extreme right" and "far right" to describe the other side.

- The media rarely (only five times) referred to Cristiani's government as "democratic" or "freely elected." And they never described the FMLN insurgency as "undemocratic."

## STUDY EXCERPT

**Reporting the War on FMLN Terms** by the Media Research Center. From *MediaWatch*, December 1989.

Consider this Latin American scenario: a democratically elected government comes under attack from a band of terrorists. The government, elected six months earlier, had won in a landslide with a higher turnout than in any national election in the U.S. over the last twenty years. The terrorists, who assassinated at least eight mayors and threatened to murder anyone who dared to vote, carried less than 4 percent of the electorate. The election was certified by international observers as one of the freest and fairest in the history of the region.

Having lost this test of the people's support, the terrorists now try to shoot their way to power. They have invaded neighborhoods in the capital city, where they hide behind innocent civilians, and then cynically blame the government's army for civilian deaths.

Does this version of events sound familiar? If not, you probably relied on major media sources for your news of the war in El Salvador. Through the subtle use of labeling and cursory reporting of rebel violence, the media indicted the country's democratic government as a harsh violator of human rights, while softpedaling the terror and violence of the Soviet-backed Farabundo Marti National Liberation Front (FMLN) insurgency that would overthrow them.

**1. Assassinations.** Several hundred civilians were killed in the mid-November FMLN offensive, but when six Jesuit priests sympathetic to the communist rebels were murdered a few days into the fighting, their deaths, immediately attributed to "right-wing death squads," quickly became the pivotal event in the unfolding news story. In typical fashion, CBS reporter Juan Vasquez portrayed the priests as martyrs for the right side of history: "The nation's archbishop said the murdered priests' only crime was being on the side of the poor, a central theme of liberation theology." Not one TV reporter bothered to mention that liberation theology is inspired by Marxism. *Time*'s Jill Smolowe found that of all the killings, the "most cold-blooded was the brutal slayings of six Jesuit priests, which seemed to symbolize all that is wrong in El Salvador." To Smolowe, "all that is wrong" are the misdeeds and alleged misdeeds of the right, and not the left.

This concern wasn't extended to the victims of left-wing violence. Only one story (in the *Los Angeles Times*) mentioned the FMLN's past assassinations of government officials and mayors while the newscasts and front pages were dominated by the Jesuit murders. Not one contrasted the priests' deaths with reports of the hospital raid in Zacatecouluca, where the rebels killed wounded soldiers in their beds, despite Assistant Secretary of State Bernard Aronson's November 17 Senate testimony on the incident.

When former Supreme Court President Francisco Guerrero was assassinated on November 28, the media demonstrated a noticeable lack of outrage. ABC didn't find it important enough to make the evening news. In reports the next day, none of the three newspapers reported the killing as part of a continuing FMLN campaign to assassinate prominent government officials and mayors. The only assassination they reported just happened to be the only one the FMLN has acknowledged, that of Attorney General Alberto Garcia Alvarado. The three newspapers cited an interview with rebel commander Joaquin Villalobos, who said, "because of his defense of death squads, he was a legitimate target." Guerrero's assassination wasn't played much differently: *The New York Times* described the killing with the subheadline "An official seen by leftists as a barrier to change is gunned down."

2. **Labels.** The media's point of view also came through in the words used to describe the two sides in the war. By employing a standard right-left road map to describe the war, reporters applied labels that implied pluralism within the FMLN, where there is none, and denied the kinds of clear comparisons (communist vs. anti-communist, democratic vs. anti-democratic) that would give the Cristiani government any form of moral advantage. In the twenty days following the onset of the guerrilla offensive, reporters never once identified the FMLN as "communist." The media's label of choice for the FMLN was "leftist," applied 123 times. That's mild enough to apply to George McGovern or Jesse Jackson. Another label, "Marxist-led," used twenty times, implies that Marxists lead some sort of broad-based coalition. [See Graph 6D]

Contrast the labeling of the FMLN with that of El Salvador's right wing. Especially in the aftermath of the Jesuit murders, the media tossed around terms such as "extreme right," the "violent right," the "far right," and "right-wing extremists" 59 times. "Far left" was invoked only twice. No reporter used "extreme left," "left-wing extremists," or "violent left" to characterize the communist guerrillas. (Although no reporter ever used the word "terrorist" to describe the FMLN, Dan Rather once used the term "rebel terror squads.") Despite assassinations attributed to both sides, a Nexis ® search of major newspapers and magazines over the last decade found that no reporter has ever used the term "left-wing death squad."

*Time* was the champion of labeling imbalance: in three weeks of stories, it never labeled the guerrillas. But in its December 11 issue, Washington reporter J.F.O. McAllister wrote that the "ultra-rightists" of

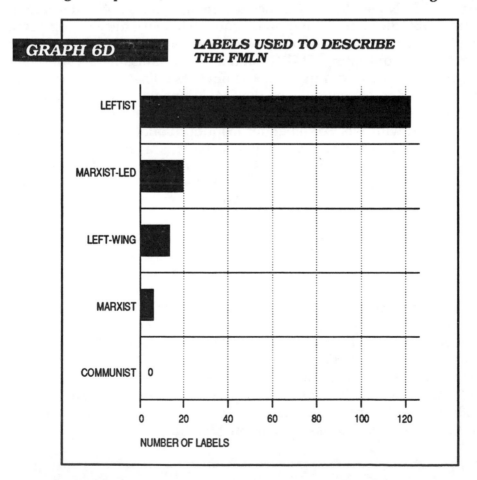

**GRAPH 6D**

**LABELS USED TO DESCRIBE THE FMLN**

NUMBER OF LABELS

the Cristiani government were "betraying distressingly fascist leanings," and concluded that "the future of El Salvador looks to be a free-for-all between a buoyant and rearmed FMLN and generals willing to make the country a boneyard."

**3. Democracy.** The Cristiani government was elected, but reporters ignored this vital point. They allowed U.S. officials to state it on a few occasions, but made it themselves only five times. Major media reporters never referred to the rebels as "anti-democratic" and refused to note that the FMLN's so-called "popular movement" got less than 4 percent of the vote. Instead, amazingly, the government was labeled undemocratic. On CBS, Juan Vasquez reported: "In a country where the powerful consider liberation theology a dangerous idea, the priests dared to speak up for social justice and, frequently, against the U.S. policy of supporting a government they saw as undemocratic." NBC's Jim Cummins repeatedly referred to the government as "military-civilian," making no distinction between the current elected government and the junta that took power in 1979.

The tenor of news coverage was best distilled in *Time*'s December 4 issue. "Washington should rethink its relationship with a democratically elected government that cannot control fanatic right-wing elements in the armed forces. El Salvador's armed forces, nourished by American dollars, bear primary responsibility for the country's scandalous human rights record. Washington should cut off military aid unless travesties like the killing of the six Jesuits are stopped."

Wrapped up in its Vietnam-driven suspicion of U.S. foreign policy and its distaste for the recipients of U.S. aid, the media crossed the line from skepticism to antagonism, refusing to concede that the Cristiani government is the legitimate voice of its people. The media reserved their harshest scrutiny for Cristiani's elected government, repeating the propaganda themes of the FMLN, which has little regard for Western democratic values.

**CHAPTER SIX, STUDY 5**

## Grenada and the Media's Anti-Liberation Line

### OVERVIEW

The October 1983 liberation of Grenada was a milestone for Ronald Reagan and American foreign policy. The vast majority of Americans wholeheartedly supported the move, which brought renewed vigor and patriotism to the American public and a new sense of purpose to U.S. policy abroad. Rolling back communism was hailed by the Grenadans as well; the overwhelming majority of the island's inhabitants welcomed the arrival of U.S. liberation forces.

But despite the jubilation of most Americans and Grenadans, the American media pushed a distinct anti-liberation line. A study by the National Conservative Foundation (NCF) which ran in the October, 1986 *Newswatch* concluded that media reports favored the opponents of the U.S. liberation of Grenada far more than its supporters.

The NCF used the Nexis ® newspaper data retrieval system to study *Washington Post, New York Times,* Associated Press (AP), and United Press International (UPI) non-opinion news stories from October 25 to November 9, 1983. To determine whether the coverage favored supporters or opponents of the military effort, stories that used the following words were analyzed: "condemn," "oppose," "protest," "criticize," "support," and "endorse."

### KEY FINDINGS

- Nearly 70 percent of the 155 stories analyzed dealt with opposition to the military action. Of the AP stories, 81 percent were about opposition to the U.S. military move, as were 70 percent of *The New York Times,* 67 percent of the UPI, and 57 percent of *The Washington Post* reports. [See Graph 6E]

- The four news sources ran only seven stories on public opinion polls in which the majority of Americans supported the military operation. In contrast, they ran 12 stories on small public protests around America. An October 27 *New York Times* article about a South

Carolina protest began: "10 people carrying signs reading 'Non-Intervention for Russia and America' and 'Marines out of Grenada -- U.S. abide by U.N. Charter' gathered across from the Federal Building to protest the invasion. 'Reagan is a cowboy' said one."

- "Invasion" was the favorite descriptive term. Other negative terms dominated the newsprint as well: "Occupation" was used by reporters twenty times. For example, the *Post* on October 29 wrote: "The officials said the Marines will probably depart within a week, leaving an occupation force of about 5,000 Army soldiers." The NCF study brought up an interesting parallel: "[The media] would never

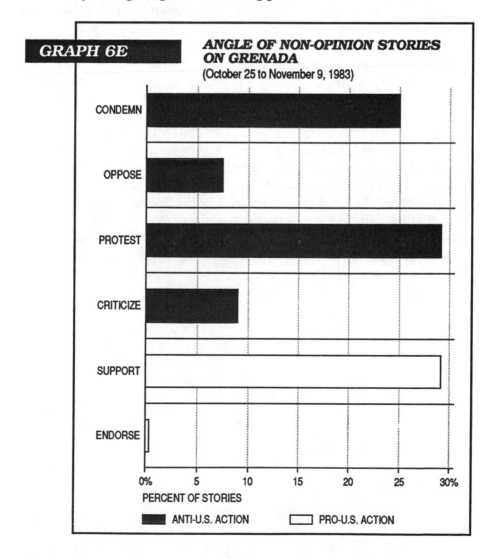

**GRAPH 6E**

**ANGLE OF NON-OPINION STORIES ON GRENADA**
(October 25 to November 9, 1983)

PERCENT OF STORIES

■ ANTI-U.S. ACTION    □ PRO-U.S. ACTION

have written that America 'occupied' France in 1944, yet the situation in Grenada was similar -- the U.S. and allied forces arrived, did battle with a third nation's troops, reinstated democratic institutions usurped by a puppet government, and withdrew as soon as feasible."

• On 19 occasions, the four outlets quoted President Reagan speaking of the "rescue mission" to save the American citizens on the island, but they themselves used the term just once in 155 news stories.

• Reporters never once used the term "liberation" unless in quotes and/or attributed to someone.

• Disgruntlement over press restrictions gained more prominence than freedom for Grenadans. Twenty-eight stories were fully devoted to the restrictions while another 25 mentioned them.

• The NCF study concluded: "In a clear conflict between a genuinely well-meaning U.S. effort to free a nation from totalitarian oppression and those opposed to the noble goal, the media chose to aim their sights not to telling of the victorious liberation of Grenada, but, instead, focused on those upset by the Soviet defeat. Unwilling to distinguish between American actions motivated by good will and Soviet actions to enslave more people, the media saw the event as an occupation or conquest just like Afghanistan."

# "The Unnewsworthy Holocaust: TV News and Terror in Cambodia"

## OVERVIEW

The xenophobic reign of terror by the Marxist Khmer Rouge from April 1975 to January 1979 in Cambodia was as brutal as that of any in history. Up to three million Cambodians died of starvation, torture or execution. But despite what George Washington University professor William Adams and research associate Michael Joblove called "the barbarism and the magnitude of the tragedy," major media outlets in the U.S. paid little attention to the tragic events.

To find out what the American public was told about the despotic reign of Pol Pot, Adams and Joblove, with the help of the Vanderbilt News Archive, studied ABC, CBS, and NBC weeknight news coverage from April 1975 through December 1978. They limited their focus to reports about "Cambodian refugees, genocide, general Khmer Rouge policies, and the reconstruction of society." They excluded reports about border clashes with neighbors, simple civil war occurrences, and the Mayaguez incident. Their statistics show that Americans who watched network news never saw the carnage and chaos that consumed Cambodia during those four years.

## KEY FINDINGS

- "Stories about the 'new society' and death in Cambodia were so sporadic that even the most constant viewers could not be expected to grasp the gravity of the Cambodian crisis." Over the four-year period of the Khmer Rouge rule, the three networks devoted less than sixty minutes on weeknights to the human rights situation in Cambodia. That averaged out to less than thirty seconds per month per network.

- Explicit discussion of genocide was heard on ABC for less than one minute and on CBS and NBC less than four minutes each during the four-year period.

- To show what little mention there was of death in Cambodia, the authors compared the coverage to time given the Jonestown murders and suicides. In the first week alone, three hours of network news detailed the cult deaths, although the death toll was at least a thousand times less than in Cambodia.

- Adams and Joblove dismissed the old network line that without pictures there is no story: "Poignant and striking footage was available without end in refugee camps all across eastern Thailand....The fact that television ignored the upheaval in Cambodia simply cannot be attributed to a dull story with poor pictures."

- The authors blamed the print media as well. "Television caricatures the front page of the prestige press" and "assignment editors rely heavily on *The New York Times*, *The Washington Post*, and the wire services to set the network agenda." So it was no surprise when the networks didn't "veer far from the pack" and "provide extensive coverage of a topic given little attention in print." Until mid-1978, little print space was given the events in Cambodia. Only when it picked up did television follow.

## STUDY EXCERPT

**The Unnewsworthy Holocaust: TV News and Terror in Cambodia** by William C. Adams and Michael Joblove. From *Television Coverage of International Affairs.*

In April of 1975, Khmer Rouge forces overran Phnom Penh. Until their fall from power in the winter of 1979, the world was witness to one of the most bizarre and brutal revolutions of this century. Costs of Khmer Rouge rule were high. An estimated one to three million of Cambodia's eight million people died by starvation, disease, or execution.

No other single episode has involved a greater loss of life during the last quarter century. Yet, despite the barbarism and magnitude of the tragedy, little public attention was directed to Cambodia. It was ignored by the U.S. media, government, and people.

The death toll was at least a thousand times greater than that of the Jonestown murders and suicides, but news coverage of Cambodia was a fraction of that given to Jonestown. Added together over the entire four-year Khmer Rouge period, all three television networks devoted less than sixty minutes on weeknights to the new society and human rights in Cambodia. Nearly three hours were spent detailing the Jonestown deaths in the first week alone.

What, if anything, were Americans told about human rights and society in Cambodia from their preferred source of international news -- early evening, network television news? To find out, we examined Vanderbilt University's *Television News Index and Abstracts* for weeknight news coverage from April 1975 until December 1978.

The Vanderbilt Archive loaned compiled videotapes of the stories we had identified from the abstracts. Stories selected were all those about Cambodian refugees, genocide, general Khmer Rouge policies, and the reconstruction of society. Excluded were purely military stories about border clashes, civil war, and the *Mayaguez*. Research was conducted at the television news studies facilities of George Washington University's Gelman Library. The findings were generally consistent for all three networks.

### A Few Sad Seconds
Stories about the "new society" and death in Cambodia were so sporadic that even the most constant viewers could not be expected to grasp the gravity of the Cambodian crises. As shown in Table 6F, from April 1975 to December 1978, NBC aired 11 stories (17 minutes 35 seconds) on life in the "new Cambodia," compared with 13 stories on CBS (28 minutes 55 seconds), and 6 stories on ABC (11 minutes 25 seconds). This averages out to less than thirty seconds per month per network on the rule of the Khmer Rouge.

ABC offered a little over four minutes in 1975, and the next year carried one human rights story about Cambodia. Two years passed before ABC returned to the subject. In April 1978, ABC viewers heard anchorman Tom Jarriel say President Carter had condemned Cambodia as "the worst offender in the world" with regard to human rights. Carter had apparently not been watching ABC News.

CBS focused on human rights in Cambodia for sixty seconds during 1975, for six minutes, ten seconds in 1976, and for the same amount of time again in 1977. CBS stepped up coverage in 1978. In April 1978, CBS ran two special reports -- each over four minutes. Later in August, after

Senator McGovern's call for armed intervention in Cambodia, CBS spent two minutes and twenty seconds on the subject of Cambodian human rights.

NBC's nearly 18 minutes of coverage over four years almost equaled a single night's coverage of the Guyana massacre. NBC did broadcast a "Segment Three" (4 minutes 30 seconds) feature on human rights in Cambodia during the evening news on June 2, 1978. Once, NBC even opened its program with a lead story on Cambodian suffering (7/20/75). The twenty-second story concerned an attempted escape of 300 Cambodians; only 12 people had survived. This story and its placement were quite exceptional. No other Cambodian human rights story was ever made the lead; the few stories that were aired were usually placed midway through the broadcast. Overall, in 1975-78, very little time was devoted to the steady stream of refugees who succeeded (or failed) in escaping what they called the "terror" of their homeland.

This accounting of air time on human rights in Cambodia does not measure the number of times when, in a story that was otherwise about a border clash with Vietnam, the regime might have been referred to as "harsh." However, the figures are actually generous because they include air time devoted to any discussion of the "new society" created by the

| TABLE 6F | WEEKNIGHT COVERAGE OF THE "NEW SOCIETY" AND HUMAN RIGHTS IN CAMBODIA (April 1975-December 1978) | | | | | |
|---|---|---|---|---|---|---|
| | ABC | | CBS | | NBC | |
| | TIME | NUMBER OF STORIES | TIME | NUMBER OF STORIES | TIME | NUMBER OF STORIES |
| April-June 1975 | 0:20 | 1 | 1:00 | 2 | 1:00 | 1 |
| July-Dec. 1975 | 4:10 | 2 | — | 0 | 2:20 | 2 |
| Jan.-June 1976 | 3:10 | 1 | 2:30 | 1 | — | 0 |
| July-Dec. 1976 | — | 0 | 3:40 | 1 | — | 0 |
| Jan.-June 1977 | — | 0 | 2:30 | 1 | 0:40 | 1 |
| July-Dec. 1977 | — | 0 | 3:40 | 2 | 4:00 | 2 |
| Jan.-June 1978 | 0:30 | 1 | 11:40 | 4 | 6:40 | 3 |
| July-Dec. 1978 | 3:15 | 1 | 3:55 | 2 | 2:55 | 2 |
| Total | 11:25 | 6 | 28:55 | 13 | 17:35 | 11 |

Khmer Rouge, some of which dismissed or ignored reports of genocide. When this "harshness" was specifically mentioned, treatment of the subject of mass murders varied wildly -- sometimes treated with skepticism, sometimes as undisputed fact, sometimes as mere rumor. The issue of genocide was explicitly addressed less than one minute by ABC, less than four minutes by CBS, and less than four minutes by NBC.

On August 21, 1978, Senator McGovern called for an international force to invade Cambodia in order to stop the genocide. The incongruity of George McGovern advocating military action in Southeast Asia was enough to attract some attention. ABC interviewed the Senator and included a follow-up clip of a refugee's personal story of tragedy. CBS covered the subcommittee meeting at which the plea was made. NBC gave minimum coverage with a twenty-second summary.

### Network Silence Despite Numerous Reports

Why was the massive loss of life in Cambodia given so little attention? It was not that the networks were uninformed about the new regime; as soon as news of the deaths reached the outside world, the networks were alerted. As early as June 24, 1975, in a speech covered by all three networks, Secretary of State Kissinger stressed that Cambodians had "suffered a terrible death toll" under the Khmer Rouge. CBS also mentioned that Freedom House had compared the Cambodian events to the Nazi annihilation of 6 million Jews.

On July 8, 1975, as eyewitness reports of barbarism were brought by escaping refugees, NBC ran a story with correspondent Bernard Kalb. According to Kalb, "the story [the refugees] have been telling is one of horror." One witness saw "1,500 bodies, all knifed to death." One refugee said people were killed "if they didn't plant rice" and said he had recently seen 1,000 dead bodies. Kalb noted that skepticism first greeted such stories, "but now there are so many that it must be true."

Somehow, this remarkable NBC story did not generate others. The fact that thousands of people were filling up refugee camps across Thailand with accounts of mass murders and starvation in Cambodia was not deemed newsworthy.

ABC's single enterprising story in 1975 was an interview with the then head of state, Prince Sihanouk. This was the only network interview with a Cambodian government official since Kissinger's speech on the massive loss of life, since the Kalb story of atrocities, and since newspaper accounts of forced labor camps and execution. Harry Reasoner was not shown questioning Sihanouk about any of these matters. Instead, the Prince was shown talking about rice production and boosting the economy.

This prompted Mr. Reasoner's "roughest" inquiry:

"Prince Sihanouk, you spoke of the necessary severe and austere government. Now I think of nothing more unlike the Cambodian people than severity and austerity. Have they changed?"

To this hard-hitting question Sihanouk answered:

"No, no, no, no. You know the Khmer Rouge, they are very nationalistic. Also, they want Cambodia to remain Cambodian. When I say severe or austere I mean that we have to walk much more than before. But Cambodians, they remain Cambodians. They like joking. They like laughing, they like singing. So they continue to do it. There is really a general way of life and there is still this way of life in Cambodia."

Sihanouk's depiction of the joking, laughing, singing Cambodian people was not seriously questioned by ABC News that year.

On January 26, 1976, CBS aired an account from reporter Peter Collins about forced evacuation from the cities, forced labor in the fields, and a refugee tale of five workers beaten to death with an iron pipe. Collins concluded that no one had been allowed to verify the refugee horror tales, "but their accounts of life across this frontier are so numerous and detailed, there seems little doubt that the new communist regime is continuing its harsh reform of Cambodia, under what refugees describe as 'a reign of terror.'" But CBS did not pursue the story. Six months passed before CBS again considered this "reign of terror."

## A Small Shift in 1978

In 1978, after two years of near total neglect, the networks ran a handful of stories about human rights in Cambodia. On January 18, 1978, CBS covered Deputy Secretary of State Warren Christopher's condemnation of the "systematic terror and grinding down of the Cambodian people." "Hundreds of thousands of human beings," he said, "have perished under this regime." (Neither NBC nor ABC made any mention of the speech, although five months had passed since NBC had told its viewers about human rights "problems" in Cambodia and nearly two years had elapsed since ABC's last report on the subject.)

A two-part "Inside Cambodia" series by CBS's Bert Quint was aired April 20 and 21, 1978. Quint made references to estimates of one million people having been killed, though he cautioned that the figure "had not been confirmed by neutral observers." "Neither," he added, had "the new rulers bothered to deny them." Refugee accounts of harsh working conditions and mass killings were also mentioned.

Also on April 20, 1978, NBC ran a retrospective on Khmer Rouge rule. John Chancellor introduced the piece:

"It was three years ago this week that the city of Phnom Penh was captured by the Khmer Rouge revolutionary movement, and since then the story of Cambodia has been a horror story: The cities emptied -- thousands killed or allowed to die in the countryside. There have been charges of genocide."

Thus, in the fourth year of its rule, the Khmer Rouge emerged on television as a nasty and tyrannical -- though still rarely newsworthy -- group that was probably implicated in the ominously empty streets of Phnom Penh. David Brinkley, having displayed little prior moral outrage on the subject, called them "iron-fisted murderous savages" in a brief 1978 commentary.

By late 1978, the occasional network stories had even begun to stop "balancing" the reports of mass execution with reports of "cleaning up the cities." Death estimates that had earlier been simple "reports of mass death" (NBC, 7/8/75) became in 1978 "stories of one million killed" (CBS, 4/20/78), "hundreds of thousands, possibly 2.5 million killed" (CBS, 8/21/78), "one hundred thousand to one million" (NBC, 6/2/78), "one to three million" (NBC, 9/21/78).

### Why Did the Networks Dismiss Cambodia?
Nightly news cannot cover everything. The criticism that broadcast news people themselves make most frequently is that the program is too brief. In this light, they note, the omissions and compression imposed by brevity are unfortunate but also unavoidable. (The subject then shifts to

affiliates which resist expansion to an hour of network news.) Nevertheless, it is difficult to understand why the tragedy of Cambodia never secured any sustained attention.

One explanation is ideological. Events in Cambodia appeared to contradict the supposed Lessons of Vietnam. The wisdom Americans were to have acquired in Southeast Asia was that leftist guerrilla insurgents were nationalistic and relatively benign, were likely improvements over the corrupt rightist regimes they replaced, and were certainly not worth any significant expenditure of U.S. diplomatic, economic, or military power. As one telling *New York Times* headline put it: "Indochina Without Americans/For Most, a Better Life" (April 13, 1975). Unfortunately, Pol Pot's epigones of Marx-Lenin-Mao had not read this particular script. Thousands of Cambodian refugees brought stories of mass death and murder, but this "unverified" news could not be easily broadcast or printed to fit the Lessons of Vietnam.

There are other possible reasons for the lack of coverage. However, some of the usual explanations are inadequate.

When television news downplays a story that would otherwise appear to merit more coverage, the reason is often that the story lacked "good pictures," lacked drama and controversy, or lacked human interest. Television news, students of the medium repeatedly note, places a premium on stories that can be made visually interesting and that create emotional involvement by showing continuing sagas of conflict, danger, irony, humor, tragedy.

Cambodia under Khmer Rouge rule should have qualified superbly for the dramaturgy of television news. Only one barrier hampered coverage: camera crews were not invited inside the borders to beam home pictures of death, executions, and the forced march into the countryside. Poignant and striking footage was available without end, however, in refugee camps all across eastern Thailand. The horrible tales of death told movingly by escaped Cambodians made Kalb's July 1975 story strong and vivid. With continuous daring escape attempts, the uprooted and terrorized families, and the vandalizing of an historic culture, human interest stories were scarcely in short supply. The fact that television ignored the upheaval in Cambodia simply cannot be attributed to a dull story with poor pictures.

An even less convincing argument for the lack of coverage is that the outside world did not really know precisely what was going on within the jungle borders. Pol Pot did not issue a press release confirming the number of deaths as 3 million or merely three hundred thousand. Nor was it announced how many of the deaths should be attributed to starvation, the forced march, disease, bullets, or being clubbed to death. Not knowing exactly, the line goes, the media prudently overlooked the subject entirely.

When presented with the network record on Cambodia, one producer at ABC News responded, incredibly enough, by repeating the "no pictures" and "no certitude" arguments. Mary Fifield (1980) wrote that the "elemental explanation" for ABC's "difficulty" in covering the "devastation in Cambodia" was that "we could not get into the country."

She said candidly:

"Since we were not able to gain entrance to Cambodia, there was no way television news could show the actual tragedy. Although there were refugees in camps along the Thai border who were willing to describe the atrocities committed by the Khmer Rouge, some reporters and editors were reluctant to use their stories because they were not always completely reliable."

So, without good inside pictures of the tragedy and with refugees who "were not always completely reliable," ABC just ignored the suspected death of thousands of Cambodians and failed to run a single weeknight story on the subject over a two-year period at the height of Khmer Rouge rule.

(Producer Fifield notes correctly that in 1979, *after* the Khmer Rouge was overthrown, the networks' coverage "improved." In 1979, with Pol Pot's terror ended, ABC's retrospectives -- presumably replete with superb pictures and the very fullest verification -- must certainly have been impressive.)

The head-in-the-sand argument is a bizarre one. Even the possibility of mass murder of thousands, let alone tens of thousands (at a time when Americans were watching *Holocaust* in prime time), should surely have triggered a sustained effort at intense and tough investigative reporting. That the dimensions of the chaos in Cambodia were not altogether clear should have prompted greater scrutiny, not less. From Three Mile Island to Jonestown to Skylab to DC-10s, uncertainty as to the possible scope of a misfortune is usually an incentive, not a deterrent, to additional coverage.

In the case of Cambodia, from the earliest days of the Khmer Rouge, there were repeated and consistent reports from refugees in camps hundreds of miles apart telling similar stories of death and murder (e.g., see Barron & Paul, 1977). Only a handful of these stories found their way onto network television.

### Silence from the White House, Post, and the Times
In addition to ideology, another plausible explanation for the low level of television news about Cambodia was the strange silence from the White House. Scholars observed a decade ago that television, even more than the print media, is obsessed with the presidency. The absence of presidential concern about Cambodia would thus be likely to decrease the prospects for network coverage still further.

Neither Carter nor Ford directed any sustained attention to events under the Khmer Rouge. Both administrations engaged in the ritual of an annual condemnation of the regime, but little more -- no major diplomatic offensives, no continual publicity efforts, no stream of speeches, and no public debate over more overt moves. With little but token gestures from the President, at least one major factor that would promote network coverage of the subject was absent. (This is also partly circular, because greater media attention would likely have stimulated more concern with the subject at the White House.)

One other explanation for the lack of concern with Cambodia is that television caricatures the front page of the prestige press. Assignment editors rely heavily on *The New York Times*, *Washington Post*, and wire services to set the network agenda. Television news usually seems afraid to veer far from the pack and is unlikely to provide extensive coverage of a topic given little attention in print. While this explanation begs the question of *Post* and *Times* coverage, it does help account for television's pattern. In fact, until mid-1978, the *Times* and the *Post* gave very little space to events in Cambodia.

In the summer of 1978, both papers began to run two or three front page stories a month relating to human rights in Cambodia. While this falls short of the attention focused on certain authoritarian regimes in the West, it exceeded the coverage given throughout 1975, 1976, and 1977 to Cambodia. In those years, only two or three news stories regarding human rights in Cambodia were run during each 12-month period. Thus, television coverage as a proportion of available time and space compares favorably to print coverage.

The problem of inattention and silence was explained in a *New York Times* editorial on July 9, 1975:

> "The picture begins to emerge of a country that resembles a giant prison camp with the urban supporters of the former regime being worked to death on thin gruel and hard labor and with medical care virtually nonexistent.
>
> The mouthing of such high-sounding objectives as 'peasant revolutions' or 'purification' through labor on the land cannot conceal the barbarous cruelty of the Khmer Rouge, which can be compared with Soviet extermination of Kulaks or with Gulag Archipelago.
>
> What, if anything, can the outside world do to alter the genocidal policies of Cambodia's hard men? Silence certainly will not move them. Were Cambodia a non-communist or non-Third World country, the outraged protests from the developing and communist countries, not to mention Europe and the United States, would be deafening.
>
> Members of Congress and others who rightly criticized the undemocratic nature of the Lon Nol regime have a special obligation to speak up. Few if any have been heard from. The United Nations is silent. That silence must be broken."

After this call for an end to silence, over three years passed before the *Times* again editorialized on the subject. Nor, as we have shown, was the silence broken by the great American networks. The "genocidal policies of Cambodia's hard men" were insufficiently newsworthy.

Reprinted with permission from *Television Coverage of International Affairs* edited by William C. Adams. Copyright © 1982 by Ablex Publishing Corporation.

**CHAPTER SIX, STUDY 7**

# Ignoring the Flight of the Boat People

## OVERVIEW

After the fall of Saigon in April 1975 and the communist takeover, Indo-China was plunged into an era of persecution and squalor, due in large part to the Marxist philosophies forced upon Vietnam, Cambodia, and Laos. More than 2 million people fled their homelands over the next decade -- a testament to the brutality that the communists brought to the region.

But the massive exodus was barely mentioned by the media when the tenth anniversary of communism in Southeast Asia rolled around. A National Conservative Foundation (NCF) study in the April, 1987 *Newswatch* found that the plight of the so-called "boat people" rarely appeared in the print media when reporters recalled Saigon's fall.

The NCF studied articles in *The New York Times*, *Washington Post*, *Time*, *Newsweek*, and the two major wire services between April 1 and May 15, 1985 that dealt with the Vietnam anniversary. These articles were checked for references to "boat people" or other refugees.

## KEY FINDINGS

- 106 news stories on the anniversary were run. Just 12 (11 percent) centered on boat people and the refugee exodus.[See Table 6G]

- *The Washington Post* found the refugee problem important enough for just one news story. *The New York Times* did only one better, allotting just 14 percent of all anniversary coverage to the problem.

- The wire services each ran 37 stories, but "boat people" coverage was limited to one story on the UPI wire and four at AP.

- *Newsweek* "managed to salvage the honor of the profession." It alone gave prominent coverage to the region's "victims of communism" in all three of its articles on the anniversary. Two articles dealt with refugees. The lead article of *Newsweek*'s special issue on the anniversary declared: "The events of the last decade -- the occupation of Cambodia, the flight of the boat people, the dreary neo-Stalinist isolation of Vietnam today -- have deflated the hopeful expectations of those who saw Ho Chi Minh as the liberator of his country."

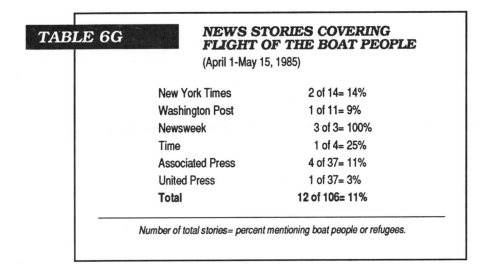

**TABLE 6G** — *NEWS STORIES COVERING FLIGHT OF THE BOAT PEOPLE*
(April 1-May 15, 1985)

| | |
|---|---|
| New York Times | 2 of 14= 14% |
| Washington Post | 1 of 11= 9% |
| Newsweek | 3 of 3= 100% |
| Time | 1 of 4= 25% |
| Associated Press | 4 of 37= 11% |
| United Press | 1 of 37= 3% |
| **Total** | **12 of 106= 11%** |

*Number of total stories= percent mentioning boat people or refugees.*

# 7 The Media & Economics: Big Brother's Best Friend?

Every election year pollsters try to determine what most concerns voters. The answer is always the same: "pocketbook issues" -- how well-off voters feel and how secure they view their economic future. Obviously, peoples' perceptions are influenced by how the media tell them the economy is performing.

Do Big Media reporters accurately portray the state of the American economy, or do journalists present a distorted picture by emphasizing negative economic developments? More to the point, is economic reporting biased against conservative policies and does this lead voters to go to the polls with an unfairly negative understanding of conservative economic policies?

The studies presented in this chapter show that reporting not only reflects "bad news bias," but also favors liberal economic policies over conservative ones.

---

**CHAPTER SEVEN, STUDY 1**

## "Television Evening News Covers Inflation"

### OVERVIEW

Inflation soared out of control in the late 1970s, prompting the Media Institute in 1980 to study what the television networks told Americans about the "most serious domestic problem" of the time. "Would the casual, or even attentive viewer," the Media Institute wanted to know, "come away from his television set with the impression that government causes inflation? Or that the private sector is to blame?" Tom Bethell, then an editor of *The Washington Monthly*, reviewed 248 television network evening news stories. The monograph, *Television Evening News Covers Inflation*, covered every 1978 and 1979 CBS story and all ABC and NBC reports in January-February 1978 and March-April 1979.

Bethell concluded that network reporters followed liberal thinking: the overwhelming percentage of pieces blamed inflation on wage and price hikes by the private sector while exonerating government policies, such as printing too much money.

## KEY FINDINGS

- "Fully 71 percent of the 200 CBS News stories tended to encourage the view that wages or price increases either led to inflation or were synonymous with it." For ABC and NBC "either wages or prices were blamed in 66.5 percent" of the stories on inflation. [See Table 7A] This usually occurred when the networks reported the latest Consumer Price Index figures issued by the Bureau of Labor Statistics which identified the items whose price had increased. Bethell concluded: "Most economists would probably agree that this is analogous to a doctor who blames his patient's fever on the excessive level of the mercury in the thermometer."

- 76 percent of CBS stories and 77 percent of ABC and NBC stories cited non-government policy reasons for inflation.

| TABLE 7A | **WAGE OR PRICE INCREASES LEAD TO INFLATION** (Percentage of Stories Listing Causes of Inflation) | | | |
|---|---|---|---|---|
| | WAGE OR PRICE | WAGE | PRICE | WAGE & PRICE |
| CBS Evening News | 71.0% | 24.5% | 61.5% | 15% |
| NBC & ABC | 66.5% | 23.0% | 62.5% | 19% |

- Every week the Federal Reserve Board makes available the money supply figure, but only 6 percent of CBS and 4 percent of ABC and NBC inflation stories even hinted "that inflation was caused by printing too much money."

# "The Vanishing Economy: Television Coverage of Economic Affairs 1982-1987"

## OVERVIEW

In 1988 Ted J. Smith III, an Associate Professor of Mass Communications at Virginia Commonwealth University, undertook probably the most extensive study ever of how television networks cover the economy. Smith reviewed 13,915 ABC's *World News Tonight*, CBS *Evening News* and NBC *Nightly News* stories on the economy aired during three one-year periods: July 1 to June 30, 1982-83, 1984-85, and 1986-87.

Smith's findings appeared in a 1988 Media Institute monograph, *The Vanishing Economy: Television Coverage of Economic Affairs 1982-1987*. The purpose of the analysis was to learn whether television news provided viewers with an accurate understanding of economic improvement as the nation rebounded from the 1982 recession. Smith concluded that "by 1986 the reduction in coverage of basic economic data was so great that it would be difficult for even the most attentive TV viewer to form an accurate perception of how the economy was performing."

## KEY FINDINGS

- "In each year of the study, the number of negative economic stories exceeded the number of positive stories by a ratio of 4.9 to 1 or more." [See Table 7B]

- "As the economy progressively improved" from 1982 to 1987, "the amount of economic coverage on network television news progressively declined" from 1,022 stories reporting economic statistics to just 373, a 64 percent drop. Coverage simultaneously grew "more negative in tone." The ratio of negative to positive stories increased as economic indicators improved, from 4.9 to 1 in 1982-83 to 7.0 to 1 in 1986-87.

- As the economic indicators got better the networks began to neglect them so they could focus more attention on unhealthy economic signs. For instance, as the unemployment rate fell from 10.6 percent to just 6 percent by 1987, the number of stories on unemployment plunged by 79 percent while reports on the growing trade deficit soared 65 percent and on the homeless jumped by 167 percent.

- "Unlike economic problems, which were often attributed directly to Reagan Administration policies," Smithy reported "economic gains seldom were linked to any causual agent: They just happened."

## STUDY EXCERPT

From a study summary by Ted J. Smith III published in the *Richmond News Leader*, November 17, 1988.

Back in the recession of '82 it was easy to find the economy. All you had to do was turn on network TV news. But things have changed since then. You don't see the economy as much there anymore, and it's hard to recognize it when you do.

That realization is based on a study I have completed for the Media Institute in Washington. The results are simple, clear, and profoundly disturbing.

Consider first the amount of economic news. By most traditional standards, the economy improved in each of the three years of study, moving from recession and early recovery to slowing growth to renewed expansion. But network coverage followed an opposite progression, dropping from 5,191 focus stories in 1982-83 to 4,357 in 1984-85 and to 3,709 in 1986-87. [Over the three periods another 658 stories mentioned economic performance.] In general, the better the performance of the economy, the less attention it received on network television. [See Table 7B]

This pattern was especially pronounced in coverage of statistical indicators, which form the basis of any sound understanding of the economy. For example, in 1982-83 unemployment hit a post-Depression high of 10.8 percent and civilian employment dropped to 99 million. In 1986-87, the situation was dramatically different: Unemployment fell steadily from 7.1 percent to 6.3 percent while employment surged from 109.7 million to 112.4 million.

The change in initial reports of monthly unemployment statistics was equally dramatic. The network provided 139 minutes of coverage in 1982-83, but a mere 29 minutes in 1986-87 -- a 79 percent reduction. In five months of the 1986-87 period, NBC didn't even bother to report unemployment data.

Nor was this an isolated instance. We tracked coverage of every recurrent economic statistic reported on network news, a total of 86 major indicators. Excluding coverage of the stock and bond markets, reports of all other indicators dropped sharply and consistently -- from 1,022 in 1982-83 to 543 in 1984-85 and 373 in 1986-87. That's a staggering 64 percent reduction in the amount of statistical information provided to TV viewers.

Few areas of the economy escaped the cuts. Of the 34 indicators reported ten times or more, coverage of 32 declined over the course of the study. By 1986-87, six had been eliminated completely -- including

| TABLE 7B | TELEVISION NEWS* VS THE U.S. ECONOMY | | | |
|---|---|---|---|---|
| | (1 year periods — July1-June30) | | | |
| | RECESSION 1982-83 | RECOVERY 1984-85 | RECOVERY 1986-87 | PERCENT CHANGE |
| **Economic Focus Stories** | | | | |
| Number | 5,191 | 4,357 | 3,709 | -28.5% |
| Hours | 119.3 | 116.7 | 95.1 | -20.3% |
| Average Stories per Newscast | 5.21 | 4.32 | 3.81 | -26.9% |
| Percent Positive | 6.0% | 6.0% | 5.0% | -16.7% |
| Percent Negative | 29.4% | 33.8% | 35% | +19.0% |
| Ratio Negative:Positive | 4.9:1 | 5.6:1 | 7.0:1 | +42.9% |
| **Economic Statistics Stories by Sector** | | | | |
| Business/Industry | 212 | 99 | 55 | -74% |
| Employment | 143 | 62 | 34 | -76% |
| Personal Income | 116 | 112 | 95 | -18% |
| Industrial Production | 28 | 13 | 13 | -54% |
| Trade Deficit | 20 | 28 | 33 | +65% |
| Homelessness | 15 | 34 | 40 | +167% |

*Nightly news broadcasts of ABC, CBS and NBC.
Source: Media Institute "The Vanishing Economy"

business failures, and sub-group unemployment. Eight others -- including capacity utilization, factory orders, personal income, and employment -- were reported five times or less across the three networks combined. In short, by 1986 the reduction in coverage of basic economic data was so great that it would be difficult for even the most regular and attentive TV viewer to form an accurate perception of how the American economy was performing.

While the amount of economic coverage declined, its tone remained much the same. In general, negative economic information was reported often, prominently, and at length. Positive information was stressed only when it offered a novel counterpoint to negative. And unlike economic problems, which were often attributed directly to Reagan Administration policies, economic gains seldom were linked to any causual agent: They just happened.

To maintain this negative tone, coverage shifted from sector to sector in a constant search for new problems. For example, as unemployment improved and the trade deficit worsened, coverage of employment issues dropped from 15 percent of all economic stories in 1982-83 to 9 percent in 1986-87, while coverage of foreign economic news increased from 15 percent to 27 percent. And of the 86 economic indicators reported on network news, only one -- the merchandise trade deficit -- got greater coverage in each year of the study.

Another factor was a sharp increase in attacks on the business sector. These doubled to 915 stories in 1984-85 alone, or about 5 percent to 7 percent of all stories on network news that year. But this only emphasized an existing trend. In each year of the study, criticism of business outweighed praise by a ratio of at least ten to one, and businessmen were more often depicted as criminals than as benefactors of any kind.

Opinions will differ on the reasons for this pattern of coverage. But one likely cause is an overemphasis by network journalists on the "watchdog" role of the press. In their protectionist zeal they have neglected the more fundamental task of informing the electorate, which requires full coverage of both problems and accomplishments. Unfortunately, the systematic exclusion of positive information -- economic or otherwise -- is nothing less than censorship. As such, it strikes at the foundations of the democratic process.

If this analysis is correct, then network journalists have a clear obligation to reorder their priorities. In the area of economic news, the first (and absurdly obvious) step is to provide regular coverage of all major economic indicators. This would require less than 30 minutes per network per month, or about one-sixth of the time devoted to the economic news in 1986-87.

But for now, the damage may already be done. Most Americans claim television as their primary source of news, and many of them lined up at the polls on Election Day. It is not a comforting prospect to think that any President is chosen by voters uninformed -- or seriously misinformed -- about basic economic facts.

Reprinted with permission, from the *Richmond News Leader*, November 17, 1988.

CHAPTER SEVEN, STUDY 3

# Whatever Happened to "Reaganomics"?

## OVERVIEW

The first two studies in this chapter demonstrated the media's tendency to focus on negative economic news while ignoring positive developments. But does this "bad news bias" have a political twist detrimental to conservative policies? To find out, in 1987 the National Conservative Foundation (NCF) utilized the Nexis ® news data retrieval system to determine when reporters from *The New York Times, Washington Post, Time, Newsweek,* Associated Press and United Press International used the tendentious term "Reaganomics" (a word coined by the media) between January 1981 and the end of 1986.

The March, 1987 *Newswatch* study discovered that the media were quick to blame Reagan's conservative supply-side policies for economic downturns but very reluctant to credit his policies with success when the economy turned healthy.

## KEY FINDINGS

- The NCF charted the unemployment rate's rise and fall over the six year period and found that the use of "Reaganomics" followed in direct proportion. [See Graph 7C]

- Throughout 1981 and 1982, as unemployment rose steadily, the print media outlets used the term 1,957 times. The number of stories referring to "Reaganomics" dramatically increased in the third and fourth quarters of 1981, when the unemployment rate jumped to 8.8 percent.

- "References kept climbing through 1982 as the election drew closer, peaking at 768 in the fourth quarter." Following the November elections reporters used the term one-fourth as often.

- The unemployment rate dropped from 10.8 percent in late 1982 to 8.3 percent by the end of 1983. Concurrently, references to "Reaganomics" plummeted 74 percent. "As the economy continued

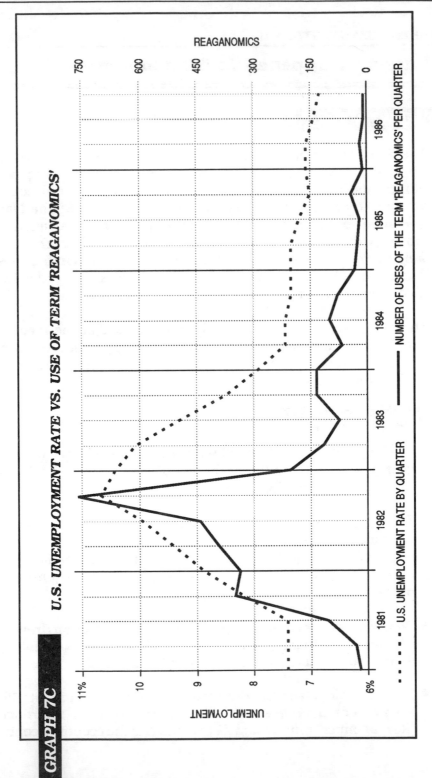

GRAPH 7C

U.S. UNEMPLOYMENT RATE VS. USE OF TERM 'REAGANOMICS'

to improve with unemployment dropping another 1.2 percent during the 1984 election year," NCF found use of the term fell "to a piddling 392 times."

- In 1981 "Reaganomics" appeared in only 121 *New York Times* stories, "but that number shot up to 354 with the onset of the 1982 recession." When the economy recovered in 1983 "the number of stories plummeted to 107." In 1982 *Times* coverage focused on "the theme that Reagan's economic policies were old, outdated, and unworkable." A January 3 news article titled "Reaganomics: The Report Card for 1981," concluded: "Instead, the blend of policies known as Reaganomics has resulted in what Allen Sinai of Data Resources Inc. called the 'old-time religion' -- a slowing of inflation by the familiar lead weights of recession and unemployment....What went wrong in 1981 is that Reaganomics met reality."

- By 1986 "Reaganomics" had nearly dropped from reporters' vocabulary; it was mentioned just 96 times.

# "TV News Covers the Budget Debate"

## OVERVIEW

How to reduce the deficit was a hotly debated issue throughout the 1980s. On the one side, conservatives urged reduction of non-defense spending, such as trimming the Social Security cost of living allowance (COLA) which automatically hikes payments to match inflation. On the other, liberals fought for Defense Department cuts. In 1985 the Media Institute decided to analyze how the television networks covered these "two most publicized options" and found "viewers were subjected to coverage which was not even remotely balanced." Network news "was overwhelmingly opposed to freezing the Social Security COLA" and "overwhelmingly opposed to increases in defense spending."

The Media Institute reviewed a total of 56 ABC, CBS, and NBC evening newscast stories aired in March, April, and May 1985, just as Reagan began his second term. After transcribing each report, analysts counted the number of lines dedicated to arguments for and against each option.

Arguments favoring a COLA freeze included:

- controlling the deficit is the top priority
- the elderly are fairly well off
- the overall package of cuts spreads the effects over the majority of the population

Arguments opposed to a COLA freeze included:

- a freeze will result in the neglect of the poor and elderly
- the elderly are being asked to bear a disproportionate amount of cuts
- Social Security represents a contract/promise that cannot be broken
- Social Security adds nothing to the deficit

Arguments favoring increased defense spending included:

- national security will be threatened if cuts are made
- the character of the defense budget is unique
- the defense budget sends a message to the Soviets

Arguments opposed to increased defense spending included:

- controlling the deficit is the top priority
- the previous military build-up was sufficient
- the Pentagon suffers from a credibility gap

## KEY FINDINGS

- Network coverage opposed freezing the COLA by almost three to one. "The networks devoted 277 lines, or 66.9 percent, to issues opposed to a COLA freeze. They devoted only 99 lines, or 22.9 percent, to issues supporting a COLA freeze." The rest were neutral. [See Graph 7D]

- "CBS presented the most balanced mix of opposing viewpoints, relatively speaking, although its coverage opposing a COLA freeze still predominated, 57 percent to 21.8 percent."

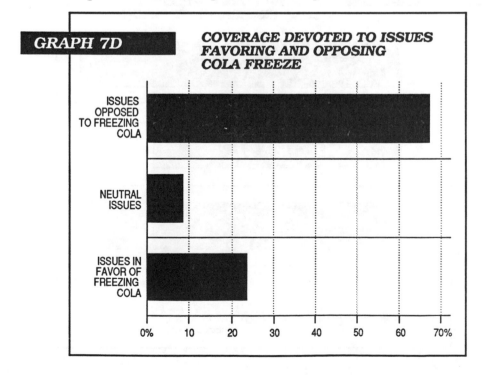

**GRAPH 7D**

*COVERAGE DEVOTED TO ISSUES FAVORING AND OPPOSING COLA FREEZE*

- "NBC's coverage was the least balanced of the three, by a 78.8 percent to 21.1 percent margin." [See Graph 7E]

- Network stories were against raising defense spending by more than two to one. "The networks devoted 192 lines, or 65.5 percent, to issues opposed to increased spending. In contrast, they devoted 91 lines, or 31.1 percent, to issues in favor of more defense spending." [See Graph 7F]

- Again, NBC was the least balanced. "Of its total coverage of defense issues, 76.4 percent of NBC's coverage was opposed to increased defense spending." In contrast, less than half of CBS coverage opposed defense spending increases. [See Graph 7G]

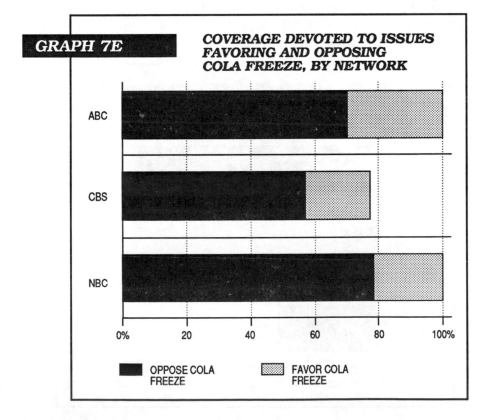

**GRAPH 7E**

*COVERAGE DEVOTED TO ISSUES FAVORING AND OPPOSING COLA FREEZE, BY NETWORK*

OPPOSE COLA FREEZE

FAVOR COLA FREEZE

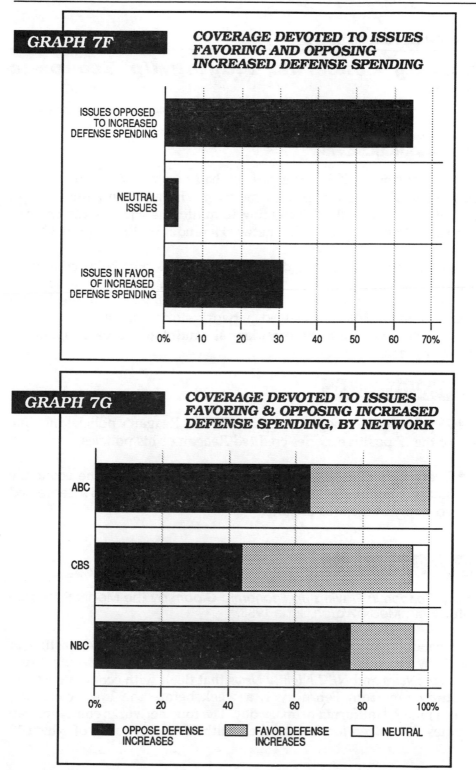

**GRAPH 7F**

**COVERAGE DEVOTED TO ISSUES FAVORING AND OPPOSING INCREASED DEFENSE SPENDING**

ISSUES OPPOSED TO INCREASED DEFENSE SPENDING

NEUTRAL ISSUES

ISSUES IN FAVOR OF INCREASED DEFENSE SPENDING

0%   10   20   30   40   50   60   70%

**GRAPH 7G**

**COVERAGE DEVOTED TO ISSUES FAVORING & OPPOSING INCREASED DEFENSE SPENDING, BY NETWORK**

ABC

CBS

NBC

0%   20   40   60   80   100%

■ OPPOSE DEFENSE INCREASES      ▨ FAVOR DEFENSE INCREASES      □ NEUTRAL

**CHAPTER SEVEN, STUDY 5**

# "Primary Concerns: Playing Up Economic Gloom"

## OVERVIEW

By the spring of 1988 Reaganomics had created 67 months of consecutive growth, a modern peace-time record. Inflation and interest rates rested at half their 1980 level, creating 15 million new jobs in the process. What kind of verdict did the TV networks render on Reaganomics?

As Study 3 of this chapter demonstrated, Big Media belittled Ronald Reagan's economic policies, using the term "Reaganomics" to describe negative -- never positive -- developments. Thus, when the Media Research Center (MRC) reviewed network stories on the economy as voters began evaluating the presidential candidates in early 1988, the findings were no surprise.

## KEY FINDINGS

- 75 percent of the negative reports blamed Reagan's policies; not one of the 17 positive stories credited Reagan or his policies.

- Every CBS and NBC economic story reporting on the economic status of regions facing presidential primaries depicted a depressed economy in the area or state.

## STUDY EXCERPT

**Primary Concerns: Playing Up Economic Gloom** by the Media Research Center. From *MediaWatch*, June 1988.

To conduct this study, *MediaWatch* examined all stories lasting at least thirty seconds on ABC's *World News Tonight*, *CBS Evening News*, *CNN PrimeNews* and *NBC Nightly News* that dealt with economic issues. The study ran from February 1, a week before the Iowa caucuses, through June 7, California primary day. The four networks combined ran 35 stories. Seventeen focused on the health of the economy, of which 13 were prompted by the release of government figures showing good news, such as falling unemployment which hit 14-year lows. Six stories included a mixture of good and bad news, or tempered the good news with warnings of an imminent downturn. Another 12 stressed perceived economic weaknesses.

CNN most closely reflected reality, running seven positive stories and refraining from airing any purely negative ones. [See Graph 7H] ABC followed a similar pattern. Serving as partisan cheerleaders for Democrats trying to disparage Reaganomics, CBS and NBC ran more than twice as many negative as positive pieces.

ABC anchor Peter Jennings' February 15 look at booming New Hampshire stood out as the only such positive story aired before a primary. Other good news stories included a May 6 piece by NBC's Irving R. Levine telling of a New York town where unemployment remained so low that businesses were concerned about the possibility of labor shortages. On the same day, CNN's Deborah Marchini reported that even formerly depressed areas, such as Texas, were rapidly creating new jobs. Mixed news stories included an April 30 ABC story by reporter Chris Bury who found both the "winners and losers of Reaganomics" in Cincinnati.

When it came to reporting on the economic status of regions facing presidential primaries, CBS and NBC political reporters found only sour economic news. CBS Chief Political Correspondent Bruce Morton weighed in with stories on weak regional economies in Ohio, Pennsylvania, and New York, each timed to air shortly before their primaries. Before the April 15 New York primary, Morton traveled to Buffalo to find the state's highest unemployment rate and union members "talking Dukakis."

From Clairton, Pennsylvania, on April 22, Morton began: "Clairton is a dying town with dying steel mills." Morton focused on a small, chronically depressed population and endorsed the Democratic agenda, declaring: "This election is about their lives." One explained: "We've suffered a lot in the valley. Three Republican regimes, and they just forgot about us." Referring to past heavy union votes for Reagan, a local Democratic leader said he believed "they learned their lesson." But Morton neglected to note the state unemployment rate rested at 4.8 percent, below the already low national average.

A week later, as the Ohio primary approached, Morton reported from the state: "Reminders of jobs lost twist slowly in the wind." Again, Morton ignored the big picture: Ohio's unemployment rate fell a whopping 1.4 percent in April alone. Two days before the "Super Tuesday" Southern primary, NBC's Douglas Kiker called 1988 a "hard times election." On March 7, Tom Brokaw profiled Georgia textile workers "hurt" by the Reagan years. Just before the March 13 Illinois primary, NBC's

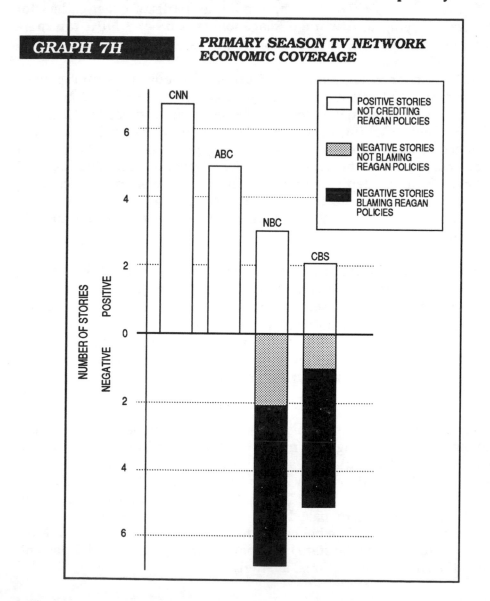

**GRAPH 7H**

**PRIMARY SEASON TV NETWORK ECONOMIC COVERAGE**

POSITIVE STORIES NOT CREDITING REAGAN POLICIES

NEGATIVE STORIES NOT BLAMING REAGAN POLICIES

NEGATIVE STORIES BLAMING REAGAN POLICIES

NUMBER OF STORIES
POSITIVE
NEGATIVE

Tom Pettit was in East St. Louis and Hillsboro, Illinois, towns described as "urban ruins" with voters eager to vote for Jesse Jackson and Paul Simon. Pettit then moved to western Pennsylvania on April 24, where he found steel workers "down and out." Reporting from Erie the next day, NBC's Ken Bode made a clear dig at the GOP's "Morning in America" slogan. "Morning," he announced, "is not what came to Erie."

**CHAPTER SEVEN, STUDY 6**

# "Tax Hike Hype"

## OVERVIEW

George Bush won the presidency on a conservative pledge of "no new taxes." But a study by the Media Research Center (MRC) found television network correspondents and anchors didn't agree. Instead, they followed a liberal economic policy agenda. Following the election, the networks spoke repeatedly of the dangers of the federal budget deficit and championed a tax increase to solve the problem.

The MRC located 22 feature-length stories on the federal budget deficit carried by ABC's *World News Tonight*, the *CBS Evening News*, *CNN PrimeNews*, and *NBC Nightly News* during the month of November 1988. Statements by reporters or those interviewed on camera were tallied in two areas: first, suggestions for tax increases versus spending cuts to remedy the deficit problem; second, placement of blame for the deficit on the White House, Congress, or both.

## KEY FINDINGS

- By a margin of nearly four to one, reporters and on-camera spokesmen called for tax increases over spending cuts to correct the budget deficit. [See Graph 7I]

- Tax increase suggestions occurred 41 times in three weeks on the four network newscasts. Nearly 60 percent came from reporters or anchors. The 11 suggestions for spending cuts were offset by ten statements discrediting the feasibility or wisdom of those cuts. No air time was given to anyone suggesting a tax cut to stimulate economic growth.

- Whom did the networks blame for the fiscal red ink? Reporters and spokesmen, echoing Michael Dukakis campaign talk, singled out the White House as solely responsible for the deficit on 31 occasions. Reporters placed the blame on Congress only twice in the same time period. Congress and the administration shared equally in the blame 13 times.

## STUDY EXCERPT

**Tax Hike Hype** by the Media Research Center. From *MediaWatch*, December 1988.

The networks wasted no time discrediting President Bush's "no new taxes" pledge. The Dow Jones Industrial average fell 47 points on November 11, just three days after the election, prompting ABC's Ted Koppel, the substitute anchor on *World News Tonight*, to blame the Bush victory: "Stocks nosedived, in part because investors are worried that George Bush's 'no new taxes' pledge may prevent him from reducing the deficit."

Ray Brady of CBS News claimed that Bush's no-tax pledge was "bothering many money men." Brady's "money men" were two unidentified stock brokers, one of whom was quick to advocate "a severe cut in the defense budget" as necessary to head off "another financial crisis." Brady didn't allow anyone to defend the Bush pledge.

NBC's Mike Jensen said markets reflected worry that Bush would ignore the recommendations of the National Economic Commission members. "Many of them want to raise taxes," and "so do a lot of other experts," Jensen warned. But Jensen's only "expert" was a Harvard University economist who urged implementation of a national sales tax. Jensen neglected to mention that Bruce Babbitt's national sales tax proposal earned him fifth place in Iowa.

NBC's Irving R. Levine kept up the chant the next day. Saturday anchor Connie Chung introduced the report with unidentified "expert" opinion: "There are experts who insist President Bush will find a way to do what he said he would never do: raise taxes." Among the "experts" Levine consulted? Democratic Congressman Dan Rostenkowski and Alice Rivlin of the Brookings Institution, both liberal Democrats. Levine offered Bush a solution: "Calling a tax by some other name may eventually provide a way for Bush to climb down from the no-tax limb."

CNN's Candy Crowley announced on November 13: "Experts say Mr. Bush's hard line [on taxes] has led investors to cast an early vote of no confidence." Crowley ran a clip of Reagan explaining he'd "given up trying to guess why the market does that. I don't think it has anything to do with George Bush." But Crowley quickly countered with this wrap-up: "Market analysts say differently," adding, they "predict that investors...will remain uncertain until they hear Mr. Bush singing harmony with Congress." ABC's Lark McCarthy gave additional credibility to the desirability of the tax increase option by warning: "Already, Democratic politicians are predicting a fiscal train wreck unless Bush does something about the 'T' word: taxes."

NBC's Levine was ready with more advice for the President-elect on November 16. He suggested Bush use the bi-partisan National Economic Commission as a cover, "enabling him to back off his no-tax pledge."

On November 17, a mere nine days after Bush's victory, CNN's Frank Sesno pronounced Bush's no new tax stance dead, dismissing it as "fun while it lasted." Indeed, "many think taming the deficit," Sesno claimed, "is all but impossible without some new taxes." His source: liberal Democratic Congressman Bill Gray.

When Bush announced his OMB and Council of Economic Advisors selections on November 21, Deborah Potter of CBS took another swipe at Bush, declaring: "With most of his economic team in place, Mr. Bush can now focus on a specific plan to lower the deficit without raising taxes, which almost everyone outside his inner circle believes is impossible." That same night, NBC's Tom Brokaw announced: "Even though Bush in-

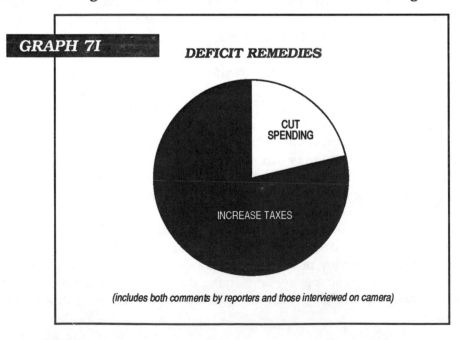

**GRAPH 7I**

**DEFICIT REMEDIES**

CUT SPENDING

INCREASE TAXES

*(includes both comments by reporters and those interviewed on camera)*

sists that he won't raise taxes, more and more prominent Americans, Republicans as well as Democrats, are urging him to do just that." Andrea Mitchell then proceeded to charge: "Bush gave the markets another case of jitters by once again saying that he was elected with a no-tax mandate, no matter what happens to the deficit." That day the Dow rose three points.

By late November, reporters were finding all sorts of impending disasters because of the Bush pledge. "With medical costs still rising, and a President who pledges 'no new taxes,'" CBS' James Hattori ominously predicted, "the outlook for federal help appears grim as hundreds of rural hospitals remain on the critical list." NBC's Levine called the savings and loan "crisis" a "ticking time bomb that could quickly force George Bush to abandon his no new tax pledge."

The Sunday after Thanksgiving NBC's Mitchell made clear Bush had quite a few economic disasters to deal with, and offered a solution. As President, "he's stuck with all the problems he avoided during the campaign; enormous deficits, a collapsing dollar, jittery markets, the need for massive cuts in defense."

The networks spent November blaming "jittery markets" on Bush's no-tax pledge. But how does that explain a big market drop on October 19 of this year, when rumors of Bush's possible political demise were circulating? Moreover, how does that explain a market recovery by early December that left the Dow higher than it had been before election day?

Could it be that investors, worried Bush would raise taxes, lost confidence in the economy, then regained it as Bush stuck to his no-tax pledge even under severe pressure? Probably no network reporter ever thought of that.

# The Media & Reagan: Were They Manipulated or the Manipulators?

The American people gave President Ronald Reagan high approval ratings throughout his presidency. At first this baffled the Washington media elite who voted overwhelmingly against him in 1980 and couldn't understand how a man with such misguided policies could remain so popular. They soon came up with an explanation: "We in the media are not doing our job. Reagan's getting a free ride." Their reasoning: the public liked Reagan only because "the great communicator" used the media brilliantly to manipulate public opinion. If the American people only knew the truth about Reagan's policies, the thinking went, they'd never buy his act.

But how accurate was this view? Did reporters really go easy on Reagan or did Americans support his conservative policies despite the media's extremely critical reporting? The following studies and a collection of quotes demonstrate that the media were anything but soft on Reagan or sympathetic to his policies.

## CHAPTER EIGHT, STUDY 1

## "With Friends Like These..."

### OVERVIEW

By 1983 numerous reporters and media critics were complaining that the Reagan Administration was not receiving its fair share of critical coverage. Michael Robinson, then with George Washington University, and two research assistants set out to determine whether the complaint was valid. Far from letting Reagan get away with anything, the press determined that "Ronald Reagan received disproportionately critical and negative press from the national media." Robinson analyzed Reagan coverage during the first two months of 1983 from *The Washington Post, New York Times, Wall Street Journal, Time, Newsweek, U.S. News & World Report* and ABC, CBS, and NBC evening newscasts.

## KEY FINDINGS

• No matter how Robinson measured coverage -- by story, by statements made, or by the number of positive and negative words -- "the results came out the same: bad press for Reagan and for his administration."

• "The ratio of bad news to good, using stories as the analytical unit, was thirteen and one-half-to-one" for the television networks.

• TV stories that treated the President favorably totaled 400 words, while unfavorable pieces added up to 8,800 words -- a staggering twenty-two-to-one negative ratio.

## STUDY EXCERPT

**With Friends Like These...** by Michael Robinson, Maura Clancey and Lisa Grand. From *Public Opinion*, June/July 1983.

It started in October 1980. A less than disinterested Jody Powell began calling around to the networks, complaining that candidate Ronald Reagan was getting a free ride from the national media.

Writing in the January 1981 issue of the *Washington Monthly*, Jonathan Alter picked up on Powell's complaint. Alter claimed that President-elect Ronald Reagan hadn't exactly been getting a free ride from the media, but that he had been paying "half fare." In 1982 journalist William Greider used *Rolling Stone* to say that Reagan was making monkeys out of the White House press corps.

Press criticism of Reagan's press coverage reached its high point in June 1983. Both the *Columbia Journalism Review* (the nation's most famous magazine about the nation's media) and *Inside Story,* (Hodding Carter's public television series about the nation's media) devoted lead pieces to the inadequacies of press coverage of Ronald Reagan. The *CJR* article, written by C. T. Hanson, unabashedly concluded that, during the first two years of the Reagan presidency, the White House press corps served as a "conduit of White House utterances and official image-mongering intended to sell Reaganomics." Hanson, who serves as *CJR*'s Washington columnist, went so far as to equate the White House press corps with the journalists at *Tass* and *Izvestia,* not because both sets of reporters were liberal, but because both acted as if they were flacking for their governments.

If anything, Hodding Carter's program went further in the direction of *mea culpa* -- the press apologizing for not getting the real Reagan story out to the people. Carter trotted out five nationally prominent journalists -- Elizabeth Drew, Sam Donaldson, Lou Cannon, Andrea Mitchell, and William Greider -- and each went on record in support of the theory that Reagan rendered the press impotent. Each reporter concluded that Reagan has proven to be a master animal trainer -- that Reagan, as President, has had greater success in controlling the media than Reagan, as movie star, had in controlling his lab monkey, Bonzo.

What makes this fascinating is that the press has been confessing to a crime it did not commit. Had members of the press corps bothered to look systematically at their own copy instead of focusing on public opinion polls, they would have found what we found -- that Ronald Reagan has received disproportionately critical and negative press from the national media. If anybody is making monkeys out of the media when it comes to covering Reagan, it's the press corps itself -- not for failing to criticize, but for failing to remember its own criticism.

### The 100 Day Story

For the past several months the Media Analysis Project at George Washington University has been analyzing press coverage of the first hundred days of 1983. Our focus involves all policy news, more specifically policy news as it appears in the "soft news" portions of the national press.

Soft news includes the editorials, columns, commentaries, and feature reports among nine of the nation's most important news sources, which provide the electorate and the government with the majority of its day-to-day news content. We looked at all the soft news about Reagan and his presidency, and all the soft news about public policies that included references to the President.

The current study concerns quantitative findings from the network evening news programs for the first two months of 1983. Still, network journalism represents no small part of the nation's daily news. And the first two months of 1983 are particularly well suited for this piece -- first because the media were doing lots of reporting about the President on the second anniversary of his presidency, and second because it was just after January and February that Reagan began his less than meteoric climb in approval polls.

The fact is, our quantitative findings for television match our qualitative findings for print. And 1983 looks to us very much like 1981 and 1982, at least in terms of White House reporting. In all cases the conclusion holds: Reagan has, with the exception of his assassination coverage, neither ridden free nor paid half fare. Reagan really has had his share of media criticism.

### About Twenty-to-One Negative
No matter how we counted, the results came out the same: bad press for Reagan and his administration.

Let's start with the *story* as the unit of analysis -- in our case the story was either a network commentary or a network feature report more than two-and-a-half minutes long. Focusing on *policy issues*, we identified just under 100 such pieces on network evening news in the first two months of the year. And among all such pieces, Reagan was mentioned or discussed in 46 items.

Most network reporting is colorless -- hard news especially. But because we concentrated on soft news coverage, we found lots of coloration -- explicit evaluation of politicians and public policies. Two-thirds of all the soft news pieces mentioning Ronald Reagan were easily classified as explicitly favorable or unfavorable.

And just how many of these stories could we classify as positive? Only two! Twenty-seven pieces were directly negative toward Reagan in one dimension or another. The ratio of bad news to good, using stories as the analytical unit, was thirteen and one-half-to-one. That statistic understates the level of criticism, because Reagan's two positive pieces were, at best, moderately favorable, and because his negative stories were often very unfavorable.

So, we went through each piece, line by line, and judged each as neutral, ambiguous, favorable, or unfavorable in its inference about the President. We then subtracted positives from negatives to reach an algebraic sum for each report. Reagan's highest score was a measly +3. His lowest was a miserable -16, indicating, we believe, just how much more willing the press had been to bury Reagan than to praise him.

Using total inferences instead of stories, Reagan came through the evening news with a net score of -133. That works out to 2.3 inferences per night on the network evening news. And these figures do not include bad news inferences made about Anne Gorsuch, Rita Lavelle, William Casey, et al., unless Reagan was specifically mentioned in those reports.

We added up the *words* in those stories which we had classified as negative, neutral, ambiguous, or positive. Then we examined the totals, and the results were dramatic [see Graph 8A].

Stories in which Reagan was treated favorably totaled 400 words, two John Chancellor commentaries of 200 words each. Stories in which Reagan was treated unfavorably totaled 8,800 words -- a ratio of twenty-two to one negative!

This ratio probably overstates the case, because many of the longest feature pieces made only one or two clear negative inferences about Reagan. But the fact that Reagan got even more bad press than ambiguous and neutral press is a stunning rebuke to those who believe that the media have somehow let Ronald Reagan get away with his presidency.

### Criticisms of Reagan

What sort of things did these correspondents and commentators criticize? Just about everything except Reagan's personality. Reporters complained most about the *results* of Reaganism. In a feature report on Reagan's first two years, Sam Donaldson and ABC superimposed the President's picture over a brightly colored visual that traced the phenomenal growth in unemployment during Reagan's term. In those same frames, ABC also used audiotape in which Reagan predicted that the recession was over. The report made it perfectly clear that Reaganomics had failed and that Reagan was out of touch with American economic reality. And Donaldson ended on a note that everybody, everywhere, would have to regard as very critical. "There is," concluded Donaldson, "plenty of room for disagreement over whether Ronald Reagan should receive a passing or failing grade for these past two years. But there is a consensus in Washington that unless he changes his game plan, economically, the grade for the next two years will almost certainly be an F."

Over at NBC, John Chancellor attacked Reagan's political judgment on several occasions, but he swung hardest on the Kenneth Adelman nomination. "There was no need," said Chancellor, "for the White House to have stumbled into the Adelman mess. Let me count the ways." John Chancellor, most prolific of the network commentators, also attacked Reagan's integrity. Speaking about the "EPA mess," Chancellor made Reagan sound like Richard Nixon:

"The White House has been acting improperly for more than two years as far as the EPA is concerned, and is in flagrant violation of the Constitution.  In December 1980, a federal law went into effect. ...It

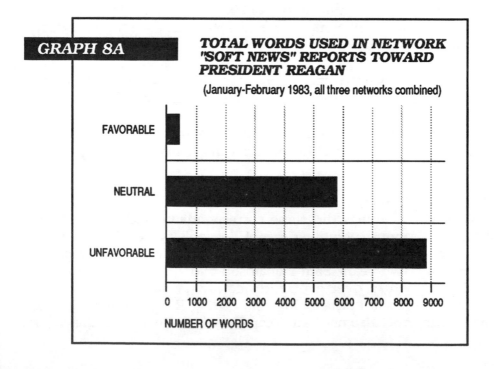

**GRAPH 8A**

**TOTAL WORDS USED IN NETWORK "SOFT NEWS" REPORTS TOWARD PRESIDENT REAGAN**

(January-February 1983, all three networks combined)

FAVORABLE

NEUTRAL

UNFAVORABLE

0  1000  2000  3000  4000  5000  6000  7000  8000  9000

NUMBER OF WORDS

orders the EPA to clean up the dumps, but the Reagan Administration has simply ignored it. The Constitution says of the President, 'He shall take care that the laws are faithfully executed.' He hasn't and that's the biggest scandal of them all."

No doubt you're wondering what happened on CBS. Nothing favorable. Unlike the other anchors, Dan Rather chose, on more than one occasion, to lead into feature reports about the failing economy by tying Reagan directly and unfavorably to the bad news.

On February 1, Rather opened a powerful four-minute feature report about the psychological impact of being unemployed with the following paragraph: "While President Reagan was in St. Louis today speaking again of an America on the mend, there was another America not far off -- an America of 12 million unemployed where the wounds are still too fresh and painful to mend. Ed Rabel looks tonight at the numbers and the faces...and he finds that losing your job involves much more than losing your paycheck."

Two weeks later, Rather gave us something on the order of an instant replay, once again tying Reagan, Ed Rabel, and the recovery together in a much less than flattering way. "At his news conference Wednesday night, President Reagan said the recovery is beginning to flex its muscles. And the latest reports....indicate recovery may indeed be just around the corner. Tonight Ed Rabel looks at some people for whom just around the corner isn't quite close enough." Rabel followed with another dramatic feature about America's new poor.

On TV in '83, even when Reagan looked good, he really looked bad. The most favorable piece on Reagan in early 1983 came from John Chancellor -- the +3 piece we discussed above. But even that commentary, concerning as it did the Nakasone visit to the U.S. in January, began with a slap, not a caress. Chancellor made sure he tempered his general approval with his first sentence. "The administration has handled the visit of the Japanese prime minister with the kind of skill and dexterity it does not always show in foreign affairs." So much for flacking on the evening news.

Is network news unique? Not really. Establishment print -- as establishment print reporters would predict -- has been tougher on Reagan than network television. And in 1983, eastern print went after Reagan on almost every ground imaginable, including grounds which at this point don't look nearly so firm.

One would expect that *The New York Times* would go after Reagan for implementing Reaganomics. But in early 1983, the *Times* went well outside supply-side theory to declare Reagan a political abomination, a total loss politically. "The stench of failure hangs over the Reagan White House" was the opening line in the lead editorial on January 9.

David Broder, the usually moderate and always respected national columnist for *The Washington Post*, pulled out most of the stops as he also wrote a political obituary for Ronald Reagan. "What we are witnessing [in 1983] is not the midpoint of the Reagan presidency, but its phase-out. 'Reaganism,' it is becoming clear, was a one-year phenomenon....What has been occurring ever since is an accelerating retreat from Reaganomics, a process in which he is more spectator than leader."

Reagan did get some good news for his work with the Social Security Commission and for the final legislative compromise. But not from *The Wall Street Journal*. "Ronald Reagan's answer to a political deadlock," said the *Journal*, "was to appoint a bipartisan commission which....will soon feed back to Congress and to the President the problem it began with. The ultimate in this style of government should be reached well before the Reagan first term ends....a bipartisan commission to study bipartisan commissions."

At the same time Norman Miller, bureau chief for the *Journal*, blasted Reagan for his recklessness in a piece labeled "Reagan's Record: An Economy Out of Control." Prestige press has been no consistent friend to Ronald Reagan, even the conservative prestige press.

### The First Two Years

William Greider has been the most consistent complainant about what he terms a "lame" press corps, one given to "impotence" as far as Reagan is concerned. But Greider admits that Reagan was roughed up in December of 1982 and January of 1983. We suspect he would declare our findings irrelevant to the other twenty-eight months of the Reagan Administration.

Let's review the "historical" record. First, some ancient history: our data from the 1980 campaign have already shown that Reagan was the second most negatively treated candidate in all of Campaign '80. Only Jimmy Carter did worse.

Since his inauguration, minus the shooting, Reagan has actually been on a press journey that Homer might have concocted for a movie-minded midwestern hero. Since 1981, the press has covered, fully and dutifully, each of the following "problems": Nancy's "little gun" problem; Nancy's china purchase; Nancy's clothing budget; the Lefever nomination; the ketchup-is-a-vegetable fiasco; the uncharitable President routine; the night Ron slept through the Libyan air war; Watt's attack on liberals; the Richard Allen scandal; the apostasy of David Stockman; General Schweitzer's declaration of inevitable nuclear war; the Bob Jones imbroglio; the Max Hugel resignation; Haig vs. Kirkpatrick; the Thomas Reed affair; the Bill Casey stock portfolio; Ron's $58,000 handyman; the ACDA flaps; Rita Lavelle's luncheon calendar; Ice Queen Annie, from Gorsuch through Burford; Watt's war on the Beach Boys; White House disarray; Watt's "fire-sale" prices on coal leases; Reagan's constant vacationing, both from Washington and from current events; and now, of course, Debategate.

Have we forgotten any? The media seem to have forgotten most of these crises, even though they covered them at the time. And note, too, that this list does not include Reagan's *policy* problems, like unemployment, like El Salvador, like MX basing, like the Russians, like the Allies, all of which came up in soft news features and hard news reports.

### Explaining Press Misperceptions

The press has spent lots of time explaining how it is that Reagan bamboozles them. In *CJR*, C.T. Hanson invokes a three-part explanation -- Reagan's charm; "the cowed opposition"; the "bovine" habits of the press. All good explanations, but for a faulty premise. The real question is why the press has insisted on wearing sackcloth and ashes for the last two years.

We see four factors at play here. First is politics. Liberal reporters probably do have a hard time accepting moderate levels of political success from a man who is so immoderately conservative. As tough as the *Journal* has been with Reagan, the *Times* has been much tougher. Right-of-center and profoundly right-of-journalism, Reagan makes it easy for journalists to see themselves as failing whenever he succeeds.

Ideology is, however, only a part of this. The press sees a free ride for Reagan because it confuses amicable relations in the White House with good press for the President. The press has mistakenly used invective as the litmus test for criticism. Because reporters smile more than they ever did with Johnson, Nixon, or Carter, they assume that they have given Reagan a free ride.

Sam Donaldson has been among the most outspoken critics of his own press reporting, blaming himself for not going after Reagan enough. But Donaldson has gone after Reagan a lot. Donaldson smiles more than he used to, but he continues to blast away at Reagan, for his frequent vacations, for his failed policies, for his false facts, and for his notions of leadership.

Third, the press is doing to the press what it does to all institutions -- accentuates the negative. Media are so preoccupied with institutional deficiencies, they insist on finding fault with themselves as well as everybody else. Our data from 1983 actually show that most press stories about the news media are critical of the media. Doubting their coverage of Reagan is one more instance of their obsession with being watchdogs.

Finally, press people are currently engaged in a magnificent irony. They have fallen into the same trap that Reagan, the Democrats, and the public have been slipping into for years -- blaming the media for whatever occurs in politics, especially the unexpected.

Journalists read polls; they see Reagan doing comparatively well in terms of public approval. But journalists neither understand nor appreciate Reagan's modest rise in those surveys. To the press, Reagan's polls must represent their own failure to get the story out. Just as Reagan foolishly, but predictably, blamed the media for the recession, journalists unpredictably blame themselves for Reagan. Journalists see an effect and assume the cause. And media are everybody's *first* cause.

For the past thirty-two months, the press has not been at Ronald Reagan's throat, but it has been consistently nipping at his heels. Reagan had a brief press honeymoon after his election and a real affair with the press right after he was shot. But the basic thesis about Reagan's power to disarm the media is mostly a myth.

And, as for media effects -- if we must assume media effects -- it's crucial to point out that Reagan is not all that popular. A number of polls show him behind his Democratic opponents. Reagan is not the Republican Rasputin, and the public does not regard him as magic. It's mostly the press that does that. In the last analysis, the nation's reporters have written or said that Reagan is dumb, lazy, out of touch with reality, cheap, senile, ruining NATO, tearing up his own social safety net, even violating his constitutional oath. What else could anybody ask these reporters to say?

We have our doubts about Reagan. After having read and watched all this reportage, how could we not? We have our doubts about the nation's press as well. But one thing we know for sure: the White House press has neither flacked for Ronald Reagan nor ignored his shortcomings -- personal or policy-related.

CHAPTER EIGHT, STUDY 2

# "It's All Meese and No Wright"

## OVERVIEW

In early 1988 Edwin Meese, the conservative Reagan Administration Attorney General, came under daily media fire for alleged ethical misconduct. The attack was prompted by allegations leveled by congressional Democrats. At the same time Republican Congressman Newt Gingrich and a few Texas newspapers were charging Speaker of the House Jim Wright, the highest ranking elected Democrat, with equally serious ethical breaches.

To see whether major print outlets and the television networks focused equally on the two men, the Media Research Center compared the number of stories on Meese that ran in January and February 1988 to the number on Wright over a 14 month period. The study found that while the news outlets jumped on any rumor of misconduct by the Attorney General, they virtually ignored questions about Wright's misbehavior.

It should be noted that Big Media reporters did not begin to take notice of Wright until several month later, when the liberal group Common Cause complained about him. The charges drove Wright from office in May, 1989.

## KEY FINDINGS

- "The print media covered Meese 17 times more often than Wright in one-seventh the time."

- ABC, CBS and NBC's evening newscasts carried 26 reports on Meese in two months, but in 14 months never once found time for a story on Wright's behavior.

## STUDY EXCERPT

**It's All Meese and No Wright** by the Media Research Center. From *Media-Watch*, March 1988.

Using the Nexis ® news data retrieval system, *MediaWatch* determined that *The New York Times, Washington Post, Los Angeles Times, Newsweek, Time,* and *U.S. News & World Report,* during just January and February of 1988, ran a total of 103 news stories focused on Meese's ethics. Another 73 made passing reference. The *CBS Evening News, NBC Nightly News* and ABC's *World News Tonight* ran 26 reports. In all of last year and the first two months of 1988, however, the print publications carried a mere six stories focused on Wright's ethical problems while 23 others made passing reference. The print media covered Meese 17 times more often than Wright in one-seventh the time. Incredibly, in the 14 months ending in February, 1988 the networks never aired one story on Wright's problems. [See Graph 8B]

Nearly 46 percent of the 103 Meese stories in the newspapers and magazines dealt with old controversies, including how he supposedly used his influence to obtain a federal contract for Wedtech and possible conflict of interest concerning stock he owned in telephone companies. So far, nothing has been proven illegal. On January 28 the *Los Angeles Times* claimed Meese may have acted improperly by not reporting that a memo from a friend made reference to a plan to "bribe" Israeli officials who opposed the oil pipeline from Iraq to Jordan. While vague, the media pounced on the story, looking for a way to turn the development into a scandal. During the following month, the print media outlets ran 56 stories exclusively on Meese's role with the pipeline, accounting for 54 percent of the Meese articles. Another 33 pipeline stories concentrated on other players, but made a passing reference to the Attorney General.

A few weeks later, ABC's Dennis Troute reported that a key player in the pipeline project said the memo "shows no technical violations of the law by the Attorney General," but Troute still didn't hesitate to pick up the anti-Meese agenda, concluding on February 12: "His critics will point to it as another example of what they call 'a blind spot to ethical concerns' on the part of Mr. Meese." When Meese released the memo on February 22 in order to clear his name, NBC reporter James Polk declared: "This is still likely to loom as the most embarrassing crisis yet for the beleaguered Attorney General."

While some of the allegations of wrong-doing against Jim Wright date back to 1979, several new ones arose in 1987. These included: (1) profiting from a business relationship with a Ft. Worth developer he helped get federal money; (2) intervening with federal officials to prevent the closing of a debt-ridden Texas savings and loan owned by a big Democratic contributor; (3) laundering campaign contributions for his personal use through a publisher who reportedly paid Wright $54,000 in book royalties while the company received $68,000 in 1986 campaign funds, a year he ran unopposed and paid just $100 in campaign staff salaries.

These questions prompted U.S. Rep. Newt Gingrich (R-GA) to call for an investigation. Virtually every media outlet ignored Gingrich's February 19, 1987 press conference, which generated just a two-paragraph story in the *Los Angeles Times* and a passing reference in an unrelated *Post* story. But the record of the networks was even more atrocious. *Newsweek* on June 29 and the *Post* on September 24 considered the allegations serious enough to merit lengthy stories. But the networks didn't pick up these pieces as they often did when it came to Meese. The only mention occurred during a January 25, 1988, NBC profile. Wright told reporter Bob Kur he never did anything worth investigating.

What might account for this disparity? At least some of the reason is institutional: the national media, especially the TV networks, consider

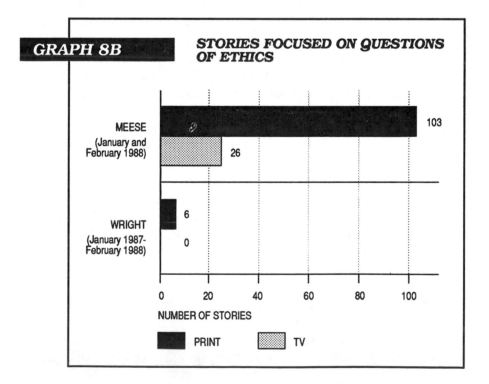

the Executive to be the most significant of the three branches of government. That's why, for instance, ABC viewers see a lot more of White House reporter Sam Donaldson than Capitol Hill correspondent Brit Hume. As Hume explained to *MediaWatch*, that short shrift naturally "leads the media to become soft on Congress, its leaders especially." But, as Meese is one of the few solid conservatives left in the cabinet, it's hard to avoid concluding a more important reason is that reporters don't mind emphasizing anything that makes the Reagan Administration look bad.

CHAPTER EIGHT, STUDY 3

# "No Single Standard for Sleaze"

## OVERVIEW

Shortly before he resigned in the summer of 1988, Attorney General Ed Meese was cleared of committing any illegal acts. But the media continued to portray him as an example of what they termed the "ethical insensitivity" of the Republican administration. Less than a year later, Speaker of the House Jim Wright, a liberal Democrat, resigned rather than face action by the House Committee on Standards of Official Conduct which had evidence that he had broken the law. But as a Media Research Center study discovered, unlike their harassment of Meese, reporters circumvented the accusations against Wright, by concentrating on concern that an "ethics war" was damaging the political process.

## KEY FINDINGS

- Major newspapers and magazines and the television networks portrayed Ed Meese as "the crown jewel of the sleaze factor," but treated Jim Wright as a "casualty of the ethics thunderstorm."

- 70 percent of print stories and 58 percent of broadcast reports blamed the "partisan" atmosphere for Wright's troubles. No television story and only 4 percent of broadcast stories blamed "partisan" action by Democrats for Meese's downfall. [See Gragh 8C]

## STUDY EXCERPT

**No Single Standard for Sleaze** by the Media Research Center. From *Media-Watch*, July 1989.

Coverage of Meese's resignation focused on his personal ethics problems, while reports of Wright's resignation focused on the fate of the House in the midst of "mindless cannibalism." The media also used differing terminologies to report the controversies surrounding Meese and Wright, focusing on the "sleaze factor" for Meese and the "ethics war" for Wright. To measure these trends, analysts investigated print reports in the *Los Angeles Times, New York Times, Washington Post, Time, Newsweek,* and *U.S. News & World Report,* and viewed ABC's *World News Tonight, CBS Evening News, CNN PrimeNews,* and *NBC Nightly News.*

**1. THEMES.** To study the dominant themes underlying both episodes, *MediaWatch* compared stories within the first four days of Meese's resignation announcement on July 5, 1988, and the release of special prosecutor James McKay's report on July 18, with the first four days following Wright's May 31, 1989 speech to the House.

**a) Continuing ethical/legal problems.** Although special prosecutor James McKay failed to indict Meese, 12 of 25 print stories (48%) and four out of nine network segments (44%) predicted further difficulties for Meese, most notably an investigation by the Justice Department's Office of Professional Responsibility. Despite possible Justice Department investigations against Wright only two of nine network stories (22%) and two of 25 print stories (8%) speculated on further troubles. Not one newspaper account touched on further ethical problems for the Speaker, focusing instead on stories like the *Los Angeles Times'* "'Liberated' Wright Explains Why He Resigned." [See Graph 8C]

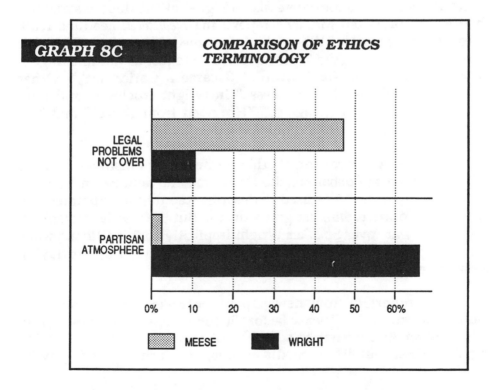

**GRAPH 8C**

**COMPARISON OF ETHICS TERMINOLOGY**

LEGAL PROBLEMS NOT OVER

PARTISAN ATMOSPHERE

0%   10   20   30   40   50   60%

MEESE       WRIGHT

**b) Partisan atmosphere**. The tenor of the Wright coverage was stringently critical of the "partisan bloodbath" that led to Wright's resignation. Twenty-one of 30 print stories (70%) and 7 of 12 broadcast reports (58%) described some form of "partisan rancor" on Capitol Hill when Wright quit. As Michael Oreskes led off coverage in *The New York Times* June 1: "The House to which Speaker Jim Wright announced today his plan to resign is a House beset with fear, one in which every rumor, every phone call from a reporter, every partisan spat could be the beginning of the end of a career." Although the investigation by the House ethics committee took more than a year to complete, the *Los Angeles Times* headlined a June 2 story, "Rush to Judge Politicians Held Damaging to Nation." Wallowing in this atmosphere, ABC's Jim Wooten could sympathetically report of Wright: "And if his moving speech today does not restore those decencies he so wistfully remembered today, then perhaps history remembered that at least he tried." But Meese got no such treatment. In 25 print stories, only one *New York Times* story (or 4 percent of articles) mentioned in passing that "old-line conservatives" thought partisanship might have been involved. None of the nine evening news stories raised the issue.

Headlines and subtitles were also a signal of the double standard. When Meese protested McKay's report, the *Newsweek* headline read, "Meese Plays the Martyr." When Wright resigned, *Time* asked, "Have We Gone Too Far?" *Los Angeles Times* subtitles were just as illuminating: in one Meese story, the *Times* wrote, "'Became a Caricature'," "Other Failures," and "'Personal Obtuseness'." In Wright articles, subtitles included "Embraced by Colleagues," "'Hounded from Office'," and "Atmosphere of Mistrust."

**2. TERMS.** A comparison of ethics terminology illustrates how the media presented the debate to the Democrats' advantage on both occasions. "Sleaze factor" was used to describe Republican appointees accused of impropriety, whether guilty or not. But the martial metaphors of an "ethics war" over Speaker Wright implicitly charged Republicans with dirty pool and excused the Democratic corruption by portraying Democrats as victims of a "partisan bloodbath."

In 1988, reporters from newspapers and magazines made unattributed reference to the "sleaze factor" 56 times, mostly as a description of the Reagan Administration's "legacy of easy ethical virtue," as *The New York Times* put it. To media minds, the term related only to

Republican ethics controversies. Thus, Senator Lloyd Bentsen's deflated ploy to charge lobbyists $10,000 for breakfast "might blunt" or "make it tougher to exploit" the Democrats' use of the "sleaze factor" instead of being an example of the "sleaze factor." In spite of all the ethics coverage, reporters used the term only six times in the first six months of 1989.

But in the aftermath of the Wright resignation, print reporters made unattributed use of a thesaurus of "ethics war" terminology (including "ethics purge," "ethics reign of terror," and "ethics epidemic") 37 times, often in headlines. *Newsweek* made "Ethics Wars" a section heading for all its Wright stories in its June 12 edition.

In contrast, conservative phrase coiners were stiffed. Only three print news stories in 1989 mentioned Newt Gingrich's pet phrase, "corrupt liberal welfare state," and when they did it came with criticism: *The Washington Post*'s Myra McPherson wrote, "Newtisms have indeed appalled members on both sides of the aisle." In fact, print stories that included the words "corrupt" or "corruption" with unattributed reference to the Democrats have appeared only 16 times so far this year, and most of them showed up in sentences like "Democrats tired of being lumped together as corrupt and venal will support Wright as a demonstration of their own self-worth." This sentence by Tom Kenworthy appeared in the only *Washington Post* news story to use the word "corrupt" anywhere near the name of Jim Wright in May or June, 1989.

Impartiality in ethics coverage requires that scandals involving liberal Democrats and conservative Republicans be covered in a balanced fashion, with a single standard. Circumstances may differ, but to tar the accused conservative Republican in one case and then assail the conservative Republican accuser in the next is proof positive of a double standard.

## CHAPTER EIGHT, STUDY 4

# What They Say About Reagan

### OVERVIEW

As Reagan's last day in office approached, members of the media began to render their verdict on his eight years. These statements collected by the Media Research Center, plus a few from earlier years, demonstrate numerous reporters had little use for Reagan personally or for his conservative policies. In short, they were glad to see him go. Here are some examples.

**Tom Brokaw**, *NBC Nightly News* anchor

"Pretty simplistic. Pretty old-fashioned. And I don't think they have much application to what's currently wrong or troubling a lot of people...Nor do I think he really understands the enormous difficulty a lot of people have in just getting through life, because he's lived in this fantasy land for so long." -- Speculating on Reagan's values in *Mother Jones*, April 1983.

**Chuck Conconi**, *Washington Post* "Personalities" columnist

"I'm one of the few people who had no tears in my eyes when that helicopter took off and Reagan was going back to California. I was going, 'Bye, hope you stay there and have a nice life.'" -- Mutual Broadcasting System's *Larry King Show*, January 20, 1989.

**Timothy Noah**, *Newsweek* reporter

"I never met the former President, and never voted for him." -- *The New Republic*, February 13, 1989.

**Lesley Stahl,** CBS News White House correspondent

"I predict historians are going to be totally baffled by how American people fell in love with this man and followed him the way we did." -- NBC's *Later with Bob Costas*, January 11, 1989.

Bill Moyers: "When it comes to visuals, do you miss Ronald Reagan?"
Lesley Stahl: "Well, I guess as a television reporter yes, but as an American citizen, no." -- Exchange on PBS' *Bill Moyers: The Public Mind*, January 22, 1990.

## Reaganomics

**Tom Brokaw,** NBC *Nightly News* anchor

"But I thought from the outset that his 'supply side' [theory] was just a disaster. I knew of no one who felt that it was going to work, outside of a small collection of zealots in Washington and at USC -- Arthur Laffer." -- interview in *Mother Jones*, April 1983.

**Bryant Gumbel,** NBC *Today* anchor

"Largely as a result of the policies and priorities of the Reagan Administration, more people are becoming poor and staying poor in this country than at any time since World War II." -- *Today*, July 17, 1989.

**Tom Mathews,** *Newsweek* Senior Editor

"As a practical matter, the homeless won't get very far unless they can persuade a Republican to break with Ronald Reagan's policies -- or elect a Democrat." -- *Newsweek*, March 21, 1988.

**Bill Moyers,** former CBS News commentator

"The documentary has held up as both true and sadly prophetic. While Congress restored some of the cuts made in those first Reagan budgets, in the years since, the poor and the working poor have borne the brunt of the costs of the Reagan Revolution. The hardest-hit programs have been welfare, housing and other anti-poverty measures. Even programs that were not cut have failed to keep up with inflation. Meanwhile, rich people got big tax breaks. And the middle class kept most of their subsidies intact. As a result, the Reagan years brought on a wider gap between rich and poor." -- After PBS re-airing of 1982 *CBS Reports* "People like Us," June 20, 1989.

**Jonathan Rowe**, *Christian Science Monitor* correspondent

"If the Mondale-Dukakis mind was wired permanently through the institutions of government, then the Reagan mind ran a solipsistic loop back to itself. Reaganite economics are the hedonism of the sixties drug culture, transferred to the economic realm." -- *Washington Monthly*, January, 1990.

**Lesley Stahl**, CBS News White House correspondent

Don Regan: "What's the bottom line of the Reagan Administration? It's a great record."
Lesley Stahl: "Bottom line. Largest deficits in history. Largest debtor nation. Can't afford to fix the housing emergency." -- Exchange on *Face the Nation*, May 15, 1988.

**Abigail Trafford**, Editor, *Washington Post*

"An unfortunate legacy of the Reagan revolution is a swelling medical underclass: alcoholics and drug addicts who deluge emergency rooms and fill prisons, AIDS babies and crack newborns in overwhelmed pediatric wards, homeless children with anemia, schizophrenics and other mental patients in shelters and jails and on the streets...While Ronald Reagan did not cause the medical underclass, his laissez-faire approach to social problems exacerbated the trend." -- *The Washington Post*, January 24, 1989.

## Reagan and Civil Rights

**Bryant Gumbel,** NBC *Today* anchor

"But Lee, blacks have looked at the past eight years and seen this administration retreat from civil rights, retreat from affirmative action, make South Africa no priority, continue to see a greater disparity economically between blacks and whites, foster a spirit of racism that hasn't been seen in 20 plus years. What makes you think blacks are going to say, okay, these [Republicans] are going to break with what used to be?" -- Question to Republican National Committee Chairman Lee Atwater on NBC's *Today*, January 19, 1989.

**Jack Nelson,** *Los Angeles Times* Washington Bureau Chief

"Now it was Rosalynn Carter who said that he makes people feel comfortable about their prejudices." -- CBS *Nightwatch*, December 30, 1988.

**Lesley Stahl,** CBS News White House correspondent

"I'm kind of surprised at President Reagan, because based on his personal history in Hollywood, I'm surprised he has not been an advocate of civil rights...I had heard that he was a very open-minded, broad-minded person, that he cared about human rights...But the record is abysmal." -- Howard Cosell's *Speaking of Everything*, April 10, 1988.

## Reagan's Legacy

**Richard Corliss,** *Time* film critic

"From its plot synopsis, *Risky Business* (1983) promised more of the lame same. An affluent high school senior has an affair with a hooker (Rebecca de Mornay), dunks the family Porsche in Lake Michigan, turns his house into a brothel and still gets into Princeton. Sounds like the Reagan era in miniature." -- *Time* Tom Cruise cover story, December 25, 1989.

**Haynes Johnson**, former *Washington Post* editor

"To the self-indulgent age of the '80s and to the characters that gave it special flavor at home -- Oliver L. North and Ronald Reagan, Michael Milken and Ivan Boesky, Jim and Tammy Faye Bakker, Arthur Laffer and his curve, the Yuppies and the leveraged buyout dealmakers -- good riddance." -- *The Washington Post*, December 29, 1989.

**Robert Maynard**, *Oakland Tribune* Publisher

"[Reagan's] obsession with freedom abroad was not matched by any sense of justice at home for millions of Americans, and it is his lack of appreciation for the issues of equality, his failure to lead the nation toward healing in that area, is indeed also a part of his legacy and an unfortunate part....

"There are more people in poverty in this country today, and I don't believe their morale was built by Ronald Reagan. There are more homeless people in the streets of America today than there were when he came to office, a shame of the nation." -- On *This Week with David Brinkley*, January 15, 1989.

**Sarah McClendon**, free-lance White House reporter

"It will take 100 years to get the government back into place after Reagan. He hurt people: the disabled, women, nursing mothers, the homeless." -- *USA Today*, February 16, 1990.

**Harrison Rainie**, *U.S. News & World Report* Senior Editor

"By 'selling the sizzle' of Reagan, as his aide Michael Deaver put it, the administration spun the nation out of its torpor with such fantasies as supply-side economics, the nuclear weapons 'window of vulnerability,' and the Strategic Defense Initiative." -- *U.S. News & World Report*, December 25/January 1, 1990.

**Roger Rosenblatt**, then *U.S. News & World Report* Editor

"I think it's a dangerous failure at least in terms of programs. A mess in Central America, neglect of the poor, corruption in government....And the worst legacy of all, the budget deficit, the impoverishment of our children." -- CBS News 1988 Republican Convention coverage.

**Terence Smith**, CBS News reporter

"Historians will note, for example, that it was Jimmy Carter who focused the nation's attention on the need for energy conservation and defined human rights as a legitimate consideration in foreign policy....But analysts will also recognize that Ronald Reagan presided over a meltdown of the federal government during the last eight years. Fundamental management was abandoned in favor of rhetoric and imagery. A cynical disregard for the art of government led to wide-scale abuse....

"Only now are we coming to realize the cost of Mr. Reagan's laissez-faire: the crisis in the savings and loan industry, the scandal in the Department of Housing and Urban Development, the deterioration of the nation's nuclear weapons facilities, the dangerous state of the air traffic control system -- not to mention the staggering deficit." -- *New York Times* op-ed piece, November 5, 1989.

**Kathleen Sullivan**, then *CBS This Morning* co-host

"In just seven weeks, the '80's will be behind us. It was a decade dominated, in politics and style, by the Reagans....While the wealthy got most of the attention, those who needed it most were often ignored. More homeless, less spending on housing. The gap between the top and the bottom grew in the '80's....The AIDS crisis began in the '80's. Some say the decade's compassion gap made it worse." -- *CBS This Morning*, November 13, 1989.

**Helen Thomas**, UPI White House reporter

"I think there is a question mark on the domestic policy: I think he left an uncaring society...a government that was not as concerned." -- CBS *Nightwatch*, December 30, 1988.

### Robert Wilson, *USA Today* book critic

"At one point of the book, [Noonan] blames activists for the homeless for the presence of a frightening street person outside the Executive Office Building. C'mon Peggy, read my you-know-whats: Mitch Snyder didn't put that man there; your old boss did." -- review of Reagan speechwriter Peggy Noonan's *What I Saw At The Revolution*, February 9, 1990.

# 9 The Media & Campaigns: Balanced Conduit or Partisan Participants?

Covering a presidential campaign is a sought after assignment for a network correspondent. It brings prestige and high visibility that can only help a reporter's career. Moreover, while on assignment the reporter becomes a central figure in an unfolding political drama. Millions of Americans go into the voting booth with views substantially molded by watching television network news stories.

This responsibility should pursuade reporters to act responsibly. As we have already seen, the studies presented in Chapter 1 showed that network news reporters have consistently supported the Democratic candidate for President since 1964. The question then is: Are these correspondents able to separate their personal preferences from their reporting? This chapter has gathered studies on the 1984 and 1988 presidential campaigns, and they demonstrate that ABC, CBS and NBC coverage favored the Democratic candidate, labeled Republicans but not Democrats, offered more criticisms of Republican than Democratic policies, and in general promoted the Democratic campaign agenda.

## CHAPTER NINE, STUDY 1

## "The Media in Campaign '84: Convention Coverage"

### OVERVIEW

Few events offer a better chance to check for media bias than the political conventions the two major parties hold every four years. Each serves as a showcase for the party and provides the media with an equal opportunity to question the party leaders and analyze the nominee's policies.

Immediately after the 1984 conventions Professor William Adams and some of his students at George Washington University set out to compare and contrast how CBS and NBC covered the July Democratic convention in San Francisco and the Republican convention in Dallas a month later. They soon discovered that the networks portrayed the Republican Party and Ronald Reagan as political extremists, far too conservative to be re-elected. The same reporters were at ease with the liberal Democratic platform, finding little to criticize or even to question.

## KEY FINDINGS

- Network coverage completely ignored what eventually led to the defeat of the Democratic ticket: the alienation of many rank-and-file Democrats from the liberal positions espoused by Walter Mondale and Geraldine Ferraro.

- 43 percent of Democrats in Congress were conservative or moderate, but the networks never interviewed a single conservative congressional Democrat. Liberals constituted 56 percent of congressional Democrats, but they represented 85 percent of those interviewed during the Democratic convention.

- CBS and NBC reporters and anchors called the Democratic party, its platform and leaders by liberal labels just 21 times. The same two networks used various conservative labels to describe the Republicans 113 times, more than five times as often. "On the average," Adams learned, "about once every six minutes from Dallas, viewers were told that the Republican Party was in the hands of 'very strong conservatives,' or 'the hard right,' with enormous power exercised by, in Walter Cronkite's words, the 'fundamentalist religious conservative right wing.'"

- Good journalists confront politicians with the strongest arguments of their opponents, but Adams determined that "questions at both conventions came overwhelmingly from the Democratic agenda."

STUDY EXCERPT

**The Media In Campaign '84: Convention Coverage** by William C. Adams. From *Public Opinion*, December/January 1985.

The last CBS News/*New York Times* poll before the San Francisco convention disclosed something startling: Just 61 percent of the Democratic rank-and-file said they intended to vote for Walter Mondale.

CBS News/*New York Times* summer polls also demonstrated that most people believed the country was better off than it had been four years earlier, and most people attributed that to the economic surge and the easing of inflation. When asked about the country's "most important problem," economic issues far surpassed everything else.

During the many hours of prime-time convention coverage, these two pivotal stories -- the defection of Democratic regulars and the political effect of the economic boom -- were given little attention by two giants of the American news media -- CBS News and NBC News. These omissions were puzzling because convention coverage was so extensive.

### Convention Significance

Conventions offer the largest dose of political coverage the networks ever broadcast. Eight convention days took up as much TV airtime as the nine-week general election campaign did on nightly newscasts.

Admittedly, the nationwide audiences for the conventions were smaller than those garnered by most prime-time fare -- Ronald Reagan's Dallas was no rival for J.R. Ewing's *Dallas* -- but these smaller audiences packed a political punch. Three-quarters of registered voters told pollsters they watched the conventions on television at least one night, and from one-fifth to one-third of the voters have said they make their candidate choices during the late summer convention periods.

One last reason for assessing convention coverage: Network news directors have complained that media analysts confine their research to the few seconds that appear on the nightly news and ignore "what we do when we have more time." With two to four hours airing each night, conventions provide an excellent opportunity to examine how network reporters conveyed key battles of American politics in 1984.

### Convention Speeches

Timothy Klein, Tonya Smith, Leslie Suelter, and I analyzed 39.5 hours of CBS News and NBC News convention videotapes from the Vanderbilt TV News Archives -- typical Central Standard Time zone versions of the conventions, with few interruptions for local news. (Limited resources prevented us from looking at all networks.) CBS News and NBC News allocated close to 40 percent of their airtime at each convention to speeches from the podium. Both networks gave the Democrats over two hours more coverage than the Republicans received, including an extra hour of Democratic oratory.

Although most convention coverage consisted of reporters and anchormen talking to one another and conducting interviews, it did offer a rare chance to hear several hours of extended, largely unedited, political speeches -- far more than any other time on ABC News, CBS News, or NBC News. (Usually only C-SPAN viewers have this chance.)

During those periods when network journalists were not talking, the major prime-time speakers naturally reflected the dominant elements of each party. Those given more than ten minutes of airtime from San Francisco were liberals: Mario Cuomo, Tip O'Neill, Jesse Jackson, Gary Hart, George McGovern, Jimmy Carter, Geraldine Ferraro, Edward Kennedy, and Walter Mondale. Those with over ten minutes from Dallas were conservatives: Jeane Kirkpatrick, Katherine Ortega, Jack Kemp, Gerald Ford, Barry Goldwater, Paul Laxalt, George Bush, and Ronald Reagan.

But the cameras used less than half their time relaying speeches from the dominant groups in each party, and the remaining hours may have been at least as important. In those hours of interviews, interpretations, and commentary, how did the networks depict the American political configuration? What issues did they elevate as most relevant to the electorate?

### Democratic Disunity

The story the networks could have told has developed over the last one hundred years. In that time, only one northern Democrat has received a majority of the popular vote for President -- Franklin D. Roosevelt. All other Democratic Presidents either won with pluralities or came from the South.

In four of the last five presidential elections, the Democrats' share of the vote failed to exceed 43 percent: Hubert Humphrey received 43 percent in 1968; George McGovern, 38 percent in 1972; Jimmy Carter, 41 percent in 1980; and Walter Mondale, 41 percent in 1984. Georgian Jimmy Carter's narrow 1976 majority was the sole exception.

Volumes have been written about the collapse of the New Deal coalition, and they have made at least this much elementary: Along with many blue-collar workers and Southerners, a wide range of people who think of themselves as Democrats, and who usually do vote for Democratic gubernatorial and congressional candidates, absolutely refuse to support undiluted, industrial-strength liberals for President.

As a result, a large share of all Democrats bolt their party and vote against liberal nominees: Over 30 percent of all Democrats voted against Humphrey in 1968; 33 percent voted against McGovern in 1972; 18 percent voted against Carter in 1976; 31 percent against Carter in 1980; and 24 percent against Mondale in 1984. With defections of this magnitude, there is no election contest.

This Democratic disaster is compounded by the Republicans' cohesiveness. Typically, only a small fraction of Republicans defect to vote for a Democrat for President. In 1984, for example, most exit polls found that fewer than 7 percent of the Republicans voted for Mondale.

That Democrats secured less than 45 percent of the vote in six of the past nine presidential elections is more than bad luck. The northern liberal Democratic candidates' failure to muster the support of less liberal rank-and-file Democrats is surely the fundamental dilemma for the party.

This may be either a sad situation, or the salvation of the Republic, depending on one's point of view, but the Democrats' divisions are no secret. How did CBS News and NBC News, each with nearly a dozen hours from the Democratic national convention, treat this historic drama?

### Missing Interviews
CBS News and NBC News produced coverage that emphasized the crucial matter of Democratic Party unity, but treated it as primarily dependent upon harmony among Walter Mondale, Jesse Jackson, and Gary

Hart. The two networks rarely talked to moderate or conservative Democrats.

Table 9A contrasts the voting records of the senators and representatives who were interviewed by NBC News and CBS News with the overall congressional voting records of each party. The index used is a composite of the *National Journal* scores for liberal-versus-conservative voting on foreign, economic, and social policy.

As do most rankings, these show that over one-third of the Democrats in Congress vote in relatively moderate fashion, while nearly

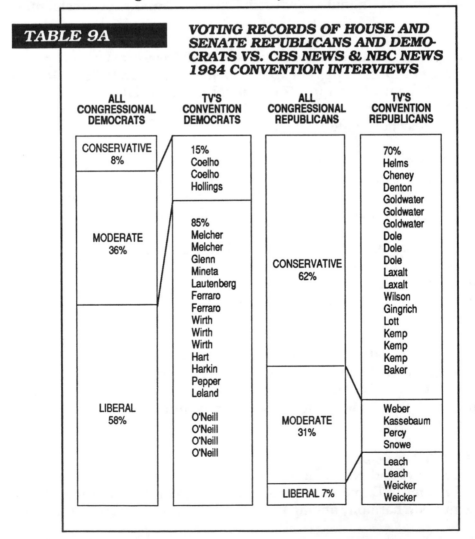

| **TABLE 9A** | **VOTING RECORDS OF HOUSE AND SENATE REPUBLICANS AND DEMOCRATS VS. CBS NEWS & NBC NEWS 1984 CONVENTION INTERVIEWS** | | |
|---|---|---|---|
| **ALL CONGRESSIONAL DEMOCRATS** | **TV'S CONVENTION DEMOCRATS** | **ALL CONGRESSIONAL REPUBLICANS** | **TV'S CONVENTION REPUBLICANS** |
| CONSERVATIVE 8% | 15% Coelho Coelho Hollings | | 70% Helms Cheney Denton Goldwater Goldwater Goldwater Dole Dole Dole Laxalt Laxalt Wilson Gingrich Lott Kemp Kemp Kemp Baker |
| MODERATE 36% | 85% Melcher Melcher Glenn Mineta Lautenberg Ferraro Ferraro Wirth Wirth Wirth Hart Harkin Pepper Leland | CONSERVATIVE 62% | |
| LIBERAL 58% | O'Neill O'Neill O'Neill O'Neill | MODERATE 31% | Weber Kassebaum Percy Snowe |
| | | LIBERAL 7% | Leach Leach Weicker Weicker |

one in ten vote as conservatives. This substantial minority of nonliberals (43 percent) was dismissed by the networks that covered the Democratic convention. They interviewed *no* conservative congressional Democrats and only two moderates -- Tony Coelho (twice) and Fritz Hollings, both liberal moderates. While liberals constituted 56 percent of all congressional Democrats, they received 85 percent of all the convention interviews conducted with senators and representatives.

A review of the noncongressional interviews reinforces this finding. We asked leaders of the Coalition for a Democratic Majority (CDM), a group of "Scoop Jackson Democrats," whether they recognized any like-minded friends among the 52 noncongressional interviewees; they spotted only one -- Governor Charles Robb of Virginia.

Another two Governors who were interviewed also have nonliberal reputations -- Richard Lamm of Colorado and Joe Frank Harris of Georgia. Altogether, these three Governors represent 6 percent of the noncongressional interviews. Most were with liberal delegates and people like Betty Friedan, Andrew Young, Patsy Mink, Joan Mondale, Harold Washington, and John Zaccaro.

When NBC's Chris Wallace interviewed Governor Robb, he asked: "As a moderate, do you feel 'odd man out?'" If he did feel out of place, it shouldn't have been with his party; in a 1982 CBS News/*New York Times* poll, a remarkable 76 percent of the Democratic rank-and-file said that they thought of themselves as moderates or conservatives, and the Democrats have a good number of moderates on Capitol Hill and in the statehouses. According to voting ratings, their Senate ranks include names like Chiles, Boren, Bentsen, DeConcini, Dixon, Exon, Ford, Heflin, and Johnston.

Moderate conservatives were by no means abundant on the floor of the Moscone Center, but under the circumstances, they might have been worth seeking. As it was, CBS News and NBC News treated moderate and conservative Democrats as less newsworthy than San Francisco's favorite transvestite, Sister Boom-Boom, and his Order of Perpetual Indulgence.

### Missing Questions

The Democrats who are most likely to rebel against their party's current incarnation of liberalism -- and those who are most likely to let a strong economy pull them into the Republican presidential column -- are overwhelmingly those whose issue inclinations and self-identification are conservative-to-moderate. One might expect that this continued spectacular revolt against liberal leaders would have prompted network inquiries about the rebels and why they again seemed unattracted to their party's product. Instead, network discussions of party unity revolved around whether various liberal (although the word "liberal" was rarely used) factions would work hard for Mondale: would Jesse Jackson rally his troops for Mondale? Would Gary Hart stump for Mondale? Would feminists energize the Democratic campaign?

Questions that explicitly pointed to the Democrats' ideological split were almost nonexistent, though there were a few notable exceptions. NBC's Ken Bode, for example, asked Tip O'Neill: "What do you tell those county chairmen in Texas who say, 'We've got two Yankee liberals on the ticket, and we need to carry the state of Texas?'"

And Dan Rather once asked O'Neill if he was worried "about putting two liberals at the top of the ticket." O'Neill assured him that there was no cause for concern. The networks, then, were not alone in overlooking the 39 percent of the rank-and-file who were unwilling to support Mondale.

Both CBS News and NBC News noted that convention participants were more liberal than the grassroots of the Democratic Party, but they left the observation largely unexplained. John Chancellor did offer a few brief insights, explaining that there were "two Democratic tribes," and that the "activist liberals" in the hall wanted the platform to appear moderate so that it would appeal to "those of you who are Democrats at home, who are more moderate than these Democrats" at the convention.

Most unity discussions returned to Mondale's camaraderie with Jesse Jackson and Gary Hart. By the final night, network pundits pronounced the party united!

After Dallas, some annoyed Republicans claimed that networks kept their cameras on liberals Lowell Weicker and Jim Leach, but the critics were wrong. CBS News and NBC News may have dismissed Democratic conservatives, but they did not neglect Republican conservatives; Weicker and Leach did not dominate the screen.

As shown in Table 9A, conservative congressional Republicans were slightly overrepresented in TV interviews. Conservatives constituted 62 percent of the Republicans in Congress, but obtained 70 percent of the convention interviews. Liberal Republicans garnered two more and moderate Republicans four fewer interviews than proportionality would have indicated, although the moderate and liberal shares were bolstered by noncongressional interviews.

Overall convention exposure -- on and off of the dais -- was dominated by the prevailing conservative voices in the Republican Party. Inattention was definitely not the problem for conservative Republicans that it was for moderate-to-conservative Democrats.

### Labeling the Republicans

Another large difference in coverage of the two conventions was that the ideological dispositions of the Republicans were frequently noticed, classified, and commented upon, while such ideological analyses of Democrats at their convention were rare. On the average of about once every six minutes from Dallas, viewers were told that the Republican party was in the hands of "very strong conservatives" or "the right wing" or "the hard right," with enormous power exercised by, in Walter Cronkite's words, the "fundamentalist religious conservative right wing."

San Francisco offered a sharp contrast. On the average of about once every hour, viewers heard Democrats mentioned as "a fairly liberal crowd" (Rather) who upheld "standard, liberal Democratic values" (Cronkite).

Several times, both CBS News and NBC News portrayed the Mondale-Ferraro approach as a move to the moderate middle: Dan Rather said Mondale wanted the party back in "the middle of the road," and he described the Democratic Party's aim for a "centrist approach" and "a rush to the middle." He also called Ferraro's speech "pretty conservative."

Together, both CBS News and NBC News called the Republican Party, its platform, or its dominant leaders by conservative labels 113 times. They called the Democrats by liberal labels 21 times and moderate labels 14 times. [See Graph 9B]

No statistical summary can quite capture the verbal disparity in ideological labeling. To get a better picture, Tables 9C and 9D list the ideological tags used by CBS News personnel to refer to party policies, groups, and all participants on the second night of each party's convention.

Republicans were measured in ideological terms, with their distance to the right discussed and calibrated. Democrats were seldom evaluated by such criteria. The terms "right wing" and "right winger" appeared repeatedly in covering Republicans; the terms "left wing" and "left winger" were never used by CBS News or NBC News reporters covering Democrats.

Ironically, it was the liberal political tradition of Walter Mondale that was suffering. Even as reporters would not speak its name, most congressional Democrats were busy running away from it and from Mondale/Ferraro. The alienation of a large chunk of the Democratic Party continued to ensure defeat. Commentators' references to Democratic flag waving and endorsements of the family never explained why the party needed to invoke those symbols. By failing to dissect the Democrats' desertions and their ideological distance from the rank-and-file, the networks missed one of the critical stories of 1984.

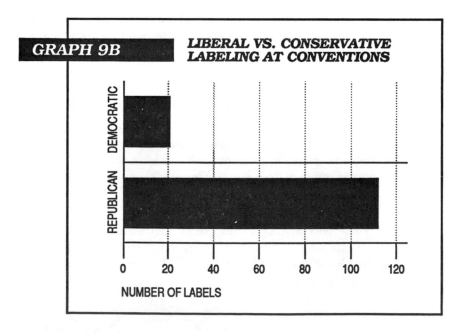

**GRAPH 9B**    *LIBERAL VS. CONSERVATIVE LABELING AT CONVENTIONS*

NUMBER OF LABELS

### *Missing Issues*

Partisans could emphasize their preferred issues when they made their podium speeches, and such speeches took up 40 percent of all convention airtime. We distilled nine major themes from each convention's major addresses and acceptance speeches.

| TABLE 9C | CBS's USE OF IDEOLOGICAL LABELS: 1984 REPUBLICAN CONVENTION (Second night) | |
|---|---|---|
| **PHRASE** | **REFERENCE** | **SPEAKER** |
| "ultraconservative platform" | Platform | Dan Rather |
| "too far to the right?" | Convention | Lesley Stahl |
| "very strong conservatives" | Platform supporters | Diane Sawyer |
| "considered narrow ideologically" | Platform | Dan Rather |
| "the right wing" | Platform supporters | Bill Moyers |
| "the fringe, the exotic radicals" | Terry Dolan and co. | Bill Moyers |
| "aim is an authoritarian Republican party of moral absolutes" | New Right | Bill Moyers |
| "party of the far right conservatives" | Republican right | Bill Moyers |
| "the hard right" | Republican right | Dan Rather |
| "the hard right" | New GOP leaders | Dan Rather |
| "billionaire . . . rightwinger" | Bunker Hunt | Bill Moyers |
| "hard right conservative" | Platform writers | Dan Rather |
| "very conservative" | Platform | Bob Schieffer |
| "too far to the right?" | Ronald Reagan | Dan Rather |
| "identify with the more conservative wing" | Jack Kemp | Dan Rather |
| "fundamentalist conservatives" | Republican element | Dan Rather |
| "fundamentalist, right-wing, conservative" | Platform writers | Walter Cronkite |
| "fundamentalist religious conservative right-wing" | Republican element | Walter Cronkite |
| "religious fundamental conservative group" | TV preachers and conservative wing | Walter Cronkite |
| maybe "Bush would be more conservative than Reagan . . ." | George Bush | Walter Cronkite |
| "fundamentalist right" | Republican element | Dan Rather |
| "populist . . . conservative . . . economic supply-sider" | Jack Kemp | Dan Rather |
| "several clicks more to the right than ever" | Platform | Dan Rather |
| "pragmatic conservatives" | Those disturbed by platform | Dan Rather |
| "on the Republican right" | Vin Weber | Bob Schieffer |

*— continued on next page*

During most of prime time, reporters had independent opportunities to select the issues they deemed worthy of attention. They and their producers decided not only whom to interview, but also which issues to

| TABLE 9C | CBS's USE OF IDEOLOGICAL LABELS: 1984 REPUBLICAN CONVENTION |
|---|---|
| *(continued)* | (Second night) |

| PHRASE | REFERENCE | SPEAKER |
|---|---|---|
| "conservatives would be proud of" | Platform | Bob Schieffer |
| "interested in the fiscal . . . side of conservatism" | Pierre DuPont | Lesley Stahl |
| "two conservative wings" | Republican party | Lesley Stahl |
| "conservative wing" | Bush opponents | Dan Rather |
| "social conservatives" | Republican majority | Bruce Morton |
| "conservative hit group" | NCPAC | Bill Moyers |
| "party of conservatives" | Republican party | Dan Rather |
| "traditional conservatives" | Goldwater and others | Bill Moyers |
| "Three main factions . . . two of them conservative" | Republican elements | Dan Rather |
| "other conservatives" | Ford and others | Dan Rather |
| "traditional conservatives" | Ford and others | Dan Rather |
| "conservatives, more conservatives, liberal, moderate" | Republican party | Dan Rather |
| "other conservative traditional wing" | Some Republicans | Walter Cronkite |
| "economic conservatives" | Some Republicans | Walter Cronkite |
| "two right wings" | Republican party | Dan Rather |
| "that endangered species, the Republican moderate" | GOP element | Dan Rather |
| "reaching out for the middle?" | Reagan's campaign | Bob Schieffer |
| "center of the party is perhaps represented by . . ." | Pierre DuPont | Dan Rather |
| "moderates" | GOP element | Dan Rather |
| "moderates" | Non-Reaganites | Dan Rather |
| "told the moderates of this party, 'get out'" | Terry Dolan | Dan Rather |
| Republican "mainstream is a dry creek" | Jim Leach, etc. | Bruce Morton |
| "the moderates have no heirs" | Jim Leach, etc. | Bruce Morton |
| "liberal-moderate" | Ripon Society | Diane Sawyer |
| "Republican liberal" | GOP element | Dan Rather |
| "represents some of the more liberal members of his party" | Jim Leach | Dan Rather |
| "liberals here are toothless, wingless, and hopeless" | GOP liberals | Bill Moyers |
| "liberals" | Republican element | Dan Rather |

highlight. We coded every question asked by a CBS News or NBC News reporter according to subject.

In light of massive Democratic defections, one would have thought newsworthy questions would have included those issues with which Republicans were apparently making headway: the growing economy, the decline of inflation, the Grenada intervention, and school prayer.

Instead, questions at both conventions came overwhelmingly from the Democratic agenda. As shown in Table 9E, policy-related questions drew on the Democrats' issues by a margin of at least seven to one. Consequently, Republicans were hit repeatedly with questions about matters the Democrats had stressed (especially arms control and E.R.A.), but Democrats rarely had to respond to the Republicans' issues.

This asymmetry meant that Democrats were almost never confronted with the possibility that the large loss from their own ranks might have something to do with preferences for the policies and performance of the opposition. In fact, Republicans were treated as if theirs was the approach that was in trouble. Some correspondents' queries from Dallas:

**Lesley Stahl**: "There was no mention of arms control in your speech....Why is that?"

| TABLE 9D | CBS's USE OF IDEOLOGICAL LABELS: 1984 DEMOCRATIC CONVENTION (Second night) | | |
|---|---|---|---|
| **PHRASE** | | **REFERENCE** | **SPEAKER** |
| "relatively conservative district" | | Ferraro's district | Morton Dean |
| "a very, very conservative district" | | Ferraro's district | Morton Dean |
| "the Archie Bunker district . . . his conservative philosophy resides there" | | Ferraro's district | Morton Dean |
| "so-called moderate black politicians" | | Black leaders not supporting Jackson | Ed Bradley |
| "left of the Democratic Party . . . he's to the left" | | Jesse Jackson | Bill Moyers |
| "Tip O'Neill of Queens" | | Geraldine Ferraro | Dan Rather |
| "a leftist politician" | | Jesse Jackson | Bill Moyers |
| "a very liberal voting record . . . one of the most liberal congresspersons | | Geraldine Ferraro | Morton Dean |

**Tom Brokaw**: "There's been practically nothing said about arms control or a nuclear freeze or the need for some kind of summit to end the madness of the nuclear arms race...."

**Chris Wallace**: "Are you concerned that there needs to be more talk about arms control and negotiations with the Soviets?"

**Tom Brokaw**: "There's not been much discussion at this convention about arms control...."

It would seem to be good journalism to confront both parties with the strongest arguments of their opposition. Even those who approve the press practice of "attacking the front-runner" must concede one thing: Shielding the underdogs from the issues that help the front-runners results in underplaying, or missing, some of the most influential factors of the campaign. The classic example of this was the economy.

### Ignored Economic Boom
Networks' summer polls showed no issue coming close to the

| TABLE 9E | PARTY ISSUES AND NETWORK QUESTIONS |
|---|---|

(Network totals combined from both conventions)

| REPUBLICAN ISSUES | QUESTIONS: CBS NEWS | NBC NEWS | DEMOCRATIC ISSUES | QUESTIONS: CBS NEWS | NBC NEWS |
|---|---|---|---|---|---|
| Democrats too liberal | 3 | 3 | Republicans too conservative | 7 | 11 |
| Soviet military threat & need for a strong defense | 2 | 3 | Need to negotiate with Soviets & need for arms control | 6 | 9 |
| Lessons of Iran and Afghanistan | 0 | 0 | Danger of war in Central America | 6 | 0 |
| Success in Grenada | 0 | 0 | Failure in Lebanon | 0 | 1 |
| Economic boom | 0 | 0 | Federal deficit | 5 | 3 |
| Inflation down | 0 | 0 | Fairness issue | 5 | 5 |
| Opportunity society | 0 | 0 | ERA and women's rights | 13 | 14 |
| School prayer | 0 | 0 | Support social welfare & moderate defense spending | 0 | 0 |
| Deregulation | 0 | 0 | Environment & EPA | 0 | 0 |
| TOTAL | 5 | 6 | TOTAL | 42 | 42 |

economy and inflation in the hierarchy of voter priorities. Large numbers of people gave the Reagan Administration some credit when they concluded the country was better off economically than it was four years earlier.

What, then, did CBS News and NBC News reporters ask convention politicos about the first postwar economic boom to increase family income and reduce unemployment without fueling inflation? Nothing. Does healthy adversarial journalism require minimizing topics that are inconvenient for the underdogs?

In nearly forty hours of convention coverage, CBS News and NBC News barely noticed two of the most powerful campaign factors of 1984: another epic defection of nonliberals from the Democratic ticket and the successful Republican appeals, most notably the booming economy. Ultimately, the summer polls correctly forecast that both factors would destroy Mondale's hopes.

# *"The Media in Campaign '84: General Election Coverage"*

## OVERVIEW

The fall campaign of 1984 offered voters a clear choice. Professor Michael Robinson and Maura Clancey, both then with George Washington University, wanted to know whether television network coverage favored the liberal Walter Mondale-Geraldine Ferraro ticket, the conservative Ronald Reagan-George Bush ticket, or neither. To learn the answer they analyzed all ABC, CBS and NBC evening newscasts between Labor Day and the November election. Robinson and Clancey documented the same double standard discovered by Adams' convention analysis. They found that the networks were friendly to Democratic issues and made far more negative comments about Reagan and Bush than about Mondale and Ferraro.

Robinson, who describes himself as a liberal, argued that liberal bias was not the cause. He attributed the anti-Reagan/Bush tilt to prejudice against incumbents and the "irritation" of "prima donna" media professionals upset by Reagan's skillful use of the media to build his positive public image, among other factors. Robinson conceded, however, that liberal bias could plausibly explain the situation.

## KEY FINDINGS

- Coding the direction of each story's "spin" -- "subjective comments about objective facts" -- Robinson and Clancey determined the number of seconds of "good press" vs. "bad press" for each candidate. "Ronald Reagan's bad press total was ten times greater than his good press total, for a ten-to-one negative 'spin ratio.'"

- Reagan got adoring coverage compared to George Bush who earned a "spin ratio that defied computation -- 1,500 seconds of bad press pieces and zero seconds of good press."

- Mondale and Ferraro, in contrast, received slightly positive spin ratios, an incredible achievement considering the normally adversarial nature of the press corps.

- Nine of the top ten campaign issues covered coincided with the Democratic agenda, including Reagan's age, controversial remarks by Bush, and the ethics of Labor Secretary Ray Donovan. "Nothing says more about the network coverage in 1984," Robinson and Clancey explained, "than this list of news topics. Neither Mondale's health problems (hypertension) nor Ferraro's confusion between 'first use' and 'first strike' made even the top twenty. Zaccaro/Ferrarogate came in surprisingly low (Number 12). In toto, the Republicans endured a bad news agenda that was about five times greater than that given the Democrats (125 stories versus 25)."

- "In 27 stories network correspondents made personal assessments implying either that Mondale had won the first debate or that Reagan had lost it," but when "Reagan won his second debate with Mondale, the network correspondents acknowledged it only twice."

## STUDY EXCERPT

*The Media in Campaign '84: General Election Coverage* by Michael Robinson and Maura Clancey. From *Public Opinion*, December/January 1985.

Starting on Labor Day and continuing through election day, a team of five sifted through tapes from all three network evening news programs, distilling from about 200 broadcasts all the news about President Reagan or his White House; about the presidential or vice-presidential race; about lower level elections or state and local referendums. All told, we analyzed 790 stories, but for this report we concentrated on the 625 news items that dealt specifically with the presidential or vice-presidential campaign.

Every piece was scored on two dozen separate dimensions, some as straightforward as length or date of the story, some as slippery as press "spin" or ideological tilt. There is no magic to what we did -- our training was collective, we used specific rules, and we reached consensus on almost every decision, despite the very different political views of our group. [1]

### Reagan's "Packaging" vs. Mondale's "Coordination"

In mid-October, Roger Mudd did a report on this year's "spin patrols" -- campaign officials or other partisans who flew to the debates and tried to put the best possible "spin" on their man's (or woman's) performance.

We were pleased that Mudd popularized the term "spin;" we had been using it as a variable since September. But to us spin means something different -- the way the correspondent interprets or embellishes the facts in a story. Spin involves *tone*, the part of the reporting that extends *beyond* hard news. On October 12, for example, Ronald Reagan's train trip through western Ohio was hard news. But when Dan Rather chose to label the ride "a photo-opportunity train trip, chock full of symbolism and trading on Harry Truman's old turf," Rather added "spin."

Throughout, we scored every story for its spin -- the positive or negative implications about the candidates contained within the reporter's own words. And we used "spin" as our first and most important test of good and bad press.

There are two important things to remember about the spin measure: First, when the reporter's subjective comments about objective facts went in both directions (positive *and* negative), we almost always judged the piece "ambiguous." Second, we *excluded* from our spin variable all references to the horse race, defining the spin as interpretations of the candidate's *quality*, not his *electability*.[2]

There may be some questions about the validity of our measure, but there can be no question about the lopsidedness of what it uncovered. Assuming that a piece with a positive spin equals "good press," and assuming that negative spin equals "bad press," Ronald Reagan and George Bush proved overwhelmingly to be the "bad press" ticket of 1984. Graph 9F contains the number of news seconds we scored as good press or bad press for each of the candidates.[3] Ronald Reagan's bad press total was *ten times greater* than his good press total (7,230 seconds vs. 730). In other words, his "spin ratio" was ten-to-one negative.

George Bush had a spin ratio that defied computation -- 1,500 seconds of "bad press" pieces and zero seconds of good press.

Walter Mondale and Geraldine Ferraro, on the other hand, had slightly *positive* spin ratios -- 1,970 seconds of good press about them-selves as people or potential leaders, and 1,450 seconds of bad press. Given what we know about the bad news bias of television, the fact that anyone, let alone any ticket, got more positive spin than negative is news indeed.

These numbers don't, however, tell us everything about spin. When Edith Efron examined news coverage of the 1968 (Humphrey-Nixon) campaign, she neglected to include news coverage that had no observable spin -- or that had ambiguous spin. [4] Efron's omission was a serious one. In 1984, 74 percent of the total time on network evening news devoted to national candidates had no clear spin, negative or positive. What we analyze here is the 26 percent that did. In fact, one of the best reasons for not getting too excited about the positive ratio for Mondale/Ferraro is that 86 percent (!) of their news coverage had no clear spin. Even George Bush, the candidate with no good press, might take some comfort from knowing that 60 percent of his news time was neutral

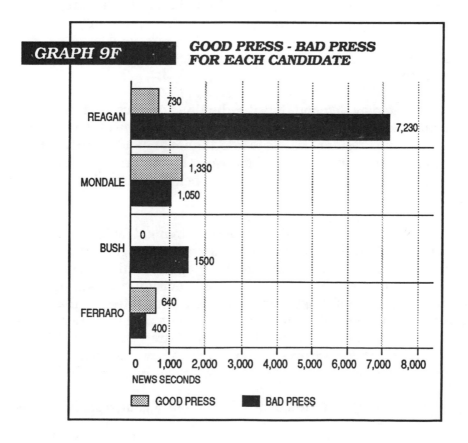

**GRAPH 9F** — **GOOD PRESS - BAD PRESS FOR EACH CANDIDATE**

REAGAN: 730 (good press), 7,230 (bad press)
MONDALE: 1,330 (good press), 1,050 (bad press)
BUSH: 0 (good press), 1,500 (bad press)
FERRARO: 640 (good press), 400 (bad press)

NEWS SECONDS

GOOD PRESS   BAD PRESS

or ambiguous. In this regard, Reagan is tied with Bush. Forty percent, precisely, of Ronald Reagan's press coverage on network television showed spin, but, as we've already seen, 90 percent of that was negative.

What did Reagan's bad press look like in qualitative terms? Commentaries, as expected, focused on his policy failures. John Chancellor, for example, blamed Reagan for the security lapses in Lebanon; George Will and John Chancellor both complained about Reagan's having injected religion into America's secular politics. Bob Simon at CBS did a powerful news analysis on the failures of Lebanon policy since Reagan first took charge, making it clear that many Americans felt the Marines in Lebanon had indeed died in vain.

In the noncommentary pieces, Reagan came in for a different kind of criticism -- a near-constant barrage of closers or interpretive remarks implying that something wasn't right with Reagan. He was hiding behind his security squad, he was cut off from the public, or he was manipulating symbols, or he was feeble-minded, or too old, or wasting taxpayers' money, or he was saying dumb things.

ABC's Sam Donaldson helped set the standard for bad tone with this mid-September piece:

"Mondale may demand deficit reduction specifics, and the President answers with one-liners. Mondale may warn of hard times ahead, and the President points to good times at hand. Mondale may issue a call to arms, and the President waves the American flag. If there are true issues in this campaign, they are being discussed but not enjoined."

And on October 4 Lesley Stahl did her quadrennial feature about the sinister nature of incumbency, focusing this time on Reagan's decision to run "a campaign in which he highlights the images and hides from the issues." Stahl told us that "the orchestration of television coverage absorbs the White House"; that "they aim to erase the negatives"; that "Mr. Reagan tries to counter the memory of an unpopular issue with a carefully chosen package (of videotape) that actually contradicts the President's policy." And Stahl even theorized about why Reagan "disappears" when things aren't quite right. "It's his gaffes," she concluded.

But NBC was at least as tough as CBS. (Table 9G suggests NBC was toughest across the board for all candidates.) And in fact, NBC did something that not only symbolizes Reagan's press problems, but also implies that Mondale did have (as our numbers indicate) an easier time of it on network news.

NBC's reporting is especially interesting because two very highly regarded correspondents essentially covered the same sort of action by Reagan and Mondale, yet treated Reagan critically, Mondale almost sympathetically.

On October 16, Chris Wallace presented a long and captious piece about (what else) Reagan's Hollywood-style, made-for-TV news campaign. The Wallace piece lasted five minutes, it linked Reagan's campaign to the Nixon gang from 1972, and its message was clear -- Reagan was all media and staging. In fact, NBC titled the piece, with logo, "Packaging Reagan."

Yet three weeks earlier, on September 27, Roger Mudd had presented a three-minute feature about Mondale/Ferraro media techniques and strategies. The Mudd piece was in no way flackery; Mudd even concluded that the Mondale "message" was not getting through. But Mudd treated the Mondale/Ferraro media machinations as a good thing. He spoke of a "coordinated message" and described the staff as "seasoned veterans." What had been "packaging" for Reagan was now "coordination" for Mondale.

## Campaign Issues

### Nine out of Ten Go Against the Republicans

News has an agenda as well as a spin. Had the networks covered *only* Geraldine Ferraro's tax and financial matters during the campaign, regardless of the spin, that would have been a very different news agenda from one that included both her controversial tax returns *and* her adoring crowds. Had the networks covered only Reagan's record on inflation and never bothered to cover his record on deficits, that news agenda would have implied something important not just about Reagan but also about press behavior.

Of course, the networks did cover Ferraro's adoring crowds and did (though very infrequently) talk about Reagan's record on inflation. News agendas *are* tricky to define and even trickier to interpret, but in

**TABLE 9G**

**SPIN SCORES OF JOURNALISTS**
(For all stories)

| JOURNALIST | SCORE |
|---|---|
| John Severson, NBC | -36 |
| Lisa Myers, NBC | -30 |
| Phil Jones, CBS | -27 |
| Lesley Stahl, CBS | -25 |
| Bob Kur, NBC | -22 |
| Chris Wallace, NBC | -21 |
| Richard Threlkeld, ABC | -19 |
| Dean Reynolds, ABC | -14 |
| George Will, ABC | -12 |
| Sam Donaldson, ABC | -11 |
| Susan Spencer, CBS | -9 |
| Carole Simpson, ABC | -9 |
| Connie Chung, NBC | -7 |
| James Wooten, ABC | -6 |
| Roger Mudd, NBC | -3 |
| Peter Jennings, ABC | -1 |
| Lynn Sherr, ABC | 0 |
| Betsy Aaron, ABC | 0 |
| Ken Bode, NBC | 0 |
| John Chancellor, NBC | 0 |
| Dan Rather, CBS | +1 |
| Tom Brokaw, NBC | +1 |
| Brit Hume, ABC | +2 |
| Bob Schieffer, CBS | +3 |
| Barry Serafin, ABC | +6 |
| Bruce Morton, CBS | +6 |
| Ted Koppel, ABC | +7 |
| Rita Flynn, ABC | +8 |
| Bill Plante, CBS | +18 |

| NETWORK | SCORE |
|---|---|
| NBC | -10 |
| ABC | -4 |
| CBS | -3 |

*Note: These numbers represent the percentage of good press pieces minus the percentage of bad press pieces for each journalist and for each network for all candidate stories. The figures include "spin" on both dimensions, "personal quality" and "horse-race favoribility." We include only those correspondents who presented at least seven stories about the campaign.*

1984 two interrelated findings about the news agenda suggest that the loser received better treatment than the winner on network news. The first has to do with what topics didn't get "normal" coverage in 1984. The second deals with the sort of topic that filled the vacuum.

### Where's the Horse-Race News?

In virtually every campaign waged in the television era, the most frequent evening news story has been the on-the-road, horse-race piece -- the reporter covers the day's campaign events and then assesses the candidate's motives and/or the electorate's possible response. In 1984, though, horse-race journalism did *not* represent the most prevalent form of campaign reporting. *Campaign issues* pieces were emphasized instead. Campaign issues are not policy issues. Policy issues involve enduring disputes about how *government* should behave; campaign issues involve short-term concerns about how *candidates* or their campaigns should behave. In 1976, for example, a major campaign issue was Ford's remark about political freedom in Eastern Europe and what it indicated about his intelligence; in 1980 it was Carter's apparent meanness.

In 1984 campaign issues surged forward as a press focus, not only passing traditional horse-race reporting but also coming to represent almost *40 percent* of the campaign coverage.

There are two plausible explanations for the networks' declining focus on the horse race and increasing interest in campaign issues. One, clearly, is that there was no horse race to cover. With Mondale/Ferraro consistently trailing in the polls, horse-race pieces became tiresome early on.

A second theory is that the media shifted to campaign issues when it became clear that emphasizing the horse race might be beneficial to the horse and jockey that were winning. If bandwagons still exist, horse-race journalism in 1984 could have been expected to help Reagan, and reporters could have been expected to know it. Again, in these terms, Reagan and Bush came up short on the evening news.

### The Agenda of Campaign Issues: Whatever Happened to John Zaccaro?

Horse-race journalism consumed less of the campaign news time in 1984, and what the networks used to fill the void made Reagan/Bush press losers again. In covering campaign issues, as opposed to policy issues, the news media were more free to pick and choose. This time, unlike 1980, they picked a news agenda that was decidedly bad for the Republicans.

Table 9H contains the twenty most fully covered "campaign issues" in the general campaign, debate coverage excepted. Nine of the top ten were campaign issues that were "bad news" issues for the GOP. Only one of the first ten was a bad news issue for the Democrats -- the imbroglio between Geraldine Ferraro and her church, especially her verbal battle with Archbishop John O'Connor.

Reagan's suggestions that the Beirut embassy bombing was Carter's fault or was akin to kitchen remodeling was the most fully covered campaign issue. The "age issue" came next: coverage of Reagan's having grown too old to debate, or maybe to think. Two nights after the debate ABC gave us three pieces in a row discussing Reagan's age: what we

| TABLE 9H | AMOUNT OF ATTENTION GIVEN TO TOP TWENTY "CAMPAIGN ISSUES"* |
| --- | --- |

| AGENDA ITEMS | NUMBER OF STORIES |
| --- | --- |
| 1. Beirut (as a campaign issue) | 17 |
| 2. Reagan's age | 15 |
| 3. Bush's "shame" remark | 12 |
| 4. Reagan's availability | 12 |
| 5. CIA assassination manual | 11 |
| 6. *Ferraro vs. O'Connor/Church* | 11 |
| 7. Reagan/Religious ties | 10 |
| 8. Reagan/Heckler ties | 9 |
| 9. Bush's campaign behavior—("kick ass" included) | 8 |
| 10. "Donovangate" | 8 |
| 11. "Meesegate" | 8 |
| 12. *Ferraro/Zaccaro finances* | 5 |
| 13. Heckling/General** | 5 |
| 14. *Mondale/Gromyko meeting* | 5 |
| 15. Vetoes of journalists/debate one** | 5 |
| 16. Bush's blind trust/Taxes | 4 |
| 17. *Ferraro's credentials* | 4 |
| 18. Barbara Bush's remarks | 3 |
| 19. Campaign ethics generally ** | 3 |
| 20. TV political ads ** | 3 |

Note:  *Debate coverage is not included here.
       **Bipartisan issues.
       The issues in italics are those that focused on the Democrats.

label the "senility trilogy." Next on the list was Reagan's "inaccessibility," one of the networks' favorites in September. Then Bush's feeble attempts to define "shame," from several dictionaries. Eventually the networks moved us on through the CIA manual controversy, the ties between Reagan and the fundamentalist preachers; the allegations concerning White House complicity in organizing hecklers against Mondale/Ferraro, and Bush's rudeness and personal behavior. The final of the top ten pieces was about "Donovangate."

Nothing says more about the network coverage in 1984 than this list of news topics. Neither Mondale's health problems (hypertension) nor Ferraro's confusion between "first use" and "first strike" made even the top twenty. Zaccaro/Ferrarogate came in surprisingly low (Number 12). In toto, the Republicans endured a bad news agenda that was about five times greater than that given the Democrats (125 stories versus 25).

## Debate Coverage

### Mondale 1, Reagan and Bush 0
The reality of the debates -- who won, who lost -- is as tricky a topic as any pundit can ponder. But nobody -- not even Reagan -- disputes that the President lost the first debate.

As for the second round, most print journalists felt that, given what he had to do, Reagan probably did win. And most polls showed that George Bush won the vice-presidential debate by either a little or a lot. The Democrats, then, won one debate by a lot, and the Republicans won two, but by much closer scores.

But this was not the picture we got from network news -- at least not from the *personal* analyses presented by the on-camera correspondents. Looking at what the reporters concluded about the debates (when they were not merely reciting polls) one finds something remarkable: in 27 stories, network correspondents made personal assessments implying either that Mondale had won the first debate or that Reagan had lost it. Not once did these reporters make any similar personal assessments about Bush's victory in his debate with Ferraro. And when Reagan won his second debate with Mondale, the network correspondents acknowledged it only twice, all the more remarkable given that Reagan's performance in the last debate probably mattered at least as much as his showing in the first. Indeed, Reagan received more than 13 times as much evening news comment for losing the first debate as he did for winning his second.

On the day following the vice-presidential debate, the networks virtually ignored Bush's on-camera performance. All three turned instead to Bush's off-color, off-camera, off-handed remark about "kicking a little ass." Bush got more coverage for his "kick-ass" comment than for any other aspect of his debate appearance.

## Horse-Race Predictions

### Finally: One for the GOP

Other than the good press Reagan got for his hurry-up meeting with Andrei Gromyko, did the networks favorably cover anything about him or his ticket? Yes, horse-race coverage was an unambiguous press victory for Reagan/Bush. Graph 9I contains the amount of newstime for each ticket devoted to pieces in which the correspondent said or implied

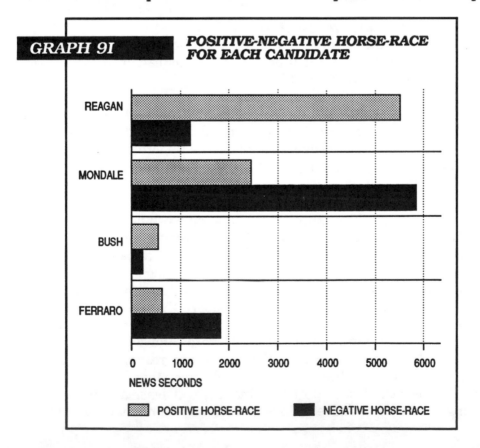

**GRAPH 9I**

**POSITIVE-NEGATIVE HORSE-RACE FOR EACH CANDIDATE**

NEWS SECONDS

☐ POSITIVE HORSE-RACE          ■ NEGATIVE HORSE-RACE

something favorable or unfavorable about the principal candidate's status in the horse-race. This measure tests whether the correspondent goes beyond citing polls and clearly implies that the campaign is going well or badly for the featured candidate. This is horse-race spin, in essence.

And spin about the horse race favored Reagan/Bush over Mondale/Ferraro. As Graph 9I indicates, horse-race assessments ran four-to-one positive for Reagan/Bush, three-to-one negative for Mondale/Ferraro.

Throughout the campaign, the Democrats complained more about press coverage than the Republicans. Democrats insisted that network correspondents were dumping on their man, their woman, and their campaign. The Democrats were right, but *only* when the "issue" was the horse race.

On the opening night of the general campaign, all three networks began what became a month's worth of poor-mouthing the Democratic chances. NBC's Lisa Myers seemed particularly hard on Mondale's political condition, something the Mondale people noticed early on. Even after the first debate, the networks failed to give Mondale much copy suggesting he could somehow win the election. Mondale, in fact, earned much less credit for winning the first debate than Reagan was blamed for losing it.

On the other side, the networks did consistently give Reagan/Bush credit for winning the race and for conducting a "masterful" campaign. Even in those pieces we've already quoted about Reagan's packaging, Reagan's hiding out, or Reagan's cynical campaign strategy, the correspondents acknowledged that all his posturing was working. The news themes throughout suggested that Reagan was clearly winning, but, if the truth were known, he shouldn't be.

### Cosmic Press Measure
Astute readers have already raised the crucial question. Was the bad press concerning Democratic chances in the race equivalent to the bad press concerning the personal qualities of the Republican ticket? We have no way of knowing how voters responded, but we do have a "cosmic" measure that combines the press spin about each candidate as a *person* with his or her press coverage of position in the race. [5]

The cosmic index, which tries to balance "horse-race" and "leadership" press coverage, was more than twice as negative for Reagan/Bush (-37) as for Mondale/Ferraro (-15). Bush got what everybody now expects -- a cosmic score worse than everybody else's (-55), one that reflected constant references to Bush's poor judgment, his intemperate behavior, his political liability to himself and Reagan. Reagan came in second to last (-33). Ferraro finished with a -28, and Walter Mondale won a Pyrrhic press victory (-10). Even with the horse-race assessments factored in, the only definitive conclusion is that the networks gave Reagan/Bush a measurably tougher time than Mondale/Ferraro.

1 In the article we provide our definitions as we go along, section by section. But one important qualification needs to be made at the outset. We analyzed the journalists, their copy, and their nonverbal gestures. We did *not* analyze the candidates or their surrogates. If Reagan smiled warmly on camera or told an hilarious joke, we excluded Reagan's performance from our assessment of news content. We scored not what Reagan said or did, but instead what Sam Donaldson, Chris Wallace, or Bill Plante et al. said or did. Our entire emphasis here is on journalism, not the comprehensive "message." And it was the *journalism* that went very much against Reagan, warm smile or one-liners notwithstanding.

2 Obviously we realize that reporters also employ "spin" in discussing the horse race. And we have a separate measure that allowed us to keep track of the way the networks treated each candidate's *chances*. But in 1980 we learned that network reporters tend to divide their news interpretations into two categories – those related to personal quality and those related to candidate status in the race. So we did the same in 1984: For us "spin" involved the reporter's remarks concerning the candidate's credibility, availability, vitality, integrity, consistency, decency, or "factuality." In essence, spin includes everything *but* "viability."

3 We scored this for the *pricipal* candidate only. If a piece dealt with two candidates equally, we divided the story, and the time, in two.

4 *The News Twisters*. Edith Efron, Nash Publishing, 1971.

5 Cosmic measures for each candidate also include scores for news *topics*. A piece about Ferraro's fight with her church gives her a negative *one*, and if the "spin" is negative also, then Ferraro gets a minus two for the piece.

The authors appreciate the support given this project by the George Washington University and by AEI. We also thank Lisa Grand, Eve Raimon, Maryann Wynne, Carin Dessauer, and Bobbie Chilcote for helping us do this research.

CHAPTER NINE, STUDY 3

# "Campaign '88: CBS' Liberal Agenda"

## OVERVIEW

Before the 1988 presidential primaries began the *CBS Evening News* profiled the contenders. Media Research Center researchers analyzed each story for positive, negative, and neutral/factual statements, from the reporter, candidate, political analysts, or people in crowds, in the following three areas: (1) Style -- the candidate's speaking ability, charisma, or character traits; (2) Policy -- anything about the candidate's political stands; (3) The horse race -- the "who's ahead" feature of each story, including not only polling data but also comments about a candidate's strategy. As in 1984, this early study found the networks much more critical of Republicans than Democrats.

## KEY FINDINGS

- Stories by CBS reporters profiling Republicans contained 13 negative and only one positive remark from a reporter about the candidate's policy views. By a five to one margin, however, these same reporters positively assessed the policies espoused by the Democrats.

- Combining the "Policy" and "Style" assessments the MRC determined that five of the six Democrats got more positive than negative comments while five of the six Republicans received more negative than positive comments.

- With seven negative remarks about his conservative policies, Pete du Pont received the most negative profile. In contrast, stories on Democrats Paul Simon and Michael Dukakis were never critical of their liberal policy proposals.

## STUDY EXCERPT

**Campaign '88: CBS' Liberal Agenda** by the Media Research Center. From *MediaWatch*, February 1988.

The TV networks, citing cost concerns, are covering the 1988 presidential race differently from previous campaigns. No longer are reporters assigned to follow each candidate. Instead, a few correspondents are stationed in key states to cover all the hopefuls as they pass through. Unable to cover every event, network officials told *The Washington Post* in January 1988 that campaign stories promise to become more "analytical" and "interpretive," a development confirmed by a *Media Watch* study of recent candidate profile stories.

As Richard Cohen, top political producer for CBS News, admitted in the *Post* article, "I think we're going to try and impose our agenda on the coverage by dealing with issues and subjects that we choose to deal with instead of parroting the candidates."

The study determined that CBS, the only network so far to air a series of candidate profiles, is using them to promote a decidedly liberal agenda. *Media Watch* analyzed "Campaign '88" presidential candidate profiles aired by *CBS Evening News* and discovered the network went out of its way to include criticisms of policies espoused by conservative Republicans, but rarely ever mentioned anything negative about ideas endorsed by liberal Democrats. Since the series skipped Dole and Jackson, and the Bush profile focused exclusively on Iran/Contra, announcement day stories for them were used instead.

In the "Policy" category, CBS failed to air even one positive statement about the political views of five of six Republicans, but issued positive judgments on policies of all but one Democrat, Michael Dukakis. Reporter Bruce Morton delivered three uncritical, straightforward summaries of his ideas.

Assessments followed a similar pattern in the "Style" category. Covering the Republicans, CBS issued nearly four times as many negative judgments as positive ones, while the Democrats got praised more often than not. Even when analyzing horse-race positions CBS found more bad things than good to say about five of the six Republicans, but came up with few reasons to believe a Democrat might not win the nomination, issuing more upbeat than negative comments on their chances.

Since horse-race positions are constantly changing, combining Policy and Style assessments gives the best measure of the slant of each story. Doing that, every Democrat but Gore, who promoted himself as a conservative on defense, received more positive than negative comments. Every Republican but Dole, whom CBS portrayed as an experienced Washington insider, received more negative than positive judgments [See Graph 9J].

Pete du Pont ended up with the most damaging profile with seven negative remarks on his conservative policies. Reporter Bob Faw introduced duPont's three central campaign themes: reduced farm subsidies, drug testing, and alternative Social Security programs and then countered each suggestion with a negative reaction from someone who claimed he or she would be hurt by the proposal. In contrast, stories on liberals Paul Simon and Mike Dukakis did not include any criticisms of their proposals to cut defense spending or raise taxes "as a last resort."

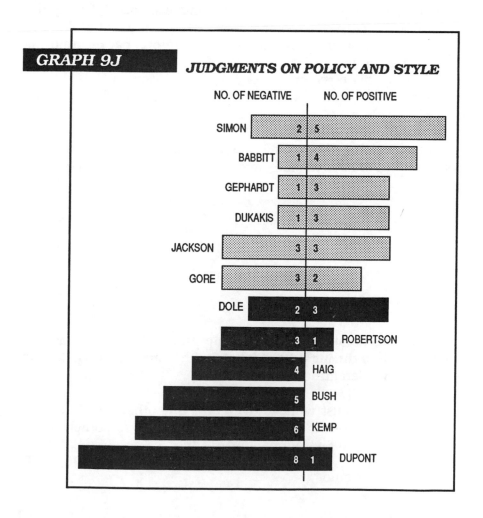

**GRAPH 9J** — **JUDGMENTS ON POLICY AND STYLE**

NO. OF NEGATIVE | NO. OF POSITIVE

| | NO. OF NEGATIVE | NO. OF POSITIVE |
|---|---|---|
| SIMON | 2 | 5 |
| BABBITT | 1 | 4 |
| GEPHARDT | 1 | 3 |
| DUKAKIS | 1 | 3 |
| JACKSON | 3 | 3 |
| GORE | 3 | 2 |
| DOLE | 2 | 3 |
| ROBERTSON | 3 | 1 |
| HAIG | 4 | |
| BUSH | 5 | |
| KEMP | 6 | |
| DUPONT | 8 | 1 |

Faw also took time to critique the supposedly dull speeches of Jack Kemp, but Bruce Morton went out of his way to portray Simon's "plainness" as an asset. In the most dubious opinionated assertion by a reporter, Faw claimed Kemp's biggest problem was his "message; he's conservative at a time when the polls show the country is moving toward the center." No CBS reporter ever blamed liberal policies for hurting any Democrat in a conservative state like New Hampshire.

With four positive policy assessments and just one negative comment on his campaign style (he lacks "razzle-dazzle"), Bruce Babbitt received the most glowing profile. Infatuated with his plans to raise taxes, Faw repeatedly praised Babbitt for "confronting issues which others fudge and sometimes offering the political equivalent of castor oil," with a platform of "common sense and sacrifice." The typical double-standard occurred between Jesse Jackson and Pat Robertson. Lesley Stahl's piece on Jackson ignored his religious background and dismissed his past praise for Castro, claiming "Jackson has shed his radical image." But in his piece on Robertson, Bruce Morton brought on a "political analyst" to explain why Robertson's "mixing of politics and religion" will hurt him.

Below is a sampling of how CBS analyzed each candidate. The listing includes examples of how virtually every report ended with an opinionated spin.

# Republicans

### George Bush
*Style*: "Bush needs to overcome the impression that he's a bad candidate: easily rattled during a 1980 debate with Ronald Reagan, too flip after a debate with Geraldine Ferraro in 1984."

*Style*: "And Bush must work to overcome one other negative -- the idea that despite his resume, and his war record, he's somehow not decisive, not forceful, not a Commander-in-Chief."
-- Bruce Morton, 10/12/87

### Bob Dole

*Style*: "Dole and his wife Liddy are Washington's quintessential power couple. When she quit her Cabinet post to go campaign for him, they found it a show that also plays well on the road."

*Style*: "Dole is also trying to soften his hatchet-man image."

*Policy*: "The keystones to his campaign are his experience on agriculture, and his vow to fight the deficit."

*Conclusion*: "If he loses [Iowa] the effort could run aground in the early months as it did in 1980."

-- Bob Schieffer, 11/9/87

### Pete du Pont

*Policy*: "Politically, du Pont has to get recognized as something more than the man who is worth $6 million or who once had a date with Jane Fonda."

*Policy*: "Du Pont's ideas are new, provocative, and not always what his listeners want to hear."

*Policy*: "Du Pont's call for a private alternative to Social Security...makes a lot of senior citizens shudder."

*Conclusion*: "He keeps raising his lance to joust with the others, even though they're convinced all Pete du Pont is doing is tilting at windmills."

-- Bob Faw, 12/1/87

### Alexander Haig

*Policy*: "On the issues, Haig is outspoken, sometimes outrageous."

*Policy*: "Many now wonder, 'can an old cold warrior lead this country into the '90s?'"

-- Richard Schlesinger, 1/8/88

### Jack Kemp

*Policy*: "Like the President, supply-sider Kemp is against abortion, against higher taxes....Still, some who listen leave unconvinced, like Michigan stockbroker Marty Gotkin, who doubts that Kemp would do enough to reduce deficits." Gotkin: "I think we're gonna, the government's gonna have to resort to some tax increases."

*Style*: "Part of the problem is the candidate. Better on the stump than he was six months ago, Kemp still quotes Hegel and Maimonides, still fails to excite crowds."

*Conclusion*: "The Republican candidate who's run the longest and hardest will try to persuade skeptics he's not just running in place."
-- Bob Faw, 10/27/87

### Pat Robertson

*Style*: "There is a downside too...because of course he was a preacher and no ordinary one, he was a charismatic Christian, a television evangelist who believed prayer could and did heal...Robertson has resigned the ministry, but that identification may hurt him."
-- Bruce Morton, 11/4/87

## Democrats

### Bruce Babbitt

*Policy*: "Is the only candidate to say how he would pay the bills, with a 5 percent national sales tax on food, medicine, and clothing."

*Policy*: "Talking straight while others seem to be blowing smoke."

*Conclusion*: Iowa "will determine if Bruce Babbitt gets into the political fast track or whether he's just been taken for a ride."
-- Bob Faw, 12/17/87

### Michael Dukakis
*Policy*: "Ideas? Dukakis has plenty. Like the other candidates, he stresses education."

-- Bruce Morton, 12/9/87

### Richard Gephardt
*Style*: "Say one thing for Gephardt, he looks the part and his family is campaign poster classic right down to the loyal dog."

*Conclusion*: "In the meantime, you have to ride a lot of planes like this [small] one before they let you ride Air Force One."

-- Bob Schieffer, 10/22/87

### Al Gore
*Policy*: "Al Gore is the only candidate...stressing his theme that he's the Democrat who's strong on defense. It is a big gamble."

*Policy*: "The candidate is widely respected for his expertise on the environment and arms control."

*Conclusion*: "The biggest question for Gore is whether a hidden block of conservative Democrats will show up at the polls, something they haven't done in more than a decade."

-- Lesley Stahl, 11/27/87

### Jesse Jackson
*Style*: "At 46, he is one of the most famous men in America, often treated like a rock star. In his second run for the presidency, Jesse Jackson is turning 'em on in White America."

*Policy*: "Jackson is getting what he always wanted: respect. This time Jackson wants to represent all victims, black and white."

-- Lesley Stahl 10/9/88

### Paul Simon

*Policy*: "A tax-and-spend Democratic liberal? Simon says no. He supports a Constitutional amendment to balance the budget."

*Style*: "One other note. Simon is a plain man. No high flown eloquence, no glitz. Plain speech. That plainness finds an echo here. A lot of Iowans are plain people too."

*Conclusion*: "The new fashion may be the old fashioned, old Democrat, warts, ideals and all. He may be an improbable dreamer, but he has some followers here [Iowa]."

-- Bruce Morton, 11/23/87

**CHAPTER NINE, STUDY 4**

# "Ducking Jesse Jackson's Left-Wing Views"

## OVERVIEW

Jesse Jackson and Pat Robertson represented opposite ends of the political spectrum among 1988 presidential candidates. When both were still viable and actively campaigning, the Media Research Center decided to see whether the networks gave equal treatment to the views each candidate held that their opponents considered outside the American political spectrum. The MRC discovered quite a contrast in coverage. ABC, CBS, CNN, and NBC depicted Robertson as an extremist by concentrating on his religious beliefs while almost totally ignoring the pro-PLO and pro-Castro comments made by Jackson.

## KEY POINTS

- Only 8 percent of primary season network stories on Jesse Jackson mentioned his pro-Palestinian Liberation Organization (PLO) views.

- Only 14 percent of Jackson pieces even alluded to his positive comments about Cuba's Fidel Castro.

- More than three-fourths of television reports on Pat Robertson negatively portrayed his past statements, allegedly controversial, including his faith healing and claim he talks directly to God.

## STUDY EXCERPT

**Ducking Jesse Jackson's Left-Wing Views** by the Media Research Center. From *MediaWatch*, April 1988.

From his embrace of Yasser Arafat and communist dictator Fidel Castro to his desire for a unilateral U.S. nuclear freeze, Democratic presidential candidate Jesse Jackson has expressed radical views that place him well to the left of liberal candidates such as Michael Dukakis. But a *MediaWatch* study has determined that the evening newscasts of the four networks rarely report Jackson's extremist positions. When it comes to conservative Republican Pat Robertson, however, the same TV reporters consider many of his beliefs "controversial" enough to report.

To conduct the study, analysts examined ABC's *World News Tonight*, *CBS Evening News*, *CNN PrimeNews*, and *NBC Nightly News* stories beginning the week before each candidate became a formidable force. For Robertson, the study ran from the week before his "surprise" finish ahead of George Bush in Iowa through his poor showing in the New Hampshire primary.

For Jackson, the study began a week before his strong Super Tuesday showing and continued to the end of March, as Jackson battled Mike Dukakis for front-runner status. After eliminating "horse-race" stories, *Media Watch* identified 13 pieces on Robertson and 37 on Jackson that entirely or predominantly focused on either candidate.

Jackson has expressed plenty of radical ideas that place him well outside the American political spectrum. These include: praising PLO terrorist leader Yasser Arafat as "educated, urbane and reasonable," calling Zionism a "poisonous weed," and standing arm in arm with Cuban dictator Fidel Castro chanting, "Long live Fidel Castro, long live Che Guevara." Only 24 percent of all stories in the month of March mentioned any controversy related to Jackson's candidacy [See Graph 9K]. Just three stories, or 8 percent, contained reference to Jackson's pro-PLO stand. Viewers may never have learned of his Arafat sympathies if not for candidate Al Gore. Two stories near the end of the month included brief clips of Gore denouncing Jackson's desire to radically alter U.S. Middle East policy.

Only 14 percent of the stories alluded in even the most obscure way to his Castro connection. Two of these five consisted of brief film clips of Jackson standing with Castro. On March 2, ABC's Rebecca Chase made passing reference to how "Jackson has practiced a form of foreign policy by photo opportunity." The same day, NBC's Bob Kur didn't see it as a negative either, referring to Jackson "meeting with world leaders." At the end of March, NBC's Ken Bode gave time to conservative Democrat Ben Wattenberg to express concern about the Castro alliance. CBS once showed Gore complaining. Only one time in any of the 37 stories did a reporter utter the name "Castro." During a March 11 interview, Tom Brokaw asked Jackson about his visit to Cuba, but let Jackson's answer go unchallenged: "Positions I have been taking in foreign policy, in Latin America, in the Middle East, are now mainstream American political thought in foreign policy."

Jackson's close ties to Muslim leader Louis Farakkhan and his "Hymietown" remark caused quite a bit of controversy in 1984, but this year the networks have practically forgotten them. Just seven stories (19 percent) mentioned either topic. This year Jackson has announced policies that go far left of anything proposed by even liberal Democrats. For instance, he has called for unilateral disarmament, saying he wants to cut defense spending by 25 percent and end production of every nuclear weapons system, from the Midgetman missile to the Stealth bomber. Only three stories (8 percent) noted his desire to radically alter American defenses, but none portrayed his cuts as anything extreme. The toughest scrutiny came from CBS' Bob Schieffer: "Jackson talks of

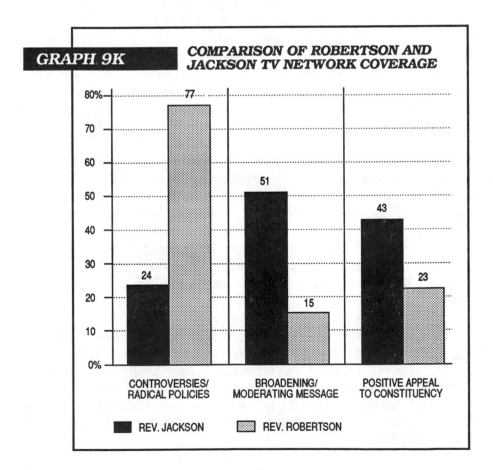

**GRAPH 9K** — *COMPARISON OF ROBERTSON AND JACKSON TV NETWORK COVERAGE*

REV. JACKSON    REV. ROBERTSON

cutting as much as $30 billion his first year from the defense budget, which would mean more than just trimming fat."

What did network coverage concentrate on? Emphasizing how he had moderated his views and broadened his base. Over half the stories dismissed concerns about Jackson's extreme and controversial views. For example, without critical comment, NBC's Dennis Murphy devoted an entire story to how Jackson was trying to "prove he [was] a mainstream, electable candidate." ABC's Peter Jennings told viewers on March 2: "It's eminently clear that the Jesse Jackson of '88 is a much different man than the Jackson that first ran in '84." Just two weeks later Jackson reaffirmed his desire to open relations with Cuba, saying on the March 17 *Nightline*: "I think in the case of Fidel Castro we would be wise to work out ways to expand our influence into Cuba."

Just over 43 percent of the reports contained statements characterizing the campaign as having a positive impact on his constituency; for instance, CNN's reference to his "promise of hope to the less fortunate." On March 15, Bruce Morton of CBS delivered this glowing assessment: "Jesse Jackson toured Chicago and brought tears and excitement wherever he went. Watch him as he walks to the Robert Taylor project, home of some of this city's poorest people. They gave him what they had, they gave him love."

Since Pat Robertson's Republican opponents refrained from criticizing his beliefs, just as Jackson's Democratic opponents did until the very end of March, you might think the media would have given them equal scrutiny. But *MediaWatch* discovered quite the opposite. In 13 stories that appeared on Robertson, ten (77 percent) spoke negatively of past Robertson statements that network reporters considered controversial. Four reports reminded viewers of Robertson's past religious life, including his faith healing, claims he talked directly to God, and "speaking in tongues."

NBC's Chris Wallace was so concerned about Robertson's past that he dug up a video tape in which Robertson said only Christians and Jews would be allowed to hold government office. Wallace declared on February 9: "Robertson may be restricted on reaching out by years of controversial statements." Unlike Jackson, who never renounced his chat with Castro, Robertson apologized for the remark. Wallace made no mention of the fact.

While they ignored Jackson's early 1988 *Nightline* comment on his desire to improve relations with Cuba, the media were quick to jump on Robertson for any statement liberals found controversial. Seven stories focused on his comments about Soviet missiles in Cuba, that Planned Parenthood was attempting to create a "master race," and that he opposed sanctions on South Africa. Jackson received almost twice as much positive coverage as Robertson; a mere three stories (23 percent) referred positively to Robertson's strong appeal among Christians. An even smaller 15 percent of the stories talked about his campaign appealing beyond its base, to Catholics, Democrats, and blue collar workers.

Fear of being charged with racism could partially explain why reporters refrained from writing stories that might hurt the Jackson campaign. One unnamed network correspondent admitted to *The Washington Post*: "It's absolutely clear to me that if Jesse were a white man, he'd probably be getting kicked around rather royally by the press." But another factor is at work. Many reporters do not see Jackson as outside the mainstream. To many in Big Media, it is Robertson who espouses radical views and they feel obligated to alert the American public.

## CHAPTER NINE, STUDY 5

# "Election Year Doom and Gloom"

### OVERVIEW

"Americans believe the state of the economy is the most important issue in the presidential campaign," announced Peter Jennings in opening ABC's *World News Tonight* in late September, less than two months before the November election. Reporter Ken Prewitt then reviewed the state of the economy, concluding: "When you look at the overall economy, the average American voter is doing fine....and that makes economic issues a difficult pitch for the Democrats."

Given the importance of economic performance in determining how Americans vote, the Media Research Center set out to analyze how well TV network news stories reflected economic reality in the months preceding the 1988 presidential election. Despite the continuing economic boom, which was an important issue for candidate George Bush, the study found that numerous network reporters depicted the economy as unhealthy and emphasized other economic themes matching the Democratic campaign pitch.

### KEY FINDINGS

- Forty of sixty stories (67 percent) stressed weaknesses in the economy.

- Only 11 (18 percent) focused on economic strengths, while another nine stories were mixed or neutral in their assessment of the economy.

- The networks aired more than three times as many negative reports reinforcing Dukakis campaign themes than positive reports echoing Bush campaign themes.

### STUDY EXCERPT

**Election Year Doom and Gloom** by the Media Research Center. From *MediaWatch*, November 1988.

From the end of the primaries in early June, through October 15, ABC's *World News Tonight, CBS Evening News, CNN PrimeNews,* and *NBC Nightly News* aired sixty economic stories. *MediaWatch* analysts classified each as mixed, negative, or positive.

Stories considered mixed included an August 5 *Evening News* look at the growing number of temporary workers. Reporter Terry Drinkwater gave both sides: "Companies say the temporaries give them flexibility; some workers agree....But for many other temporaries, the insecurities are so severe, they use their free time to look for a permanent job." CNN's Chris Abel gave a mixed picture of the economic impact of dropping oil prices, concluding: "There are ten states hit hardest by the oil slide....But while the economies in oil-producing states worsen, experts say the oil price drop will mean good news for consumers."

Forty percent of the negative pieces emphasized themes pushed by Dukakis, such as the supposed growth of low pay jobs at the expense of

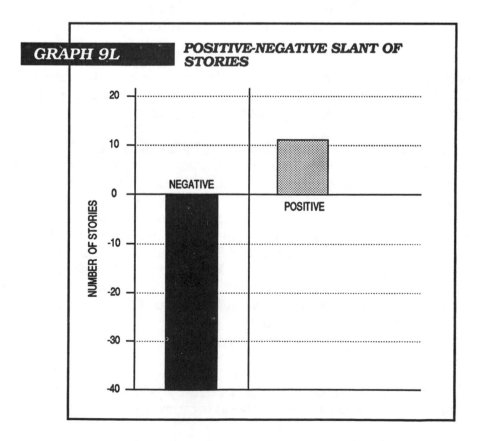

higher-paying ones, increasing income inequality, the inability of the middle class to afford a home, and the shaky foundation of the economic recovery. For instance, ABC's Kathleen DeLaski vigorously attacked the Reagan legacy on August 31. She announced the census report showing an increase in family income to $31,000 per year. DeLaski quickly tried to dampen the good news, adding, "most of the additional income went to those who were already well off." After interviewing Bob Greenstein of the liberal Center for Budget and Policy Priorities, DeLaski highlighted the 15.5 percent poverty figure, concluding that "the report gives Michael Dukakis some evidence that the poor and middle class are losing ground."

Three days later DeLaski was at it again, featuring a group of economic "losers": this time, "urban migrants," workers who have only been able to find jobs far away from home. "So they are being forced to the great outdoors, because their paychecks cannot put a roof over their heads." Her examples included a man who claimed he could not afford housing for his family on an $11 per hour construction income. Not surprisingly, DeLaski explored only liberal solutions: "public or sub-sidized housing."

Back on June 7 ABC aired back-to-back stories on how "the dream of owning a home is fading in the 1980s" as values increase far faster than incomes, a theme repeated two months later by CBS.

A trade deficit study from the Economic Policy Institute (EPI) on October 15 prompted CNN's Patricia Ochs to warn: "One of Ronald Reagan's thorniest economic problems has cost millions of jobs in manufacturing and related industries." With a clear political angle that echoed Dukakis's promise of "good jobs at good wages," Ochs continued: "The jobs lost are good ones; about half pay more than $400 a week." Ochs didn't mention that Labor Department figures show more than two-thirds of the jobs created since 1982 paid $20,000 (about $400 a week) per year or more. Ochs wrapped up with a leading conclusion: "The study is expected to fuel arguments by...Michael Dukakis and other Democrats that the trade deficit is a growing burden on the U.S. economy, and Americans are already paying."

Viewers could have put the story in better perspective if Ochs had mentioned a key fact about EPI: It is headed by Jeffrey Faux, listed by *Business Month* as an advisor to the Dukakis campaign.

Even when the news was unequivocably good, CBS and CNN managed to add a sour note. On October 7 Dan Rather quickly reported the unemployment rate had fallen by 0.2 percent to 5.4 percent, but then turned to Ray Brady who spent a minute and a half bemoaning the relative decreasing productivity of the American worker. The next day CNN's Dan Blackburn worried about the future of the American economy. Blackburn lamented in tones that sounded like Dukakis speeches: "Many of the jobs are in the clerical field, or they may involve the hiring of laborers on a daily basis..." Blackburn concluded with this gloomy assessment: "For most American workers...the unemployment figures offer at least some assurance. But many economists warn that the 1990s could bring trouble."

Other negative stories did not overtly reflect major Dukakis themes, though a few quoted him. An increase in the discount rate, said Ray Brady, "is the kind of move that is seldom made during an election year, and today Michael Dukakis blamed it on the economic policy followed by the administration." CNN's Lou Waters chimed in: "The move is meant to curb consumer spending and it could pose political problems for Vice President Bush if voters blame Republicans for tighter credit." CBS' Ray Brady took a sensationalist approach to food price hikes, declaring on August 23 that consumers "are suffering from 'supermarket shock,'" as food prices were "skyrocketing."

NBC, however, was the gloomiest network, with all six of its feature-length economic reports accentuating the negative. For reporter Irving R. Levine, the modest 0.2 percent increase in unemployment for August was an opportunity to tell voters what he termed the "reality" of the situation. If the Labor Department counted discouraged workers and those who "work part time because they can't find a full-time job" as out of work, "the unemployment rate would not be 5.6 percent," but much more.

A more realistic picture occasionally slipped through. On October 7 ABC's Ken Prewitt offered viewers a rare positive analysis of the employment situation. Prewitt explained that one in six people counted as unemployed are briefly unemployed between permanent jobs while about half find jobs in less than six weeks. Five of the eleven positive stories analyzed reinforced themes like this, topics Bush highlighted: the record percentage of people employed, low inflation and rising family income. On October 5, Brady offered this encouraging assessment:

"Labor experts say, if you're just starting out...this is the best time to be looking for work in twenty years."

A CBS News/*New York Times* poll showed voters by a margin of 51 to 38 percent preferred Bush over Dukakis as the man to help the economy most and a September Gallup poll showed 54 percent of Americans believed they personally would be better off a year from now. But with the media distorting and misrepresenting the national picture, small wonder that only 24 percent believed the country as a whole would be better off.

CHAPTER NINE, STUDY 6

# 1988 Democratic and Republican Convention Contrasts

## OVERVIEW

William Adams thoroughly documented the liberal bias CBS and NBC displayed in covering the 1984 political conventions (Chapter 9, Study 1). Did the television networks take note and take steps to hold their bias in check before traveling to Atlanta for the July 1988 Democratic National Convention and a month later to New Orleans for the Republican National Convention?

Using the Adams study as a model the Media Research Center (MRC) analyzed the 1988 covention coverage not only of CBS and NBC, but ABC and CNN as well. After examining over one hundred hours of tape, the MRC found that the 1988 network coverage was almost a mirror image of what viewers saw in 1984.

## KEY FINDINGS

- Republicans were tagged as conservative two and a half times more often than Democrats were described as liberal. The 86 labels attached to Democrats were split about evenly between liberal and conservative. At the Republican gathering, however, 85 percent of the labels were conservative.

- The networks interviewed far more liberals than conservatives at both conventions.

- Republicans had to respond to Democratic agenda issues on 128 occasions, more than twice as often as Democrats were challenged by Republican themes.

- Republican controversies, from the Iran/Contra affair to the "sleaze factor," were raised 32 times. Questions about Dan Quayle's background were highlighted another 471 times. By contrast, in Atlanta, reporters were silent about controversies that dogged Dukakis in the months before the convention.

## STUDY EXCERPT

**Coddling Democrats and Discrediting Republicans** by the Media Research Center. From *MediaWatch*, September 1988.

In mid-August, Republicans from across America arrived in New Orleans to nominate George Bush as their candidate for President of the United States. But reporters for the four television networks repeatedly portrayed the Republicans as extreme and on the fringe of the American political spectrum: in other words, simply out of tune with average Americans. How? By incessantly labeling convention goers as conservative ideologues and attacking Republicans all they could -- on issues including opposition to abortion, ERA, the plant closings bill, and the Civil Rights Restoration Act.

When looking at the Democratic Convention coverage a month earlier, a media double standard became evident. Reporters in Atlanta fawned over the Democrats and their policies. Viewers at home saw presidential nominee Michael Dukakis portrayed as a competent manager and political moderate, not an ideological liberal. In fact, network anchors and reporters labeled Michael Dukakis a moderate about as often as they tagged him liberal. The networks avoided substance as much as possible. Any controversies surrounding the Democrats and criticism of Dukakis' liberal record were all but ignored.

To conduct the study, analysts evaluated ABC, CBS, CNN, and NBC News coverage of the two political conventions in a variety of areas, including labeling, ideology of those interviewed, ideological agenda of questions posed, and the controversies in the two parties highlighted or ignored.

### 1. Labeling

During the Democratic convention, the networks used descriptive labels a total of 86 times. In New Orleans, Republicans were labeled 214 times. At the Atlanta convention, labels attached to Democrats were split: 52 percent liberal, and 48 percent moderate or conservative. During the GOP gathering, 15 percent of labels were "moderate" or "liberal," while 85 percent were "conservative," or harsher.

In a total of 49.5 hours of coverage in Atlanta, the networks identified Mike Dukakis as a "liberal" or "progressive" just 13 times, or approximately once every 3.8 hours. For Jackson, the numbers were even more remarkable: he was tagged "liberal" just nine times, or once every five and one half hours.

Reporters lost such restraint when it came to Republicans. On 182 occasions in New Orleans, the networks used the term "conservative," more than four times as often as they bothered to note the liberal views held by Democrats a month earlier.

Barraged viewers heard a conservative label nearly four times an hour, about once every fifteen minutes. ABC's Lynn Sherr managed to issue a label six times in the space of just thirty seconds. "This is clearly being seen as a great night for the conservatives. But, the delegates here are much more conservative than the country as a whole," Sherr told Senator Thad Cochran (R-Mississippi) on the second night. "But it is a very conservative platform, Senator, and the country is not that conservative...Do you believe that by moving toward the right, by staying very

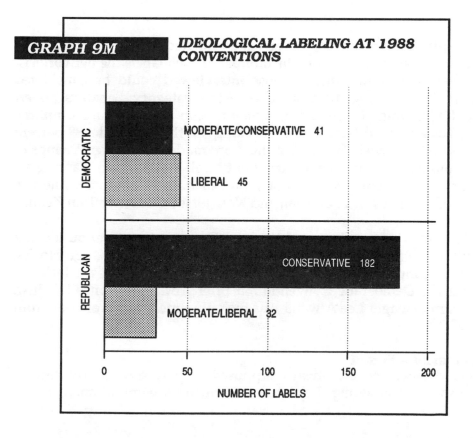

**GRAPH 9M**    *IDEOLOGICAL LABELING AT 1988 CONVENTIONS*

DEMOCRATIC
MODERATE/CONSERVATIVE 41
LIBERAL 45

REPUBLICAN
CONSERVATIVE 182
MODERATE/LIBERAL 32

0    50    100    150    200

NUMBER OF LABELS

conservative, that's the way to keep the Reagan Democrats in your column?"

The harshest descriptive adjective used on the Democrats was the word "liberal." But some reporters were not satisfied just labeling Republicans "conservative." Dan Rather and Walter Cronkite became quite creative, referring to "hard right conservatives," "hard rock conservatives," and "hard right people." CNN's Mary Tillotson smelled a "conservative odor" in the Superdome. Other terms used: "the religious right," "far right wing," and "right flank."

## 2. Interviews
At both conventions the networks demonstrated a preference for liberals and moderates when it came to whom to interview on the air. In Atlanta the four networks aired 112 interviews with Senators, Congressmen, Mayors and Governors. The vast majority (76 percent) came from the liberal wing of the Democratic Party, such as New York Governor Mario Cuomo, Walter Mondale, and Senator Edward Kennedy.

Despite the fact that conservatives dominated the New Orleans convention, at least judging from the number of such labels the networks issued, less than two-thirds of those interviewed could be considered conservative. Among the politicians in this category: Senators Robert Dole, Phil Gramm, Orrin Hatch, Alan Simpson and Gordon Humphrey as well as Reverend Jerry Falwell. Seeking out the other side, 39 percent of those interviewed represented the more moderate or liberal wings of the Republican Party, such as Senators Lowell Weicker and Nancy Kassebaum, Congressmen Silvio Conte, Jim Leach, and Claudine Schneider, Illinois Governor Jim Thompson and New Jersey Governor Tom Kean.

ABC also gave plenty of time to Democrats to denounce the Republican efforts. Viewers heard from NAACP head Benjamin Hooks, Dukakis campaign chairman Paul Brountas and even Jesse Jackson. During the Democratic Convention, a brief ABC appearance by Bush campaign manager Lee Atwater was the only time granted anyone from the GOP.

## 3. Questions Posed
Good newsmen are always supposed to play devil's advocate to those they are covering. Reporters and anchors were adamant about

maintaining this mandate when covering the Republicans, but skirted their responsibility in Atlanta.

The Republicans had already attacked Mike Dukakis as a social liberal who was soft on crime and defense, but ABC, CBS and CNN rarely raised these issues. In total, Republican agenda issues were raised in only 49 questions throughout the Democratic Convention.

NBC stood apart from the other networks by putting Republican concerns to Democratic delegates. For example, Chris Wallace challenged Senator Al Gore: "You campaigned against Dukakis and your other opponents, saying they're soft on defense. Aren't Republicans this fall going to be able to use that same argument?"

From day one of the Republican convention, network anchors and reporters echoed Democratic campaign themes and demanded that Republicans respond. In total, reporters challenged Republicans two and one half times more often than they did Democrats -- on 128 occasions.

Some examples: NBC's Tom Brokaw demanded of Senator Dan Quayle: "You're opposed to abortion in any form. You also have opposed the ERA, and you're opposed to increasing the minimum wage, which is important to a lot of women out there. Aren't you going to have a hard time selling Dan Quayle to the women of this country?" A few days earlier, Brokaw went to the floor to get the views of three pro-abortion Congresswomen.

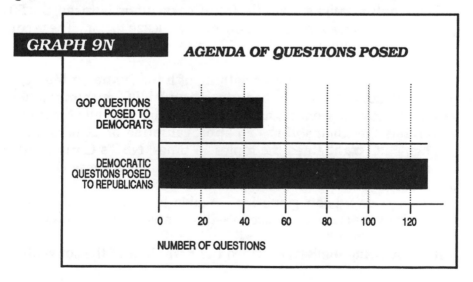

**GRAPH 9N** — **AGENDA OF QUESTIONS POSED**

GOP QUESTIONS POSED TO DEMOCRATS

DEMOCRATIC QUESTIONS POSED TO REPUBLICANS

0    20    40    60    80    100    120

NUMBER OF QUESTIONS

CNN's Frank Sesno asked a black delegate one night: "Bush and Quayle opposed the extension of the Voting Rights Act -- or balked on it. And opposed Grove City. Two very large, important civil rights bills. How do they overcome that stigma within the minority community?"

As in 1984, the conservative policies espoused by Republicans particularly concerned correspondents. For instance, Lesley Stahl of CBS News asked unsuccessful presidential candidate Pete du Pont: "Is there any concern on your part that this ticket might just be a little too conservative? It's to the right of most Americans in the country right now."

### 4. Controversies

The Republicans sent a truth squad to Atlanta hoping to prompt the networks to cover some of the many controversies plaguing Democrats and Dukakis. The networks didn't bite, but they didn't need any prompting to highlight controversies of the Reagan-Bush years.

CBS and NBC never once mentioned the ethical conduct questions surrounding House Speaker Jim Wright. ABC briefly raised the issue on two occasions and CNN only discussed the issue once during prime-time. Controversies dogging Dukakis in the months before the convention were completely ignored. Viewers heard nothing about the Dukakis policy of furloughing first degree murderers, his prison site controversy or criminal investigation of a high official in his administration.

But in New Orleans, the networks had no problem focusing on Republican controversies such as the Iran-Contra affair, Noriega, the Bitburg cemetery flap, the Beirut bombing or the "sleaze factor." These controversies were highlighted a total of 32 times.

"In this hall tonight you'll hear nothing of Iran/Contra, or Meese, or Deaver, or Nofziger, or the tragedy in Beirut," NBC anchorman Tom Brokaw began coverage one night, complaining that, "for all of that I just ticked off, this President still has an approval rating of 52 percent." In two nights, NBC highlighted the topics 14 times. NBC's Chris Wallace echoed the Dukakis campaign theme, asking Senator Alfonse D'Amato, "When George Bush talks about Michael Dukakis' inexperience in foreign policy, isn't it fair game for Dukakis to talk about Bush's experience in Panama, his experience in selling arms to the Ayatollah?"

Instead of airing the Reagan video the first night of the convention,

ABC's Sam Donaldson talked about the Bitburg cemetery controversy, the "secret scheme to divert money to the Nicaraguan Contras," and the "sleaze factor."

Questions about Bush's choice of Senator Dan Quayle as his running mate began as a trickle, but by the third night of the convention had practically become the media's sole concern. ABC opened its Tuesday night coverage with reporter Lynn Sherr complaining that Quayle might not have "much substance." ABC subsequently questioned Quayle's stands on civil rights, the economy, and his millionaire status. Already, ABC had given viewers a negative impression of the relatively unknown Quayle.

The other three networks reacted no differently. NBC's Chris Wallace asked Bush Chief of Staff Craig Fuller whether Quayle was too inexperienced and untested. His wealth and his inexperience proceeded to dominate virtually every interview thereafter. The networks, as well, immediately began to weigh in with criticism of Vice President George Bush, with reporters from all networks characterizing the Bush choice as a "cosmetic" attempt to lure women with his good looks. It was a move

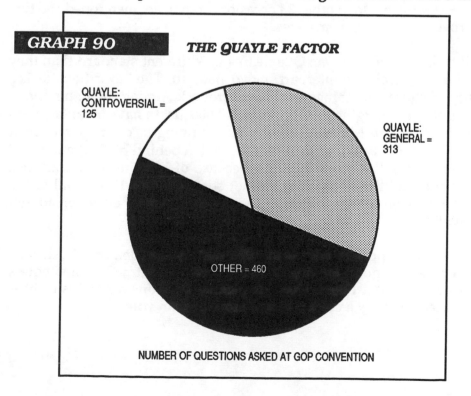

**GRAPH 90** — **THE QUAYLE FACTOR**

QUAYLE: CONTROVERSIAL = 125

QUAYLE: GENERAL = 313

OTHER = 460

NUMBER OF QUESTIONS ASKED AT GOP CONVENTION

several reporters condemned as an insult and one which would not work. They proceeded to attack Quayle's voting record as out of touch with women's issues.

But the questions of Quayle's military record and never substantiated suggestions of involvement with a lobbyist who later posed for *Playboy* quickly became predominant. Every network interviewed Quayle. While no concrete proof existed about any impropriety in his military service or his involvement with the Washington lobbyist Paula Parkinson, the media nonetheless allowed the supposed controversies to dominate their interviews. Evidently feeling that viewers did not need to learn anything about Quayle's policy views, CBS' Dan Rather asked only about the two episodes. CNN and NBC did much the same. Only ABC treated the military service and Parkinson affairs with proper perspective. Anchors Peter Jennings and David Brinkley never raised the Parkinson affair.

Of the 898 questions at the Republican convention, almost half of them -- 438 -- dealt with Quayle. Of those, 125 -- 14 percent of all the questions -- specifically concerned the issue of the lobbyist or his National Guard service. On another 33 occasions, reporters mentioned the two controversies among themselves.

But the media held Dan Quayle to a far different standard than they did his Democratic counterpart, Lloyd Bentsen. The Texas Senator has plenty of interesting things in his background. Among them: his short-lived policy of charging PAC officials $10,000 just to have breakfast with him. Even though Michael Dukakis was running a "clean government campaign" and was trying to attract those "left behind by Reaganomics," Bentsen's huge PAC contributions, because of his Finance Committee role and his millionaire status, did not stir reporters. During all of the Democratic Convention coverage the networks never even considered the matter.

The same reporters who were offended by the idea that Bush may have chosen the good-looking Quayle in order to attract women voters were silent about a liberal Dukakis picking someone far to his right -- considered by many a crass political move to gain votes.

# 10 Does the Liberal Tilt Extend to Hollywood?

These past pages have presented studies demonstrating the liberal tilt of the news media. But what about the television entertainment shows and movies Americans watch every day? Do they advance any particular values -- conservative or liberal? Can the people who produce and write them be characterized as liberals or conservatives? The following study answers the question; it shows that the Hollywood elite are even more liberal than their brethren in the media.

---

**CHAPTER TEN, STUDY 1**

## "Hollywood and America: The Odd Couple"

### OVERVIEW

Chapter 1 began with Stanley Rothman and Robert Lichter's in-depth survey of the political views held by members of the media elite. They determined that Big Media staffers held liberal social and economic opinions; more concretely, the media elite voted overwhelmingly for the Democratic presidential candidate between 1968 and 1980. A few years later the two professors, with the help of Linda Lichter, posed similar questions to 104 of Hollywood's best, those who control the content of TV shows and movies at theaters -- executive producers, producers, writers, and heads of independent production companies.

### KEY FINDINGS

- Almost all of the Hollywood elite come from cosmopolitan areas, especially California and the Boston-Washington corridor. "Very few," the poll found, "have roots in middle America."

- 93 percent "seldom or never" attend religious services.

- 97 percent believe abortion should remain legal.

- In the presidential elections between 1968 and 1980, the Republican never received more than 25 percent of their vote.

- 75 percent consider themselves liberal.

- 66 percent of the Hollywood elite think "TV should promote social reform" in order to "move their audience toward their own vision of the good society."

## STUDY EXCERPT

***Hollywood and America: The Odd Couple*** by Linda Lichter, S. Robert Lichter and Stanley Rothman. From *Public Opinion*, December/January 1983.

Conservatives and liberals harmonize on few issues, but they are, at least, equally vehement in criticizing television entertainment. On the liberal side, women and minority groups claim that television's unflattering portrayals of them perpetuate negative stereotypes. Conservatives object to the loose morality which they view as undermining the traditional American values of family, hard work, and patriotism. And myriad groups, from the PTA to the National Institutes of Mental Health, worry that pervasive television violence is breeding aggressive individuals or even criminals.

Disagreements over the political messages of television programs and their relation to the "politics" of their creators have been sharp, although little hard evidence exists to bolster either side. Typical of those who view television as a conservative voice is a researcher at the prestigious Annenberg School of Communication who concludes, "The basic reality of the television world is the reality of the American middle-class establishment; its morality is the conventional and rigid Sunday-school morality of the middle class."[1]

For many who adhere to this line of thought, the personal politics of television writers and producers are similarly conservative or of small consequence because their product inevitably supports conservative values. In this view, "The production and manufacture of television drama are rooted to business interests in the United States. Consequently, the content must be produced by people who are either willing to suppress deep-seated dissident values or by people who are fundamentally in agreement with the system."[2]

On the flip side of this question, Michael Robinson writes that television programs reflect the liberal values of program creators on such topics as homosexuality, interracial marriage, and the social position of women and minorities.[3]

Similarly, Ben Stein claims that television has an antipathy toward "establishment figures" and an accompanying sympathy for the poor and minorities. Based on interviews with Hollywood writers and producers, he concludes that "...the attitudes of the people who create television coincide almost exactly with the picture on television."[4]

### Profiling Hollywood's Elite
Who are the creators of TV entertainment? What are their backgrounds? What do they think about American society, and how do they react to the criticisms leveled against their product? To find out, we interviewed 104 of Hollywood's most influential television writers, producers, and executives, as part of a larger study of elite groups. Since formal titles mean little in this field, we constructed a sample based on reputation by asking industry "insiders" for the names of key people.

We selected only names on whose importance our sources were agreed. We eliminated those who had not been associated with the development, production, or selection of two or more successful prime-time series. The final list consisted of approximately 350 names, from which we sampled randomly. Of 172 individuals who were contacted, 104 (60 percent) agreed to be interviewed.

The 104 individuals interviewed represent the cream of television's creative community. The sample includes 15 presidents of independent production companies, 18 executive producers, 43 additional producers, 26 of whom are also writers, and 10 network vice-presidents responsible for program development and selection. The remainder gave such titles as executive story consultant, program director, and story supervisor. Among those surveyed are some of the most experienced and respected members of the craft. Many have been honored with Emmy Awards, and a few are household names. Most important, this group has had a major role in shaping the shows whose themes and stars have become staples of our popular culture.

### Demographics

The social and personal backgrounds of the television elite are summarized in Table 10A. This group is populated almost exclusively by middle-aged white males.

By and large they represent an urban and cosmopolitan sector of society. Very few have roots in middle America; instead, they were raised in big cities on the east and west coasts. Seventy-three percent hail from either California or the Boston-Washington corridor, with over one in three coming from New York State alone. Eighty-two percent grew up in large metropolitan areas, leaving fewer than one in five who made the fabled journey from small town America to Hollywood.

In many other ways, however, television's top creators have traveled far from the world of their youth. Relative to their parents (and to the average American), they are well educated, extraordinarily well paid, have adopted secular outlooks, and are politically very liberal.

They come from diverse socioeconomic backgrounds, although few

| TABLE 10A | BACKGROUNDS OF THE HOLLYWOOD ELITE |
|---|---|
| White | 99% |
| Male | 98 |
| From metropolitan area | 82 |
| From Northeast corridor | 56 |
| Father voted Democratic | 68 |
| Father graduated college | 35 |
| Raised in Jewish religion | 59 |
| College graduate | 75 |
| Family income $200,000+ | 63 |
| Political liberal | 75 |
| Religion "none" | 45 |
| Regular churchgoer | 7 |

were forced to start at the bottom of the ladder. Only 15 percent come from blue-collar backgrounds, and the largest number, 42 percent, say their fathers were businessmen. A minority of their fathers, 47 percent, had some college training, and only 35 percent obtained a degree. When asked to rate their family's economic circumstances during their youth as below average, average, or above average, they were evenly divided, with about one-third in each category.

Not surprisingly, these writers, producers, and executives are much better educated than their parents. Over nine out of ten attended college, three-fourths received degrees, and 31 percent had some graduate training. These educational advances pale before the dramatic rise in their economic status. Of those who responded, one in four reported a 1981 family income in excess of half a million dollars, and almost two-thirds (63 percent) earned over $200,000. Only 4 percent reported incomes of less than $75,000.

The television elite have traversed considerable distances in their attitudes, as well as their circumstances. In the sphere of religion, they have moved toward a markedly more secular orientation. Ninety-three percent had a religious upbringing, the majority (59 percent) in the Jewish faith. An additional 25 percent were raised in some Protestant denomination, and the remaining 12 percent as Catholics. Currently, however, 45 percent claim no religious affiliation whatsoever, more than six times the number of those who were not raised in any religious tradition. This is also greater than the proportion who currently profess to any particular religion. Defections have occurred from all religions, so that only 38 percent now call themselves Jews, 12 percent remain Protestants, and 5 percent have retained their Catholic faith. Moreover, most of those remaining affiliations appear to be purely nominal. Ninety-three percent say they seldom or never attend religious services.

Politically, the television elite are drawn from liberal and Democratic backgrounds. Whether or not their parents imparted their own commitments, a large majority of the television elite now consider themselves liberals and regularly vote Democratic. Seventy-five percent describe themselves as left of center politically, compared to only 14 percent who place themselves to the right of center. This contrasts sharply with the national picture. In a 1982 national poll, only 27 percent of the general public classified themselves as liberal, 32 percent termed themselves conservatives, and the remainder called themselves moderates. In response to similar poll questions over the past two decades, self-described conservatives have always outnumbered liberals, and the latter have never accounted for more than 29 percent of those questioned.

The television elite's ideological self-descriptions are reflected in their political behavior. Graph 10B shows how they have voted in presidential elections since 1968. In the past four elections, among those voting, Democrats outpolled Republicans by margins that never dropped below three to one and rose above five to one. No Republican presidential candidate received more than 25 percent of this group's votes. In 1972, Nixon racked up 62 percent of the vote nationwide, but among the television elite the landslide flowed in the other direction. They supported McGovern by a margin of 82 to 15 percent. In 1980, there were substantial defections from the Democratic ranks here as elsewhere, and Carter received only 49 percent of their votes. But the beneficiary was not Ronald Reagan, who polled only 20 percent of this group. Instead, the disillusioned Democrats switched to John Anderson, whose 27 percent total put him well ahead of Reagan.

### Social and Political Attitudes
The television elite's liberal self-image and presidential selections are consistent with their attitudes on social and political issues, as Table 10C reveals. We questioned them on four kinds of topics: economic issues,

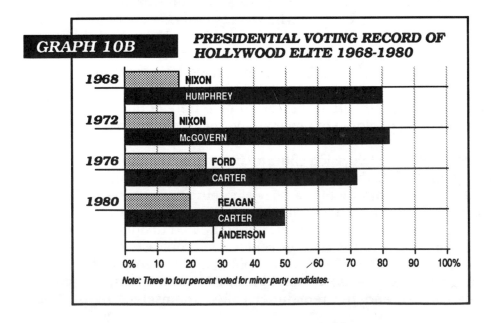

**GRAPH 10B**    **PRESIDENTIAL VOTING RECORD OF HOLLYWOOD ELITE 1968-1980**

1968  NIXON
       HUMPHREY
1972  NIXON
       McGOVERN
1976  FORD
       CARTER
1980  REAGAN
       CARTER
       ANDERSON

0%  10  20  30  40  50  /60  70  80  90  100%

*Note: Three to four percent voted for minor party candidates.*

| TABLE 10C | HOLLYWOOD ELITE ATTITUDES ON SOCIAL ISSUES | | | |
|---|---|---|---|---|
| **Economics** | STRONGLY AGREE | AGREE | DISAGREE | STRONGLY DISAGREE |
| Government should redistribute income | 24% | 45% | 16% | 14% |
| Government should guarantee jobs | 8 | 37 | 26 | 30 |
| Big corporations should be publicly owned | 6 | 13 | 14 | 66 |
| Private enterprise is fair to workers | 18 | 51 | 25 | 6 |
| Less regulation of business is good for U.S. | 20 | 45 | 25 | 11 |
| People with more ability should earn more | 62 | 32 | 5 | 1 |
| **Political Alienation** | | | | |
| U.S. institutions need complete overhaul | 8 | 35 | 28 | 29 |
| Structure of society causes alienation | 16 | 46 | 25 | 12 |
| U.S. legal system favors wealthy | 39 | 37 | 16 | 8 |
| Public officials don't care about average man | 23 | 42 | 32 | 3 |
| People in authority know best | 0 | 18 | 39 | 43 |
| **Disadvantaged Groups** | | | | |
| Women are better off at home | 0 | 8 | 17 | 75 |
| Women should get preference in hiring | 4 | 24 | 39 | 33 |
| Blacks lack education to advance | 28 | 45 | 20 | 7 |
| Blacks lack motivation to advance | 1 | 17 | 19 | 63 |
| Blacks gains come at white expense | 2 | 1 | 19 | 78 |
| Blacks should get preference in hiring | 4 | 39 | 32 | 25 |
| Whites and nonwhites should not marry | 2 | 13 | 23 | 62 |
| Discrimination can be ended | 5 | 8 | 23 | 64 |
| Poor people are victims of circumstance | 13 | 48 | 31 | 8 |
| **Sex and Morality** | | | | |
| Woman has right to decide on abortion | 91 | 6 | 1 | 2 |
| Homosexuality is wrong | 5 | 15 | 31 | 49 |
| Homosexuals shouldn't teach in schools | 6 | 9 | 20 | 66 |
| Adultery is wrong | 16 | 33 | 32 | 19 |

*Note: Figures in tables do not always add up to 100% because of rounding.*

political and social authority, disadvantaged groups, and sex and morality.

In the realm of economics, these wealthy liberals do not reject the private enterprise system, although many favor expansion of the welfare state. Seven out of ten believe that the government should substantially reduce the income gap between the rich and the poor, a policy which would surely reduce their own incomes, and 44 percent think the government should guarantee employment to anyone who wants a job.

For most, however, economic liberalism does not shade over into radicalism. They support the private enterprise system that has been so good to them. Ninety-four percent support the notion that people with more ability should earn more; 81 percent reject public ownership of corporations; indeed, almost two-thirds believe less government regulation of business would be good for the country. Finally, over two out of three see the American private enterprise system as fair to workers.

### Rebels With Causes

The television elite pledges allegiance to capitalism, but it is far more skeptical about the social and political institutions allied to this economic system. Three out of four say our legal system favors the wealthy, and nearly two-thirds believe that the very structure of American society causes people to become alienated from it. They are just as critical of those in positions of authority. Just under two-thirds agree that public officials are not interested in the average citizen, and 82 percent reject the notion that those in authority know best. Almost half disagree strongly that one should defer to those in authority, and not a single person expressed strong confidence in authority.

Given their widespread rejection of both American social institutions and their guardians, one would suspect that many in the television elite would like to see substantial changes in our society. In fact, a substantial minority of 43 percent endorses a complete overhaul of American institutions. In short, their acceptance of the economic system is tempered by a deep-set alienation from the social and political system.

If the television elite's political alienation contrasts sharply with their moderate economic views, it is quite consonant with their social liberalism. They express strong support for the social advancement of women and blacks, and they picture society as unfair to blacks, whose underprivileged position is seen as no fault of their own. Such strong sentiments notwithstanding, a majority reject preferential hiring as a means of assisting women's or blacks' advancement. Seventy-two percent reject this type of affirmative action for women, and 57 percent reject it for blacks. Perhaps reflecting the difference between sentiment and policy, most are not sanguine that social discrimination can be ended. Only 13 percent believe that racial and religious discrimination can be ended in their lifetimes.

The television elite's social liberalism is also evidenced by their views on sex and morality, another focal point for television's critics. On such issues as abortion, homosexual rights, and extramarital sex, their views diverge sharply from traditional values. Ninety-seven percent believe that a woman has the right to decide for herself whether to have an abortion; even more striking, 91 percent agree strongly with this position. Four out of five do not regard homosexual relations as wrong. Only 5 percent feel strongly that homosexuality is wrong, compared to 49 percent who disagree strongly. An even greater proportion, 86 percent, support the rights of homosexuals to teach in public schools. Finally, a majority of 51 percent refuse to condemn adultery as wrong. Moreover, the majority of those who feel strongly about this issue take a permissive stance; only 17 percent strongly agree that extramarital affairs are wrong. From this evidence, it would be difficult to overestimate the clash of values when television's creative community confronts fundamentalist Christian critics like the Moral Majority or the Coalition for Better Television.

### Different Strokes
These findings suggest that the television elite's political alienation is rooted in social rather than economic issues. It is their social liberalism that most clearly distinguishes them from the general public. To probe this topic more deeply, we inquired into their hopes for the future, as well as their assessments of the present. We asked them to choose goals for America to pursue for the next decade, by selecting the most important and least important from the following six choices:

1. Maintaining a high rate of economic growth
2. Making sure that this country has strong defense forces
3. Seeing that the people have more say in how things get decided at work and in their communities
4. Progressing toward a less impersonal, more humane society

5. The fight against crime
6. Progressing toward a society where ideas are more important than money

For the past decade, political scientist Ronald Inglehart has been presenting such choices to subjects in America and Western Europe. He classifies economic growth, national defense, and crime as traditional "instrumental" values. A humane society, participation, and placing ideas above money, on the other hand, are "expressive" or "post-bourgeois" values that are gaining strength among new elite sectors in post-industrial societies.

In most major social groups, "post-bourgeois" choices still represent a minority position. Among leading journalists we interviewed, a very liberal elite on most issues, only one in three chose "post-bourgeois" goals as most important. Corporate executives, a more conservative elite, rejected such goals by an eight-to-one margin. In sharp contrast, the television elite prefers "post-bourgeois" or "expressive" values over "instrumental" ones by almost two-to-one, as Table 10D indicates.

The television elite's strong preferences for expressive over instrumental social goals explain why many feel alienated from tradition-

| TABLE 10D | HOLLYWOOD ELITE CHOICES AND GOALS FOR AMERICAN SOCIETY | |
|---|---|---|
| **GOALS** | **MOST IMPORTANT** | **LEAST IMPORTANT** |
| National defense | 5% | 37% |
| Economic growth | 19 | 13 |
| Fight crime | 13 | 11 |
| Humane society | 43 | 6 |
| Ideas, not money | 14 | 14 |
| Community participation | 6 | 20 |
| Totals | | |
| Instrumental | 37% | 61% |
| Expressive | 63 | 40 |

al social and political institutions -- their value orientation is fundamentally different from that of the general public.

This elite seeks new directors as well as new directions for American society. We asked them to rate ten leadership groups in terms of the influence each wields over American life. Then we asked them to rate the same groups according to the amount of influence each *should* have. The groups included such traditional forces in American life as business and labor, government agencies, the military, and religion, along with such rising contenders as the news media, blacks, feminists, intellectuals, and consumer groups. We calculated the average influence rating assigned to each group on a scale ranging from "1" meaning very little influence, to "7" representing a great deal of influence.

The findings confirm the impression that the television elite is deeply dissatisfied with the direction our society is taking and would like to alter it in profound ways. As can be seen in Table 10E, they perceive America's power structure as dominated by the media and business, who finish in a virtual tie at the top of the heap. Blacks and feminists are at the bottom. When this group is asked for their preferences, the picture changes dramatically. The new kingpins would be consumer groups and intellectuals, followed by blacks and feminists. Business and the media

| TABLE 10E | HOLLYWOOD ELITE RANKS OF INFLUENCE AMONG LEADERSHIP GROUPS | |
|---|---|---|
| | **PERCEIVED INFLUENCE** | **PREFERRED INFLUENCE** |
| | 1. Media | 1. Consumer Groups |
| | 2. Business | 2. Intellectuals |
| | 3. Government agencies | 3. Blacks |
| | 4. Unions | 4. Feminists |
| | 5. Military | 5. Business |
| | 6. Consumer groups | 6. Media |
| | 7. Religion | 7. Unions |
| | 8. Intellectuals | 8. Government agenices |
| | 9. Blacks | 9. Religion |
| | 10. Feminists | 10. Military |

fall from the top to the middle of the pack. Lowest in the pecking order would be government, religion, and the military. It would be hard to imagine a more thorough indictment of the social order.

Our results seem all of a piece. Television creators emerge as upholders of the "new liberalism" that surfaced among upper status cosmopolitan groups in the 1960s. The crucial question is whether this perspective influences their work. In short, does this social portrait of television's creators tell us anything about their artistic output? Ultimately, this can only be determined by systematic analysis of television entertainment. For example, we found that businessmen were mainly bad guys in TV entertainment; this is consistent with the attitudes held by the people who create these shows. But much work remains before we have an overall picture of television's social message. In the interim, we asked members of the creative community what they thought about the social implications of their work. Did they see themselves as pure entertainers, or as educators, or even social reformers? Did they necessarily disagree with complaints that sex or violence permeated prime-time?

The results shown in Table 10F are clear and consistent. The television elites believe they have a role to play in reforming American society. They reject conservatives' criticisms of TV entertainment, while giving credence to liberals' complaints of television violence. First, television's creators make clear their preference for realism over escapist fantasy. Fully three out of four believe that TV should portray society realistically, and those who feel strongly agree by more than a three-to-one margin. Moreover, two out of three believe that TV entertainment

| TABLE 10F | TV ELITE ATTITUDES TOWARD TV ENTERTAINMENT | | | |
|---|---|---|---|---|
| | STRONGLY AGREE | AGREE | DISAGREE | STRONGLY DISAGREE |
| TV should promote social reform | 21% | 45% | 21% | 13% |
| TV should be realistic | 37 | 39 | 12 | 12 |
| TV is too critical of traditional values | 1 | 11 | 32 | 56 |
| There is too much sex on TV | 10 | 20 | 32 | 38 |
| There is too much violence on TV | 21 | 38 | 27 | 14 |

should be a major force for social reform. This is perhaps the single most striking finding in our study. According to television's creators, they are not in it just for the money. They also seek to move their audience toward their own vision of the good society.

Thus, they reject the criticism that television is too critical of traditional values by an eight-to-one margin. A majority strongly disagrees with this argument, and only one person strongly endorses it. Similarly, 62 percent disagree that there is too much sex on TV, as fundamentalist Christian groups have charged. By contrast, nearly 60 percent agree that television is too violent.

In sum, they view TV entertainment largely as we might expect on the basis of their social attitudes. Like many other liberal, cosmopolitan, upper status Americans, they believe sex is less of a problem than violence on television, and they see the medium as a source of needed social reform. The difference is that they are the creative force behind that very medium.

1 Larry Gross, "The Real World of Television," *Today's Education*, vol. 63, Jan./Feb. 1974, p. 86.

2. Muriel Cantor, *Prime-Time Television* (Beverly Hills, Cal.: Sage, 1980), p. 19.

3 Michael Robinson, "Prime-Time Chic," *Public Opinion*, vol. 2, Mar./May 1979, pp. 42-47.

4 Ben Stein, *The View from Sunset Boulevard* (New York: Basic Books, 1975), p. 105.

# *The Revolving Door*

The "Revolving Door" describes the Media Research Center's ongoing project of tracking the movement of people between political and media positions. This appendix is divided into two sections: Liberals & Democrats and Conservatives & Republicans.

As explained in Chapter 2, Study 2, which contained a representative list of Revolving Door examples, far more liberals than conservatives passed through the Revolving Door in recent years. As of April, 1990 the MRC had identified 178 liberals or Democrats, but just 57 conservatives or Republicans.

Another measure provides an even better indication of the disproportionate influence exercised by those in the liberal/Democratic list: One-time liberal or Democratic activists are far more readily accepted into media jobs than those who used to work for conservatives or Republicans. More than 70 percent of those on the liberal/Democratic list jumped from politics to the media, but more than half of the conservatives/Republicans moved from the media to politics.

**SECTION ONE:** *List of Liberal & Democratic Connections to the News Media*

1) *Alise Adde* Director of News Information, ABC News, 1988-1990

   - Assistant Press Secretary to Senator J. Bennett Johnston (D-LA), until 1982

   - Manager, News Information, ABC News, 1987-88
   - Press Representative, ABC's *World News Tonight*, 1985-87

- News Information Coordinator, ABC News Washington bureau, 1983-85

2) **Ira Allen**  Press Secretary, Congressman Chester Atkins (D-MA), 1988-1989

- Reporter, United Press International, 1970-1988

3) **Jodie Allen**  Editor, *Washington Post* "Outlook" section, 1990-; Deputy Editor of "Outlook," 1987-1990

- Deputy Assistant Secretary of Labor for Policy Evaluation and Research, Carter Administration

- Editorial writer, *The Washington Post*, 1980-85

4) **Jonathan Alter**  Senior Writer, *Newsweek*, 1987-; General Editor and Associate Editor, 1983-87

- Author, profile of John Anderson in "Selecting a President: A Citizen's Guide to the 1980 Election," distributed by Ralph Nader

- an editor, *Washington Monthly*, 1981-83

5) **Scott Armstrong**  Executive Director, National Security Archive, 1986-89

- Senior Investigator, Senate Select Committee on Presidential Campaign Practices, 1973-74

- Reporter, *The Washington Post*, 1977-1984

6) **David Axelrod**  Media Adviser, Paul Simon for President, 1987-88

- Political reporter, *Chicago Tribune* until 1984
- Manager, Paul Simon Senate campaign, 1984

7) **Michelle Baker** Associate, Podesta Associates (a Democratic political consulting firm), 1990-

- Researcher/reporter, *Chicago Tribune* Washington bureau, 1987-89

8) **Kenneth Banta** Senior Correspondent, *Time* magazine London bureau, 1989-; Eastern Europe bureau chief, Vienna, 1985-89

- Issues adviser, Gary Hart for President, 1984

- Reporter, *Time*, 1981-1984

9) **Michael Barone** Senior Writer, *U.S. News & World Report*, 1989-

- Editorial writer, *The Washington Post*, 1982-89

- Vice President, Peter Hart Research Associates, a Democratic polling firm, 1974-81

10) **Bob Beckel** Conus Communications commentator during the 1988 campaign

- Campaign Manager, Mondale-Ferraro, 1984

11) **Elizabeth Becker** Visiting fellow, Institute for Policy Studies (IPS), early 1980's

- *Washington Post* Asia reporter, until early 1980s

12) **Rebecca Bell**   Press Secretary, Senator John Glenn (D-OH), 1989-

- Director of affiliate news services for NBC News, 1986-89
- Paris Bureau Chief, NBC News, 1977-85

13) **Wendy Benjaminson**   Press Secretary, U.S. Rep. Barbara Kennelly (D-CT), 1989

- Capitol Hill editor, political editor, metro writer, UPI Washington bureau, 1984-1989

- Virginia Statehouse reporter, *The Washington Times*, 1983-84

14) **Douglas Bennet**   President and Chief Executive Officer, National Public Radio, 1983-

- Director, Agency for International Development (AID), 1979-1981
- Assistant Secretary of State for congressional relations, 1977-79
- Administrative Assistant to Senator Abraham Ribicoff (D-CT), 1973-74
- Administrative Assistant to Senator Tom Eagleton (D-MO), 1969-1973
- Assistant to Vice President Hubert Humphrey, 1967-69

15) **Lowell Bergman**   Producer, CBS News *60 Minutes*, 1983-

- Founder, Center for Investigative Reporting, 1977

- Producer, ABC News *20/20*, 1978-1983

16) **Sidney Blumenthal**   *Washington Post* political and "Style" section writer, 1985-1989

- Senior Editor, *The New Republic*, 1990-

* Political correspondent, *The New Republic*, 1984
* Boston correspondent, *In These Times,* a socialist newspaper, late 1970s
* writer for *The Progressive,* and *The Nation,* mid 1970s

17) **Ken Bode**  Chief Political Correspondent, NBC News, 1979-1989

* Aide to Morris Udall's presidential campaign, 1976
* Politics Editor, *The New Republic*, 1975-79
* Author, McGovern Commission Democratic delegate reform rules, 1972

* Contributing White House correspondent, CNN Special Investigation Unit, 1990-
* Director, Center for Contemporary Media at DePauw University, June 1989-

18) **Raymond Bonner**  *New York Times* El Salvador reporter, 1980-83

* Litigator/attorney for Ralph Nader groups, 1970s

* Author, *Weakness and Deceit: U.S. Policy and El Salvador*, 1984

19) **Elizabeth Brackett**  National Correspondent, *MacNeil-Lehrer NewsHour*, 1984-

* Reporter, WLS-TV Chicago, 1983-84
* Reporter, WGN-TV Chicago, 1979-83
* Researcher, WBBM-TV Chicago, 1977-79

* Candidate, 43rd Ward Democratic Committeeman in Chicago, 1975
* Advance staff, Democratic Alderman Bill Singer for Mayor of Chicago campaign, 1975
* Candidate for delegate to the Democratic National convention, 1972

20) **John Brademas**  former Member, RCA (former owner of NBC) Board of Directors

- U.S. Representative (D-IN), 1959-1981

21) **Harold Brown**  Member, CBS Board of Directors, 1981-

- Secretary of Defense, Carter Administration

22) **Jack Burby**  Editorial writer, *Los Angeles Times*, 1989-

- Special Assistant to Transportation Secretary Alan Boyd, 1966-68
- Press Secretary to Governor Edmund (Pat) Brown, until 1966

- Deputy Editorial Page Editor, *Los Angeles Times*, 1983-89
- Reporter, *San Francisco Chronicle*, *Honolulu Advertiser*, and United Press International, 1950s

23) **Tom Burgess**  Administrative Assistant and Press Secretary to U.S. Representative Jim Bates (D-CA), 1990-

- Investigative reporter on military issues, *The San Diego Union*, 1986-90

24) **David Burke**  President, CBS News, 1988-1990

- Chief of Staff to New York Governor Hugh Carey (D), 1975-77
- Chief of Staff, Senator Ted Kennedy, 1965-1971
- Assistant to Secretary of Commerce Luther Hodges; Assistant to Secretary of Labor Willard Wirtz, 1961-65
- Executive Secretary, President's Advisory Committee on Labor Management Policy, 1965

- Executive Vice President, ABC News, 1986-1988
- Vice President for planning and Assistant to the President of ABC News, 1977-1986

25) **Kathryn Bushkin**  Director of Editorial Administration, *U.S.News & World Report*, 1985-; Vice President for Corporate Affairs, 1984-85

  • Press Secretary, Gary Hart presidential campaign, 1983-84

26) **Margaret Carlson**  Senior Writer, *Time* magazine, 1988-

  • Special Assistant to the Chairman of Consumer Product Safety Commission, 1977-81

  • Washington correspondent, *Esquire*, 1985-87

27) **Hodding Carter**  Commentator, ABC's *This Week With David Brinkley*; Contributor, *PBS MacNeil-Lehrer NewsHour*

  • State Department spokesman, Carter Administration

28) **Wally Chalmers**  Director of Broadcast Research, CBS News, 1984-86; CBS News Political Editor, 1984

  • Executive Director and Chief of Staff, Democratic National Committee, 1986-88
  • Executive Director of Nuclear Freeze Foundation and Fund for a Democratic Majority, early 1980s
  • Kennedy for President, Midwest and Southern coordinator, 1980
  • Assistant Secretary, Dept. of Health, Education and Welfare, Carter Administration
  • Udall for President, Northeast coordinator, 1976

29) **John Chancellor**  *NBC Nightly News* commentator 1982-; anchor, *NBC Nightly News*, 1972-1982

  • Director of the Voice of America, Johnson Administration, 1966-67

30) **Roger Colloff** Vice President and General Manager, WCBS-TV New York, May 1984-

- Special Assistant to Secretary of Energy, James R. Schlesinger, and a senior staff member, the U.S. Office of Energy Policy and Planning during the Carter Administration, 1977-79
- Staff member, Carter campaign transition office, 1976-77 legislative aide to Sen. Walter F. Mondale, early 1970s

- Vice President for policy and planning, CBS Broadcast Group, mid 1983-mid 1984
- Vice President CBS Television Stations division, 1983
- Vice President and Director of Public Affairs broadcasts, CBS News, (*Face the Nation, 60 Minutes* etc.), 1981-1982
- Vice President and Executive Assistant to the Executive Vice President of CBS News, Bill Leonard, in the Washington Government Affairs office, 1979-81
- Director of Government Affairs, CBS Inc., 1972-75

31) **Elizabeth Colton** Press Secretary to Jesse Jackson, January-March 1988; Jesse Jackson campaign consultant, April-June 1988

- Reporter, National Public Radio, 1986-87
- Middle East correspondent, *Newsweek*, 1983-85
- Producer, ABC News, early 1980s

- Media Adviser, Sen. Terry Sanford (D-NC), 1987
- Author, *The Jackson Phenomenon: The Man, The Power, The Message*, 1988

32) **Mike Connolly** Press Secretary to U.S. Representative Ed Markey (D-MA) and the Energy and Commerce Subcommittee on Telecommunications and Finance, 1989-

- Washington reporter for the *San Francisco Examiner*, 1988-89
- Reporter, Gannett News Service, 1977-1984

33) **Richard Cotton** Executive Vice President and general counsel, NBC, Inc., 1989-

- Special Counsel to Deputy Secretary of Energy John Sawhill, 1979-80
- Executive Secretary to Secretary of Health, Education and Welfare, Joseph Califano, 1977-79

34) **Myra Dandridge** "Metro" section news aide, *The Washington Post*, 1990-

- Legislative Correspondent to U.S. Representative Sam Gejdenson (D-CT), 1987-1990

35) **Donna Dees** Manager of Communications, CBS News, New York, 1987-

- Assistant Press Secretary, Senator Russell Long (D-LA), 1980-83
- Assistant Press Secretary, Senator Bennett Johnston (D-LA), 1979-80

36) **Diane Dewhirst** Assistant to the Political Director, ABC News Washington bureau, 1984-85

- Press Secretary, Senator George Mitchell (D-ME), 1987-
- Communications Director, Democratic Senatorial Campaign Committee, 1985-87
- Deputy Director of Communications, Democratic National Committee, 1983-84

37) **John Dinges** Foreign Desk Editor, National Public Radio, 1986-

- Part-time assistant editor at *The Washington Post*, while simultaneously an Institute for Policy Studies Associate Fellow, 1980-82

- Co-author, with Institute for Policy Studies Senior Fellow Saul Landau, *Assassination on Embassy Row*, 1980

- Chile correspondent, *Time*, *The Washington Post* and ABC Radio, 1972- 1980

38) **Tom Donilon** Dukakis and Bentsen debate coach, September-November 1988

- Consultant to CBS News for campaign coverage, January-August 1988

- Senior adviser, Joe Biden for President Committee, 1987
- Deputy Manager, Mondale-Ferraro campaign, 1984
- Chief of Staff, Mondale campaign plane, 1984
- Chief Delegate Counter, Carter-Mondale, 1980

39) **Hedley Donovan** Editor-in-Chief, Time Inc, 1964-1979

- Senior Adviser to President Jimmy Carter, 1979-1981

40) **Richard Dougherty** NBC News Manager, New York, 1973-1974

- Press Secretary, 1972 McGovern presidential campaign

41) **Richard Drayne** (late) Director, Press Relations, CBS News Washington, 1980-87

- wrote Geraldine Ferraro speech, 1985 Gridiron Club Dinner
- Press Secretary and speechwriter, Kennedy presidential campaign, 1980
- Press Secretary, Senator Ted Kennedy, 1965-75

42) **William Drummond** Reporter, National Public Radio, 1979-1983

• Assistant Press Secretary, Carter White House, 1977-78

• Associate Dean, School of Journalism, University of California at Berkeley, 1983-
• Reporter, *Los Angeles Times* , 1978-79

43) ***Ervin S. Duggan***  Federal Communications Commission Commissioner, 1989-

• Metro and features reporter, *The Washington Post*, 1964

• Member, State Department Policy Planning staff, 1979-1981
• Special Assistant (speechwriter) to Secretary of Health, Education and Welfare, Joseph Califano, 1977-79
• Special Assistant to Senator Adlai Stevenson (D-IL), 1971-77

44) ***Erik Eckholm***  Projects editor, *The New York Times*, 1990-

• Staff member, State Department Policy Planning, Carter Administration, 1979-80

• Managing Editor of *The New York Times* "Week in Review," February 1989-1990
• Science and health editor, *The New York Times* , until 1989

45) ***Christopher Edley Jr.***  Issues Director, Dukakis-Bentsen for President Committee, 1988

• Editorial writer, *The Washington Post* , 1983-84

46) ***Jeanne Edmunds***  Producer, CBS News *Face the Nation*, 1986-87

• Staff member, Carter transition team, 1980

• Associate Producer, *CBS Morning News*, Washington bureau 1985-86

47) **Anne Edwards**  Senior Editor, National Public Radio (NPR),
   1987-

   - Mondale-Ferraro campaign scheduler, 1984
   - Director, White House Television Office, Carter Administration, 1977-1980

   - Assignment Editor, CBS News Washington bureau, 1980-84

48) **Steven Emerson**  Senior Editor, *U.S. News & World Report*,
   1985-89

   - Investigator, Senate Foreign Relations Committee, 1978-1981
   - Executive Assistant (speechwriter) for the late Senator Frank Church (D-ID), 1978

49) **Bob Ferrante**  Executive Producer of morning news,
   National Public Radio, 1989-

   - Director of Communications, Democratic National Committee, 1986- 1988

   - Senior Producer, CBS Election News unit, 1984-85
   - Executive Producer, *CBS Morning News*, 1983-84
   - Executive Producer, CBS News *Nightwatch*, 1982-83

50) **Mary Fifield**  Producer, CBS News *Face the Nation*, 1985-86

   - Press Officer, Carter campaign plane 1976
   - Press Secretary, Massachusetts Governor Michael Dukakis, 1974-75

   - Associate Producer, CBS News *Nightwatch*, 1984
   - Assistant Producer, ABC News *20/20*, late 1970s

51) **R.H. Fleming**  (late)  ABC News Washington Bureau Chief,
   early 1960s

• Deputy Press Secretary for President Johnson

52) **Doug Foster** Contributor/developer of story ideas for CBS News *60 Minutes* while editor at the Center for Investigative Reporting, 1981-85

 • Editor, *Mother Jones*, 1987-

 • reporter and editor for PBS affiliate KQED TV of San Francisco, occasionally contributed stories to the *MacNeil-Lehrer NewsHour*

53) **Jo Franklin-Trout** Producer, *MacNeil-Lehrer Report*, 1975-1980

 • Speechwriter, Hubert Humphrey's 1968 presidential campaign

 • Producer, *Days of Rage*, on PBS, 1988

54) **Martin Franks** Vice President, CBS Inc. Washington, 1988-

 • Executive Director, Democratic Congressional Campaign Committee, 1981-86
 • Issues Director, Carter-Mondale Re-election Committee, 1980

55) **Ken Friedlein** Press Secretary to U.S. Senator Terry Sanford (D-NC), 1990-

 • Executive National Editor, *The Charlotte Observer*, 1989-1990
 • Metro editor, *The Charlotte Observer*, 1987-89
 • Government and Politics editor, *The Charlotte Observer*, 1984-87
 • Assistant business editor, *The Charlotte Observer*, 1982-84
 • City Editor, *Winston-Salem Journal*, 1974-78

56) **Betty Furness**  Contributor to NBC's *Today*

  - Special Assistant to the President for Consumer Affairs, 1967-69
  - Chairman, New York Consumer Protection Board, 1970-71

  - Consumer Reporter, WNBC-TV early 1970s

57) **Leslie Gelb**  Deputy Editor, Op-Ed page, *New York Times*, 1988-

  - Deputy Secretary of State for Political-Military Affairs, Carter Administration, 1977-79
  - Press officer, Department of Defense, Johnson Administration
  - Aide to Senator Jacob Javits, 1960s

  - Deputy Editor, *New York Times* editorial page, 1986-1988; National Security Correspondent, 1982-86

58) **Katherine Gibney**  Press Secretary, Congressman Ben Jones (D-GA), 1989-

  - Editor and reporter, *Atlanta Journal* and *Atlanta Constitution*, 1984-1989

59) **Jo-Anne Goldman**  Assistant Press Secretary to U.S. Senator Frank Lautenberg (D-NJ), 1990-

  - Freelance news writer and producer, CNN and National Public Radio in Washington, 1989-90

60) **Tom Goldstein**  Press Secretary, New York City Mayor Ed Koch, 1979-1982

  - Legal affairs reporter, *The New York Times*, late 1970s

- Dean, Graduate School of Journalism, University of California at Berkeley, 1988-

61) **Martin Gottlieb** Projects editor, *The New York Times*, 1990-

- Editor, the *Village Voice*, 1986-1988

- Reporter, *The New York Times*, 1983-86
- Reporter, New York *Daily News*, 1976-1983

62) **Jeff Gralnick** Vice President of ABC News for special events/political coverage

- Press Secretary, Senator George McGovern, 1971

- Executive Producer, 1988 campaign coverage
- Executive Producer, *Jennings-Koppel Report*, 1987
- VP and Executive Producer, specials, 1985-
- Executive Producer of ABC's 1984 campaign coverage
- Executive Producer, political broadcasts, 1983-85
- Executive Producer, ABC's *World News Tonight*, 1979-83
- CBS News producer and Vietnam reporter, 1959-1971

63) **Rex Granum** Southern Bureau Chief, ABC News, Atlanta, 1986-; Podium Producer, Democratic National Convention, 1988

- Deputy Press Secretary to President Carter

64) **William Green Jr.** Senior Assistant to Senator Terry Sanford (D-NC), 1986-89

- Ombudsman, *The Washington Post*, 1981

65) **James Greenfield** Assistant Managing Editor, *New York Times*, 1977-; and Editor, *New York Times Magazine*, 1987-

- Assistant Secretary of State, Johnson Administration, 1964-66
- Deputy Assistant Secretary of State for Public Affairs, Kennedy Administration

- Foreign News Editor, *New York Times*, 1969-77
- Chief Diplomatic correspondent for *Time* magazine, late 1950s

66) **Jeff Greenfield**   Media reporter, ABC News *Nightline*; political correspondent, ABC News, 1983-

- Speechwriter, Senator Robert Kennedy, 1967-68

- Media critic, CBS News *Sunday Morning*, 1979-1983

67) **Bettina Gregory**   ABC News Washington Correspondent

- Campaign Manager for husband John Flannery, Democratic opponent to U.S. Rep. Frank Wolf (R-VA), 1984

68) **John Hanrahan**   Executive Director of the Fund for Investigative Journalism, 1988-

- Washington reporter, UPI, 1984-87
- Senior Editor of *Common Cause* magazine, 1982-1983
- *Washington Post* reporter, 1968-1976

69) **Seymour Hersh**   *New York Times* Washington correspondent, 1973-76

- Press Secretary, Eugene McCarthy presidential campaign, 1968

70) **Sheila Hershow**   Reportorial producer, ABC's *Prime Time Live*, 1989-

• Investigator, House Government Operations Subcommittee on Government Activities and Transportation, chaired by Rep. Cardiss Collins (D-IL), 1987-89

• CNN special assignment reporter, 1983-86

71) **Hendrik Hertzberg** Editor, *The New Republic*, 1989-

• Chief Speechwriter for President Carter, 1977-81

• Special Political Correspondent, *The New Republic*, 1987-89
• Editor of *The New Republic*, 1981-1985
• *Newsweek* San Francisco correspondent, 1966-67

72) **Harrison Hickman** Consultant to CBS News, 1988-

• Partner in Hickman-Maslin Research, a polling and political consulting firm. Past clients include:

Paul Simon presidential campaign, 1988
Gary Hart presidential campaign, 1988
National Abortion Rights Action League, 1987
Barbara Milkulski for Senate campaign, 1986
Terry Sanford for Senate campaign, 1986
John Glenn presidential campaign, 1984

73) **Kwame Holman** Washington correspondent, *MacNeil-Lehrer NewsHour*, 1987-; Denver correspondent, 1983-87

• Press Secretary to Marion Barry (D), Mayor of the District of Columbia, 1980

74) **Mari Hope** Production Coordinator, ABC News *Prime Time Live*, 1989-; Production Coordinator, ABC News Washington bureau, 1983-89

- Deputy Administrative Assistant to U.S. Rep. Ron Wyden (D-OR), 1983
- Aide, 1980 Carter-Mondale campaign

75) **Debbie Howlett**   Reporter, *USA Today*, 1988-

- Press Secretary to Oregon State Senator Margee Hendrickson (D), 1983

76) **David Ignatius**   Foreign Editor, *The Washington Post*, 1990; Associate Editor, in charge of "Outlook" section, 1986-1990

- lobbyist for Ralph Nader, 1973

- Reporter, *Wall Street Journal*, 1976-86

77) **Rick Inderfurth**   ABC News Moscow correspondent, 1989-

- Deputy Staff Director for political and security affairs, Democratic controlled Senate Foreign Relations Committee, 1979-80
- Special Assistant to the National Security Council Director, Carter White House, 1977-79
- Legislative Assistant in mid-'70s for Senators George McGovern and Gary Hart

- National Security Affairs correspondent, ABC News, 1984-89
- Pentagon correspondent, ABC News, 1981-84

78) **Michael Janeway**   Editor, *The Boston Globe*, 1985-1986

- Special Assistant to Secretary of State Cyrus Vance, Carter Administration
- Aide to Senator Lyndon Johnson

- Dean, Medill School of Journalism, Northwestern U., 1989-
- Executive Editor, Houghton-Mifflin, 1986-89

79) **Susan Jetton** Press Secretary to Harvey Gantt, Democratic Candidate for Senate, North Carolina, 1990

- Political Reporter, *San Diego Union,* 1979-1986
- Reporter, *The Charlotte Observer,* 1966-1978

- Press Secretary to California House Speaker Willie Brown, 1986-89

80) **Deborah Johnson** Executive Producer, CBS News *Nightwatch,* 1986-

- founder, *Mother Jones* magazine, 1975

- Foreign Producer, *NBC Nightly News,* 1984-86
- Executive Producer, NBC News *Overnight,* 1983-84

81) **W. Thomas Johnson** President, Cable News Network, 1990-

- Executive Assistant to former President Johnson, 1969-71
- Special Assistant to President Johnson, 1968-1969
- Deputy Press Secretary to President Johnson, 1967-68
- Assistant White House Press Secretary, 1966-67

- *Los Angeles Times* Publisher and Chief Executive Officer and Vice Chairman, The Times Mirror Company, 1987-1990
- Publisher and Chief Executive Officer, *Los Angeles Times;* Group Vice President, The Times Mirror Company and Senior Vice President, The Times Mirror Company, 1980-86
- President and Chief Operating Officer, *Los Angeles Times,* 1977-80
- Publisher, *Dallas Times Herald,* 1975-77
- Executive Editor, *Dallas Times Herald,* 1973-75

82) **Sherry Jones** Senior Producer, PBS *Frontline*

- Press aide to Senator Fred Harris (D-OK), 1971

83) **Fred Kaplan** National Security Affairs reporter, *The Boston Globe* Washington bureau, 1982-

- Legislative Assistant for defense to U.S. Rep. Les Aspin (D-WI), 1978-1980
- Author, *Dubious Specter*, Institute for Policy Studies published book that took a skeptical look at the Soviet Union's military build-up, 1977

84) **Mickey Kaus** Senior Writer, *Newsweek*, 1987-88

- Speechwriter for Senator Ernest Hollings (D-SC), 1983-1984

- Senior Editor, *The New Republic*, 1989-

85) **Charles Kenney** Staff Writer, *Boston Globe Magazine*, 1984-89; *Boston Globe* reporter, until 1984

- Speechwriter for Paul Guzzi (D), Massachusetts Secretary of State, 1975

86) **James Killpatrick** Press Secretary, Paul Simon for President, 1987-88

- Senior Editor, *U.S. News & World Report*, until 1987

87) **Stephen Kinzer** Eastern European reporter, *The New York Times*, 1990-

- Aide in Mike Dukakis campaign for Massachusetts Governor, 1974

- Central America reporter, *The New York Times*, 1979-89

88) **John (Jack) Kole** Senior Writer/Press Aide, Rep. David Obey (D-WI), 1989-

• Washington Bureau Chief, *The Milwaukee Journal*, 1964-1989

89) **Charles Krauthammer** Syndicated columnist; panelist, *Inside Washington*

• Speechwriter for Vice President Mondale, 1978-1980

• Senior Editor, *The New Republic*, 1982-1989

90) **Joyce Kravitz** Director, ABC News Information Washington, 1985-88

• Press Aide, Democratic National Committee and Carter White House

• Director of Public Relations, WJLA-TV, Washington, 1989-

91) **Jay Kriegel** CBS Inc. Senior Vice President for external relations, 1987-

• Chief of Staff, New York City Mayor John Lindsay, early 1970s

92) **Polly Kreisman** Washington Bureau Chief for Ackerley Communications Inc., 1989-

• Press Secretary to U.S. Representative Mel Levine (D-CA), 1985

• Washington correspondent, Group W/Westinghouse Broadcasting stations, 1986-89
• Reporter, WBAL-TV Baltimore, 1985
• Washington correspondent, KRON-TV San Francisco, 1984

93) **Robert Krulwich** *CBS This Morning* economics reporter

• Reporter for Pacifica Radio, mid-1970s

94) **Charles Lane**  San Salvador Bureau Chief for *Newsweek*, 1987-

- Associate Editor, *The New Republic*, until 1987

95) **Jonathan Larsen**  Editor-in-Chief of the *Village Voice*, January  1989-

- Senior Editor, *Life* magazine, early 1980's
- Saigon Bureau Chief, *Time*, 1970-71

96) **Deborah Leff**  Senior Producer, ABC's *World News Tonight*, 1989-

- Director of Public Affairs, Federal Trade Commission, 1979-80
- Trial Attorney, U.S. Department of Justice, 1977-79

- Senior Producer of ABC's *Nightline*, New York bureau, 1989
- Senior Producer of ABC's *Nightline*, London bureau, 1988-1989

97) **Tamar Lewin**  National Affairs reporter, *The New York Times*, 1987-; "Business Day" reporter, 1982-87

- Investigative researcher, Common Cause, 1977

98) **Christopher Little**  President, *Newsweek*, 1986-89

- Top aide, U.S. Rep. Bob Eckhardt (D-TX), 1968-70

- President, Cowles Magazine, Inc., February 1989-

99) **Joe Lockhart**  Traveling Press Aide, Michael Dukakis for President, 1988

- Assignment Manager, ABC News Chicago Bureau, 1985-88

- Press Secretary to Sen. Paul Simon (D-IL), 1985
- Assistant Press Secretary, Walter Mondale for President, 1983-84

100) **Dotty Lynch** CBS News Political Editor, 1985-

- Chief pollster, Gary Hart for President, 1984
- Pollster, Mondale-Ferraro campaign, 1984
- Polling Director, Democratic National Committee, 1981-82
- Polling Director, Ted Kennedy for President, 1980
- Deputy Pollster for the 1972 McGovern campaign

- Researcher, NBC News, 1971

101) **Paula Lyons** Consumer affairs reporter, *Good Morning America*, 1989-

- Press Secretary to Boston Mayor Kevin White (D); Assistant Director of the Mayor's Office of Communication; Deputy Director of the Office of Federal Relations, 1974-78

- Consumer reporter, WCVB-TV, Boston, 1979-89

102) **George Mair** Chief Press Officer to Speaker of the House Jim Wright, 1987-89

- CBS News reporter, 1960s

103) **Frank Mankiewicz** President, National Public Radio, 1977-1983

- Top aide in George McGovern presidential campaign, 1972
- Press Secretary, Robert Kennedy campaign, 1968

104) **Charmayne Marsh** Press Secretary to House Speaker Jim Wright, 1981-88

- Washington bureau reporter for UPI, Reuters and the *Dallas Morning News*

105) **Christopher Matthews**   *CBS This Morning* Political columnist 1988-

- Chief of Staff, Speaker of the House Tip O'Neill, 1981-86
- Speechwriter for President Carter

- Washington Bureau Chief for *San Francisco Examiner*, 1988
- Campaign commentator/analyst, Mutual Broadcasting System, 1987-
- Columnist, King Features syndicate, 1987-

106) **Deborah Matthews**   Press Secretary to Senator Wyche Fowler (D-GA), 1989-

- Reporter, *Atlanta Constitution* and *Journal*, 1988-89
- Assignment Editor, Atlanta ABC affiliate WSB-TV, mid-1980s
- Assignment Editor, CNN, 1980

107) **Susana McBee**   Associate Editor, *U.S. News & World Report*, 1981-86

- Assistant Secretary for Public Affairs for the Department of Health, Education and Welfare, Carter Administration

- *Washington Post* reporter and editor, 1964-1977

108) **Colman McCarthy**   Staff writer and columnist, *The Washington Post*

- Member, *Progressive* magazine editorial advisory board

109) **Mark MacCarthy**   Capital Cities/ABC Vice President for Government Affairs in Washington, 1988-

• Professional Staff Member for communications policy, House Energy and Commerce Committee under Congressman John Dingell (D-MI), 1981-88

110) **Max McCarthy** Washington Bureau Chief, *The Buffalo News*, 1978-1989

• Member, U.S. House of Representatives, 1960s-early 1970s

111) **Robert McNamara** Board Member, The Washington Post Company, until 1989

• Secretary of Defense, Kennedy and Johnson Administrations

112) **Sharon Metcalf** Director of Press Relations, NBC News Washington Bureau, 1984-87

• Deputy Press Secretary to President Carter

113) **Judith Miller** Editor, for media company news, *New York Times* "Business Day" section, 1989-

• Washington reporter in mid '70s for *The Progressive* magazine

• Deputy News Editor, *New York Times*, Washington Bureau, 1986-88
• Reporter, National Public Radio, 1978

114) **Newton Minow** CBS Board Member, 1983-

• FCC Chairman, Kennedy and Johnson Administrations

115) **Wilson Morris** Information Director, House Democratic Steering Committee, 1983-89

* *Washington Post* reporter, 1972-78

* Information Director, House Budget Committee, 1980-83

116) **Keith Morrison**  Legislative Director for U.S. Rep. Thomas Foglietta, (D-PA), 1988-

* Assignment Desk Assistant, National Public Radio, Washington bureau, 1984-85
* Researcher, NPR Los Angeles bureau, 1984

117) **Susan Morrison**  *MacNeil/Lehrer NewsHour,* off-air Capitol Hill reporter, 1987-88

* Deputy Communications Director, Bush for President, 1979-1980
* Director of Communications, Democratic National Committee, 1978-79
* Field Director, Frank Church for President, 1976

* Assignment Manager, CBS News Washington Bureau, 1984-85
* Assignment Editor, ABC News Washington Bureau, 1981-84
* *Washington Post* researcher, 1977-78

118) **Bill Moyers**  Commentator and reporter, Public Broadcasting Service, 1985-

* Press Secretary to President Johnson

* CBS News commentator and reporter, 1976-1986

119) **Paul Myer**  Vice President and Director of government relations for Capital Cities/ABC Inc., 1977-1988

* Associate Director for congressional relations, White House Domestic Policy Council, Ford Administration
* aide to U.S. Representative Herman Badillo (D-NY), mid

1970s
- Director of Legislation for the American Federation of State, County and Municipal Employees, early 1970s


120) **Warren Nelson** Professional staff member, House Armed Services Committee, 1983-

- Reporter, United Press International, 1967-1975

- Legislative Assistant and Administrative Assistant to U.S. Representative Les Aspin (D-WI), 1975-1983


121) **Timothy Noah** Washington correspondent, *The Wall Street Journal*, 1990-

- Issues Director for Democrat Kathleen Kennedy Townsend campaign for U.S. House seat from Maryland, 1986

- *Newsweek* congressional reporter, (covered 1988 campaign), 1986-89
- Assistant Op-Ed Page Editor, *The New York Times*, 1982-83


122) **Patricia O'Brien** National affairs and congressional reporter, Knight-Ridder Washington bureau, 1984-87

- Press Secretary to Michael Dukakis for President campaign, April-November 1987


123) **Maria Lourdes Pallais** Reporter for the Sandinista Party radio station, Managua, Nicaragua

- Interpreter for CBS News *60 Minutes*, early 1980s
- Editor, Associated Press Latin America Service and Associated Press New York Reporter, August 1978-November 1979


124) **Ike Pappas** Director, "Convention Satellite News Service"

for the Democratic National Convention, 1988

- CBS News Correspondent, early 1960s-1987

125) **Jane Pauley**  Correspondent and anchor, NBC News, New York, 1990-

- Administrative Assistant, Indiana Democratic State Central Committee, 1972

- Co-host, NBC's *Today*, 1976-1989
- Anchor, *NBC Nightly News* on Sundays, 1980-82

126) **Linda Peek**  Press Secretary to Sen. Robert Byrd (D-WV), and Director of Communications, Senate Democratic Steering Committee, 1983-87

- Director of Public Affairs, *USA Today*, 1982-83
- Director of Pubic Affairs, Gannett Satellite Information Network, 1980-82

- Director of Communications, Carter/Mondale Re-election Committee, 1979-80
- Special Assistant, White House Office of Media Liaison, 1977-79

127) **Jay Peterzell**  Reporter, *Time* Washington bureau, 1987-

- Attorney and Research Associate, Center for National Security Studies (sponsored by the American Civil Liberties Union), 1982-87

128) **Bonnie Piper**  Press Secretary to U.S. Representative Bob Traxler (D-MI), 1989-

- Production Assistant, National Public Radio *Morning Edition*, 1980-84

129) **Richard Pollock** Washington Segment Producer, ABC's *Good Morning America*, April 1988-

 • Director of Critical Mass, an anti-nuclear power group formed by Ralph Nader, 1977-1981

 • Richard Pollock Associates (merged into Arnold & Porter, May 1987)

130) **Jody Powell** Commentator, ABC's *This Week With David Brinkley*

 • Press Secretary for President Carter

131) **Lanie Pryles** Press Secretary to U.S. Representative Doug Barnard (D-GA), 1989-

 • News writer, CNN Atlanta, 1983

132) **Harrison (Lee) Rainie** Assistant Managing Editor, *U.S. News & World Report*, 1988-

 • Chief-of-Staff to Senator Patrick Moynihan, (D-NY), 1987

 • Associate Editor for political coverage, *U.S. News & World Report*, 1987-88
 • Reporter, New York *Daily News*, Washington bureau , 1979-87

133) **Dina Rasor** Founder and Director, Project on Military Procurement, 1981-89

 • Editorial Assistant, ABC News Washington bureau, 1978-79

134) **Bill Ritz** Communications Director, Senator Herb Kohl (D-WI), 1989-1990

- Reporter, *Denver Post*, 1978-1984
- Reporter, Associated Press, 1974-78

- Communications Director, Senate Committee on Aging, 1987-89

135) **Sharon Percy Rockefeller** President and Chief Executive Officer, WETA-TV and radio, Washington, D.C., 1989-

- Member, Democratic National Committee, until 1989

- Member, Corporation for Public Broadcasting (CPB) Board of Directors, 1977-1987 (appointed by President Carter); Chairman of the CPB Board, 1981-1984
- Chairman, WETA Board of Directors, 1987-1989

136) **Thomas Rogers** President, Consumer News and Business Channel, a division of NBC, 1988-

- Senior Counsel to the House Subcommittee on Telecommunications and finance, chaired by U.S. Rep. Tim Wirth (D-CO), 1981-86

- NBC Vice President for Policy Planning and Business Development, 1986-1988

137) **Marla Romash** Press Secretary to Senator Al Gore (D-TN), 1989-

- Reporter WFSB-TV, Hartford, Conn. 1985-88
- Associate Producer, (booker) ABC's *Good Morning America*, Washington bureau, April 1984-February 1985

- Director of Issues and Communications, Sen. Joe Lieberman for Senate Committee, 1988

• Press Secretary to Sen. Christopher Dodd (D-CT), 1980-84

138) **Elizabeth Rose** Press Secretary to Senator Jay Rockefeller (D-WV), 1989-

    • Editorial Associate, Public Broadcasting Service (PBS), 1986-87

    • Wisconsin Press Secretary, Dukakis presidential campaign, 1988

    • Press Secretary to U.S. Representative Tom Downey (D-NY), 1987

139) **Jack Rosenthal** Editor, *New York Times* editorial page, 1986-; Deputy Editor, 1977-86; Washington reporter, 1969-73

    • Executive Assistant to the Undersecretary State, Johnson Administration, 1966-67

    • Assistant Director, Public Information, U.S. Department of Justice, 1961-66

140) **Thomas Ross** Senior Vice President, NBC News, 1986-89

    • Assistant Secretary of Defense for Public Affairs, Carter Administration

    • Washington Bureau Chief, *Chicago Sun Times*, 1970-77

141) **Carl Rowan** News America Syndicate columnist; *Inside Washington* panelist; Member, Gannett Company Board of Directors, 1990-

    • Ambassador to Finland, Johnson Administration

    • Director, United States Information Agency, Kennedy Administration

142) **Jonathan Rowe** *Christian Science Monitor* staff reporter, 1985-

   - Special Assistant to U.S. Rep. Byron Dorgan (D-ND), 1983
   - Co-author *Tax Politics*, Ralph Nader book
   - Lawyer, Citizens for Tax Justice, 1980

   - an editor, *Washington Monthly*, 1983-85

143) **Mary Russell** Capitol Hill reporter, *The Washington Post*, mid-1970s

   - An editor of *Party Line* newsletter published by the Democratic National Committee at its 1988 convention

144) **Mike Russell** Press Secretary to U.S. Rep. Bill Ford (D-MI), 1989-

   - Assignment Manager, ABC's WXYZ-TV, Detroit, until 1980
   - Press Secretary to Sen. Don Reigle (D-MI), 1980-89

145) **Tim Russert** NBC News Vice President and Washington Bureau Chief, 1989-; NBC News Vice President, 1984-88

   - Counselor and media strategist for New York Governor Mario Cuomo, 1983-84
   - Chief-of-Staff to U.S. Senator Patrick Moynihan, until 1983

146) **Pierre Salinger** ABC News Chief Foreign Correspondent, 1983-

   - U.S. Senator, (D-CA), 1964
   - Press Secretary for President Kennedy

147) **Van Gordon Sauter** Co-Executive Producer, the *Jesse Jackson Show*, weekly television talk show, 1989-

- President, CBS News and Executive Vice President, CBS Broadcast Group, 1985-86
- Executive Vice President, CBS Broadcast Group, 1983-86
- President, CBS News, 1981-83

148) **Albert Scardino**  Press Secretary to New York Mayor David Dinkins, 1990-

- Reporter, *New York Times* "Business Day" section, 1985-89
- Reporter, Associated Press, West Virginia, early 1970s

149) **Kristy Schantz**  Deputy Press Secretary to Sen. Herbert Kohl (D-WI), 1989-

- News writer CNN Headline News channel, 1986-89

150) **Robert Scheer**  *Los Angeles Times* reporter, 1976-

- Editor, *Ramparts* magazine, mid to late 1960s

151) **Charles Seigel**  Press Secretary to U.S. Representative Steny Hoyer (D-MD), 1989-

- Reporter, Denver's *Rocky Mountain News*, 1980-83

- Press Secretary to Delaware Lt. Governor S.B. Woo's (D) campaign for Senate, 1988

152) **Eileen Shanahan**  Assistant Secretary for Public Affairs, Dept. of Health, Education and Welfare, 1977-79

- Reporter, *Congressional Quarterly*, 1986
- Assistant Managing Editor, *Pittsburgh Post-Gazette*, 1981-84
- Assistant Managing Editor, *Washington Star*, 1979-81

- Reporter, *New York Times* Washington bureau, 1962-77
- Pulitzer Prize Jury, 1973, 1982, 1983

- Special Assistant to Assistant Secretary of Transportation for Public Affairs, 1962

153) **William Shannon** (late) Columnist, *The Boston Globe*, 1981-88

- U.S. Ambassador to Ireland, Carter Administration

- Editorial writer, *The New York Times*, 1964-1977
- Washington correspondent, *New York Post*, 1951-1964

154) **Robert Shapiro**  Vice President, Progressive Policy Institute, 1989-

- Associate Editor, *U.S. News & World Report*, 1985-88

- Deputy Director for Issues, Dukakis for President Committee, 1988
- Legislative Director for Senator Patrick Moynihan, 1981-85
- Fellow, Institute for Policy Studies, 1972-73

155) **Walter Shapiro**  Senior Writer, *Time* magazine, (covered the 1988 campaign), 1987-

- Speechwriter, President Carter, 1979
- Press Secretary for Labor Secretary Ray Marshall, Carter Administration, 1977-78

- General Editor, national affairs, *Newsweek*, 1983-87
- Staff writer, *Washington Post Magazine*, 1980-83

156) **Mark Shields**  *Washington Post* Writers Group columnist

- Political analyst, PBS *MacNeil-Lehrer NewsHour*

• Speechwriter, Senator Robert Kennedy

157) **Maria Shriver** Co-Host, NBC's *Sunday Today*, 1988-89

• worked for Ted Kennedy's presidential campaign, 1980

• Co-host, *CBS Morning News*, 1985-86

158) **Leon Sigal** Editorial writer, *The New York Times*, 1989-

• Special Assistant to the Director, State Department Bureau of Politico-Military Affairs, 1979-81
• Author of two books on arms control in conjunction with the Brookings Institution

159) **Peggy Simpson** Washington Bureau Chief, *Ms.* magazine, 1988-

• Economics reporter, Hearst Newspapers Washington bureau, 1982-1988
• Associated Press Washington reporter, late 1970s

160) **Amanda Spake** Senior Editor, *The Washington Post Magazine*, 1986-

• an editor, *Mother Jones*, 1977-1982

161) **Lesley Stahl** White House Correspondent, CBS News, 1989-; Moderator, CBS *Face the Nation*, 1983-

• worked in late 1960s for New York City Mayor John Lindsay

• National Affairs Correspondent, CBS News, 1982-86

162) *Neil Strawser*  CBS News correspondent, 1952-1984

- Director of Communications, House Budget Committee, majority staff, 1987-88
- Press Secretary, Democratic controlled Joint Economic Committee, 1986-87

163) *Virginia (Ginny) Terzano*  Press Secretary, Democratic National Committee, 1989-

- Political researcher, CBS News Election Unit, 1988

- Press aide, Senator Al Gore presidential campaign,1987-88
- Deputy Press Secretary, Gary Hart presidential campaign, 1987

164) *Damon Thompson*  Press Secretary to Senator David Pryor (D-AR), 1986-

- Washington Bureau Chief, *Arkansas Democrat*, 1985-86

- Press Secretary for Senate campaign of U.S. Rep. Ed Bethune (R-AR); 1984

165) *Claudia Townsend*  Assistant Editor, *The Washington Post*, early 1980s

- Associate Press Secretary and White House News Summary Editor, Carter White House, 1977-81

- Reporter, Cox Newspapers Washington Bureau, mid-1970s
- Reporter, *The Atlanta Constitution*

166) *Cyrus Vance*  Member, New York Times Company Board of Directors, 1980-

- Secretary of State, Carter Administration

167) **Arnot Walker**  Press Representative, ABC's *World News Tonight*, 1990-

- Advance staff, Ferraro for Vice President campaign, 1984
- Deputy Press Secretary, John Glenn for President, 1984
- Advance staff, Frank Lautenberg for Senate (D-NJ), 1982
- Advance staff, Jim Florio for Governor of New Jersey, 1981
- Advance staff, Office of Vice President Mondale

168) **Karolyn Wallace**  Press Secretary to Sen. Don Riegle (D-MI), 1989-

- General Assignment reporter, KABC-TV, Los Angeles, 1986-89
- Reporter, WJRT-TV, Flint, Michigan, 1981-83

169) **Douglas Waller**  *Newsweek* foreign affairs reporter, Washington bureau, 1988-

- Legislative Assistant to Senator William Proxmire (D-WI), 1985-88
- Legislative Director, U.S. Representative Ed Markey (D-MA), 1983-85

170) **Mary Williams Walsh**  Toronto Bureau Chief, *Los Angeles Times*, 1989-

- Associate Editor, *The Progressive*, 1979-1982

- Asia correspondent, *The Wall Street Journal*, 1986-89
- Mexico City Bureau Chief, *The Wall Street Journal*, 1983-85

171) **Ben Wattenberg**  Contributing Editor, *U.S. News & World Report*

- Chairman, Coalition for a Democratic Majority
- Adviser, Senator Henry Jackson presidential campaign, 1972, and 1976

- Adviser, Senator Hubert Humphrey re-election campaign, 1970
- Speechwriter for President Lyndon Johnson, 1966-68

- Senior Fellow, American Enterprise Institute
- Spectrum commentator, CBS Radio Network

172) **Jim Weighart**  Editor, New York *Daily News*, 1982-84; Washington Bureau Chief, 1975-1981

- Chief-of-Staff to Senator Ted Kennedy, 1986-87

- Chairman, Department of Journalism, Central Michigan University, September 1989-
- National Political Correspondent, Scripps Howard Newspapers, 1984-86

173) **Jacob Weisberg**  *Newsweek* reporter, Washington and London bureaus, 1987-88; *Newsweek* intern, Summer of 1987

- Alternate delegate to the 1984 Democratic National Convention

- Associate Editor of *The New Republic*, 1989-
- Reporter/researcher, *The New Republic*, 1986-87

174) **John C. White**  Press Secretary to District of Columbia Mayor Marion Barry (D), 1987-89

- Director of Investigations, WJLA-TV, Washington, D.C., 1989-

- City Hall reporter, *Philadelphia Daily News*, until 1987
- Reporter, *Chicago Tribune*, 1980s and *Washington Star*, 1970s

175) **Michael Whitney**  Press Secretary, U.S. Representative Robert Matsui (D-CA), 1987-88

• National News Editor, United Press International Washington bureau, until 1987

176) **Roger Wilkins**  Chairman, Pulitzer Prize Board, 1987-88; Member, Pulitzer Prize Board, 1981-89

• Senior Fellow, Institute for Policy Studies

• Senior Adviser, Jesse Jackson presidential campaign, 1984
• Assistant Attorney General, Johnson Administration

177) **Charles Woolsey**  Director of Communications for Senator Jeff Bingaman (D-NM), 1989-

• Executive Producer for news, KOB-TV, Albuquerque, NM, 1986-88
• Producer, WRC-TV, Washington, 1988-86
• Assistant News Director, WTTG-TV, Washington, 1983-85
• Special Projects Producer, ABC News, Washington bureau, 1981-83

178) **Bob Zelnick**  ABC News Pentagon correspondent, 1986-; Tel Aviv correspondent, 1984-86; Moscow Bureau Chief, 1982-84

• Legislative Researcher for U.S. Rep. Henry Reuss (D-WI), 1972

• Deputy Washington Bureau Chief, ABC News, 1981-82
• Director of News Coverage, ABC News Washington, 1978-81

**SECTION TWO:** *A List of Conservative & Republican Connections to the News Media*

1) *Cissy Baker* Managing Editor, Cable News Network, 1984-

- Republican candidate for U.S. House seat from Tennessee, 1982

- Washington correspondent, CNN, 1983-84
- Assignment Editor, CNN Washington bureau, 1980-81

2) *Haley Barbour* Conus Communications commentator during the 1988 campaign

- Deputy Political Director, Reagan White House, 1983-87
- Republican candidate for U.S. Senate in Mississippi, 1982

3) *Jean Becker* Deputy Press Secretary for the First Lady, 1989-

- Reporter, *USA Today*, 1985-88

4) *David Beckwith* Press Secretary to Vice President Dan Quayle, January 1989-

- Correspondent, *Time*, 1971-78, 1980-88
- Reporter, *Legal Times*, 1978-80

5) *William Beecher* Washington Bureau Chief, *The Minneapolis Star Tribune*, 1987-

- Deputy Assistant Secretary of Defense for Public Affairs, Nixon Administration, 1973-1975

- Chief Diplomatic Correspondent, *The Boston Globe*, 1975-1987
- Military Correspondent, Washington Bureau, *The New York Times*, 1966-1973

- National Security Affairs Correspondent, *The Wall Street Journal*, 1960-1966

6) **Joanna Bistany** Vice President and Assistant to the President, ABC News, 1985-

- Special Assistant to the President for Communications, Reagan Administration, 1981-1983

- Director, News Information, ABC News, 1983-1985

7) **Robert Bork Jr.** Special Assistant for Communications, Office of the U.S. Trade Representative, 1990-

- Associate Editor, *U.S. News & World Report*, covering economics, 1987
- Managing Editor, *Regulation* magazine, 1986-1987
- Business Writer, *Forbes* magazine, Houston Bureau, 1983-1986

- Speechwriter for Senator Gordon Humphrey (R-NH), 1988-89
- Visiting Journalism Fellow, The Heritage Foundation, 1987-88

8) **Jim Boyle** Press Assistant, NBC News *American Almanac*, 1985-1986

- Press Secretary, U.S. Rep. Frank Wolf (R-VA), early 1980s

9) **Patrick Buchanan** Co-host, CNN's *Crossfire*, 1982-85, 1987-

- Director of Communications, Reagan White House, 1985-87
- Speechwriter, Nixon White House

10) **John Buckley** Director of Communications, National Republican Congressional Committee, 1988-89

- CBS News political campaign coverage consultant, 1988-

• Chief spokesman for the Jack Kemp for President Committee, 1987-1988

11) **Richard Burt**  Chief strategic arms negotiator in Geneva, February 1989-

• National Security Affairs Reporter, *New York Times*, 1977-1981

• Ambassador to the Federal Republic of Germany, 1985-1989
• Assistant Secretary of State for European and Canadian Affairs, 1982-85
• Director, State Dept. Bureau of Politico-Military Affairs, 1981-82

12) **Richard Capen, Jr.**  Vice Chairman for business information and cable television properties, Knight-Ridder, 1989-

• Deputy Assistant Secretary of Defense and Assistant Secretary of Defense for legislative affairs, 1969-1971

• Publisher, *Miami Herald*, 1983-89

13) **Eugene Cowan**  Vice President, Washington, Capital Cities/ABC Inc., 1971-1990

• Deputy Assistant to the President for congressional relations, 1969-1971

14) **Catherine Crier**  Co-anchor, CNN's *World Today*, 1989-

• Judge (elected on Republican ticket), Texas civil district court, 1984-89

15) **Ed Dale**  Director of External Affairs, Office of Management and Budget, 1989-

  • *New York Times* correspondent, 1970s

  • Assistant Director for Public Affairs, Office of Management and Budget, 1981-87


16) **Sid Davis** Director of Programs, Voice of America, 1987-

  • Washington correspondent, NBC News, 1982-87
  • Washington Bureau Chief, NBC News, 1979-1982
  • White House Correspondent, NBC News, 1977-1979
  • Washington Bureau Chief, Group W/Westinghouse, 1966-1977


17) **David Fox** Press Secretary, Rep. Lynn Martin (R-IL), 1989-

  • Associated Press reporter, 1979-89


18) **Jack Fuller** Editor, *Chicago Tribune*, 1989-

  • Special Assistant to Attorney General Edward Levi, 1975-76

  • Executive Editor, *Chicago Tribune*, 1987-89
  • Editor of the editorial page, *Chicago Tribune*, 1981-87
  • Editorial writer, *Chicago Tribune*, 1978-81
  • Washington correspondent, *Chicago Tribune*, 1977-78


19) **David Gergen** Editor, *U.S. News & World Report*, 1985-88; Editor-at-Large, 1988-

  • White House Communications Director, Reagan Administration


20) **Kimberly Timmons Gibson** Deputy Director of External Affairs and spokeswoman, Office of Management and Budget, 1989-

- Associate Producer, *Good Morning America*, ABC News Washington bureau, 1986-88

- Researcher, surrogate campaign department, Bush for President, 1988
- Researcher, White House speechwriting department, 1984-86

21) **Henry A. Grunwald** Ambassador to Austria, 1987-89

- Member, Time Inc. Board of Directors
- Editor-in-Chief, Time Inc., 1979-1987
- Managing Editor, *Time*, 1968-77

22) **Michael Healy** Legislative Assistant, Sen. John Chafee (R-RI), April 1989-

- Political Researcher, CBS News Election Survey unit, 1986-88

- Staffer, Sen. John Chafee (R-RI), 1985-86
- Researcher, National Republican Senatorial Committee, 1984

23) **Lawrence Higby** President, *Los Angeles Times* Orange County edition, 1989-

- Deputy Assistant to President Nixon

- Senior Vice President for marketing and sales, Times Mirror Cable Television, until 1989

24) **Smith Hempstone** U.S. Ambassador to Kenya, 1989-

- Editor-in-Chief, *The Washington Times*, 1984-85
- Reporter, Associate Editor and Editor of the editorial page, *The Washington Star*, 1967-1975
- Foreign correspondent, *Chicago Daily News*, mid-1960s

25) **Bernard Kalb** State Department Spokesman, 1981-1986

- Former NBC News correspondent

26) **Henry Kissinger** Member, CBS Board of Directors, 1989-

- Secretary of State, Nixon and Ford Administrations

27) **Herbert Klein** Editor-in-Chief of Copley Newspapers

- Director of Communications, Nixon Administration

28) **Margie Lehrman** Deputy Washington Bureau Chief, NBC News, 1989-

- Press Assistant to Sen. Robert Griffin (R-MI), late 1970s

- Washington Producer, NBC's *Today*, 1983-89

29) **Robert Lindsey** Writer, Ronald Reagan memoirs, 1989-1990

- West Coast Bureau Chief, *The New York Times*, 1977-88

30) **Bob McConnell** Vice President for Government Relations, CBS Inc., Washington, 1984-1988

- Assistant Attorney General, Office of Legislative Affairs, Justice Department, Reagan Administration, until 1984

31) **Bill McGurn** Washington Bureau Chief, *National Review*, 1989-

- Deputy Editorial Page Editor, Asian edition of *The Wall Street Journal*, 1986-89

    • Editorial writer, European Edition, *The Wall Street Journal*
    • Writer, *The American Spectator*

32) **Jim Miller** Associate Producer, *CBS Morning News*, Washington Bureau, 1984-1986

    • Speechwriter for Senator Howard Baker, 1982-1984

33) **Loye Miller** Director of Public Affairs, Justice Department, 1988-89

    • National affairs reporter, Newhouse news service 1979-85
    • Knight-Ridder reporter in Washington, mid 1970s

    • Press Secretary to Secretary of Education Bill Bennett, 1985-88

34) **Rex Nelson** Press Secretary for campaign for Governor by U.S. Representative Tommy Robinson (R-AR), 1989-1990

    • Washington Bureau Chief, *Arkansas Democrat*, 1986-89

    • Press Secretary to Republican congressional campaign of Judy Petty, 1984

35) **Ron Nessen** Vice President for News, Mutual Broadcasting System

    • Press Secretary to President Gerald Ford

36) **Peggy Noonan** Speechwriter for George Bush, 1988-1989

    • Writer, Dan Rather radio commentary, 1981-1984
    • Writer/Editor CBS Radio News network, 1977-1981
    • Newswriter, WEEI Radio Boston, 1974-1977

    • Speechwriter for President Ronald Reagan, 1984-87

37) **Richard Perle** Contributing Editor, *U.S. News & World Report*, 1987-

- Assistant Secretary of Defense, 1981-86

38) **Burton Yale Pines** Executive Vice President, The Heritage Foundation, 1982-

- Associate Editor and correspondent, *Time* magazine, 1966-1981

39) **Wes Pippert** Senior Adviser to U.S. Representative Paul Henry (R-MI), 1989

- Reporter, United Press International, 1959-1989

40) **Andy Plattner** Special Adviser to the Assistant Secretary of Education for educational research and improvement, 1990-

- Associate Editor, *U.S. News & World Report*, 1985-1990

41) **Rob Rehg** Executive Director to U.S. Representative Bill Schuette (R-MI), 1989-

- Washington correspondent for Hearst Newspapers, 1988-89
- Hearst Newspapers correspondent, 1981-88

42) **Scott Richardson** Manager of News Information, ABC News, 1990-

- Deputy Press Secretary for Sen. Bob Dole, 1982-88

- Press Representative, ABC's *World News Tonight*, 1988-90

43) **Ed Rollins**  Conus Communications commentator, 1988

- Executive Director, National Republican Congressional Committee, 1989-
- Manager, Jack Kemp for President Committee, 1987-88

44) **David Runkel**  Director of Public Affairs, Department of Justice, 1988-1990; Communications Director, 1990-

- Washington reporter, *Philadelphia Bulletin*, 1980-82
- City Hall reporter, *Philadelphia Bulletin*, 1978-80
- State Capital reporter, *Philadelphia Bulletin*, 1974-77

- Press Secretary to Pennsylvania Governor Richard Thornburgh, 1984-87

45) **William Safire**  *New York Times* columnist

- Special Assistant/Speechwriter, Nixon Administration

46) **Diane Sawyer**  Co-anchor, ABC's *Prime Time Live*, 1989-

- Press Assistant, Nixon Administration, 1970-1974

- Co-Editor, *60 Minutes*, 1984-1989
- Co-host, *CBS Morning News*, 1981-84
- State Department correspondent, CBS News, 1980-81

47) **John Scali**  ABC News Senior Correspondent, 1974-

- U.S. Ambassador to United Nations, 1973-74
- Special White House Adviser, President Nixon, 1971-73

- ABC News Correspondent, 1961-71
- Associated Press reporter, 1943-61

48) **Ernie Schultz** Director of Communications, Senator Don Nickles (R-OK), 1990-

- President, Radio-Television News Directors Association, 1981-1990
- Reporter, Producer, Anchor, News Director, KTVY-TV, NBC affiliate in Oklahoma City, 1955-1981

49) **David Shapiro** Press Secretary, Sen. Richard Lugar (R-IN), 1989-

- Off-air national security affairs reporter, *MacNeil/Lehrer News-Hour*, 1983-89

50) **Dorrance Smith** Executive Producer, *Nightline*, 1989-; Executive Producer, *This Week with David Brinkley*, 1981-1989

- Staff Assistant, Advance Office, Ford White House

- Producer, ABC News Washington bureau, 1977-1981

51) **William F. Smith** U.S. Attorney General, 1981-1983

- Former RCA (NBC) Board Member

52) **Kristin Clark Taylor** White House Director of Media Relations, 1989-

- *USA Today* editorial board member and reporter, 1982-87

53) **Chase Untermeyer** Personnel Director, Bush Administration 1988-

- Reporter, *Houston Chronicle*, 1972-74

- Executive Assistant to Vice President Bush, 1981-83
- Texas legislator, 1977-81
- Intern in the office of U.S. Representative Bush, 1966

54) **Gerald L. Warren**  Editor, *San Diego Union*, 1975-

- Deputy Press Secretary to President Nixon, 1969-75

- Reporter, *The San Diego Union*, 1956-1969

55) **George Will**  Commentator, ABC's *This Week with David Brinkley*, 1982-

- Washington Editor, *National Review*, early 1970s

- Aide to Senator Gordon Allot (R-CO), early 1970s

56) **Stanley N. Welborn**  Director of Public Relations, Brookings Institution, 1989-

- Speechwriter, Dole for President Committee, 1987-88
- Press Secretary to Mrs. Dole during Sen. Dole's presidential campaign, 1988

- Senior Science Editor, *U.S. News & World Report*, 1980s

57) **Claudia Winkler**  Chief Editorial Writer, Scripps-Howard Newspapers, Washington, June 1989-

- Publications Editor, American Enterprise Institute, 1975-82

- Editorial Page Editor, *Cinncinati Post*, 1985-89

# B Sources and Media Organizations

## Sources of Studies

**Ablex Publishing Corporation**
355 Chestnut Street
Norwood, NJ 07648

Ablex published William C. Adams' book *Television Coverage of International Affairs* in 1982, from which Chapter 6, Study 6 was reprinted. The volume is available ($37.50) from the publisher.

**American Enterprise Institute (AEI)**
1150 17th St. NW
Washington, D.C. 20036

AEI was publisher of *Public Opinion*, from which studies in chapters 1, 2, 8, 9 and 10 by William C. Adams, S. Robert Lichter and Michael Robinson were reprinted.

In 1990 AEI ceased publication of *Public Opinion* and began publishing *The American Enterprise*, a bi-monthly magazine of articles on public opinion, political policy making and media issues. $5.00 per copy. Subscription: $28.00 for one year. Write: *The American Enterprise*, P.O. Box 6827, Syracuse, NY 13217.

**American Society of Newspaper Editors (ASNE)**
P.O. Box 17004
Washington, D.C. 20041

ASNE published "The Changing Face of the Newsroom," from which Chapter 1, Study 7 was drawn. Copies of this report by the ASNE's Human Resources Committee are available for $9.50 each.

**The Brookings Institution**
1775 Massachusetts Avenue, NW
Washington, D.C.  20036

Published Stephen Hess' book *The Washington Reporters* in 1981. Findings from this book were included in Chapter 1, Study 3. The book is still available in paperback from Brookings for $9.95.

*The Journalist and Financial Reporting*
82 Wall Street, Suite 1105
New York, New York  10005

*The Journalist and Financial Reporting*, a twice monthly newsletter on business news reporting, conducted a poll in 1988 which was the basis for Chapter 1, Study 8. The newletter is available for $549.00 a year. The poll, "The TJFR 150 Survey of America's Top Business and Financial Journalists," is available for $49.00.

*Los Angeles Times*
Times Mirror Square
Los Angeles, CA  90053

More information on the *Los Angeles Times* poll summarized in Chapter 1, Study 5 can be obtained by writing the above address.

**The Media Institute**
3017 M Street, NW
Washington, D.C.  20007

Published studies by Ted J. Smith III Chapter 5, Study 1 and Chapter 7, Study 2; and one by Tom Bethell Chapter 7, Study 1.

**Media Research Center (MRC)**
111 S. Columbus Street
Alexandria, VA 22314

The MRC published this book; many of its studies first appeared in the MRC's newsletter *MediaWatch*. (See page 338 for more information on the MRC.)

**National Conservative Foundation**
618 S. Alfred Street
Alexandria, VA 22314

Published the newsletter *Newswatch* in which the complete versions of Chapter 4, Study 1; Chapter 5, Studies 2 and 3; Chapter 6, Studies 1,2, 5, and 7; and Chapter 7, Study 3 were originally published.

*Washington Journalism Review* **(WJR)**
2233 Wisconsin Avenue, NW
Washington, D.C. 20007

WJR published the Linda Lichter and S. Robert Lichter study on journalism school students in Chapter 1, Study 9.

Published by the University of Maryland College of Journalism ten times a year, WJR articles focus on the media's coverage of political issues and current events.

Subscriptions are $23.97 a year. A sample issue is available for $2.95 plus $1.50 shipping and handling.

# Media Monitoring Organizations

### Accuracy In Media (AIM)
1275 K Street, NW, Suite 1150
Washington D.C.  20005

Founded over 20 years ago by Reed Irvine, AIM is the oldest media monitoring organization. Published twice monthly, *The AIM Report* newsletter deals with issues of liberal bias in the news media. Subscriptions are $20.00 a year for third class delivery, $30.00 per year for first class.

### *between the lines*
325 Pennsylvania Avenue SE
Washington, D.C.  20003

Published twice monthly, *between the lines* tracks liberal bias in the news media and Hollywood. A one year subscription is $29.00.

### Center for Media and Public Affairs (CMPA)
2101 L Street NW, Suite 505
Washington, D.C.  20037

Co-directed by S. Robert Lichter and Linda Lichter, authors of several studies reprinted in this book, the CMPA conducts content analysis of television network coverage of political issues.  The center's findings are published in *Media Monitor*, which appears 10 times a year. Subscription rates are $50 (corporate) or $25 (individual) a year. Back issues are $3.00, a sample issue is available for free.

### Media Research Center (MRC)
111 S. Columbus Street
Alexandria, VA  22314

The MRC, which published *And That's The Way It Is(n't)*, also publishes three newsletters. *Notable Quotables* provides a bi-weekly compilation of outrageous or humorous quotes from the liberal media ($19 a year). *MediaWatch*, the MRC's monthly newsletter on media bias, offers readers a more detailed analysis of the content of the news, including a monthly study, the "Janet Cooke Award" for the worst story of the month, and "The Revolving Door," an on-going examination of the movement of liberals and conservatives between the media and politics ($29 a year). *TV etc.* reports bi-monthly on the activities of the Hollywood Left and political themes in television shows and movies ($35 a year).

**Times Mirror Center for The People & The Press**
1875 I Street NW, Suite 1110
Washington, D.C.  20006

Formed in late 1989, the new Times Mirror Center publishes a monthly News Interest Index which tracks how closely the public follows issues and people in the news. The center also analyzes major media coverage of current events. To be added to the complimentary mailing list, write to the address above.

# 3 GOOD REASONS TO READ
## MW MediaWatch.

**Every month, *MediaWatch*, published by the Media Research Center, will give you examples, quotes, studies, and analysis exposing the liberal bias in the media, especially the TV networks.**

"Every month when I receive *MediaWatch* I can just see and hear the leftwingers in the major media gnashing their teeth. Bravo to *MediaWatch* for exposing the hypocrisy in so much of what's going on among the 'news' business in our time."

-- *Senator Jesse Helms*

"*MediaWatch* is crucial, it's pointed, it's witty, and it's lethal."

-- *William F. Buckley, Jr.*

"Almost every day I receive letters from American citizens outraged over slanted liberal coverage of major news events. My response to these people: read *MediaWatch* and learn the truth."

-- *Congressman Robert Dornan*

"Its research is first-rate: meticulous, comprehensive, and always on target. *MediaWatch* provides necessary exposure of liberal bias in the Fourth Estate."

-- Boston Herald's *Don Feder*

# Who's Watching Hollywood?

**The makers of *MediaWatch* introduce *TV, etc.*, the Media Research Center's bi-monthly review of the entertainment industry and the Hollywood Left.**

Through *TV, etc.* you'll learn:

■ Which rock stars donate concert proceeds to the far-left Christic Institute.

■ Which far-left celebrities supported Hollywood's *Housing Now!* march and NOW's pro-abortion *March for Women's Lives*.

■ Which popular TV shows consistently slam conservatives.

■ How much money the entertainment community has poured into the campaign warchests of liberal Congressmen and Senators.

What opinion leaders say about *TV, etc.* newsletter:

"Each story is enlightening and leaves no doubt of the need to track ultra-liberal political messages tucked neatly into situation comedies and other shows watched by young people."

*-- Lee Atwater, Chairman, RNC*

"I want this stopped before it really gets started."

*-- Leftist actor John Randolph*

# MRC Publications Order Form

❑ Additional Copies of *And That's The Way It Is(n't)*

1-9 Copies @ $14.95 each

10-49 Copies @ $12.95 each

50+ Copies @ $9.95 each

_____ Number of Copies @ _____ each = _____

❑ Subscription to *MediaWatch*

$29 for 1 Year

$49 for 2 Years

*MediaWatch* Total = _____

❑ Subscription to *TV, etc.*

$35 for 1 Year

$60 for 2 Years

*TV, etc.* Total = _____

❑ Subscription to *Notable Quotables*, the MRC's bi-weekly compilation of the latest outrageous quotes in the liberal media.

$19 for 1 Year

$35 for 2 Years

*Notable Quotables* Total = _____

❑ Subscriptions to all 3 MRC Newsletters

$64 for 1 Year

$120 for 2 Years

All Three Newsletters Total = _____

TOTAL = _____

Send to:
Media Research Center (MRC)
111 South Columbus Street
Alexandria, VA 22314
(703) 683-9733

Name _____

Address _____

_____

❑ Check Enclosed
❑ VISA  ❑ MasterCard
Card No. _____
Expires _____

# MRC Publications Order Form

❏ Additional Copies of *And That's The Way It Is(n't)*

  1-9 Copies @ $14.95 each

  10-49 Copies @ $12.95 each

  50+ Copies @ $9.95 each

  _____ Number of Copies @ _____ each = _____

❏ Subscription to *MediaWatch*

  $29 for 1 Year

  $49 for 2 Years

  *MediaWatch* Total = _____

❏ Subscription to *TV, etc.*

  $35 for 1 Year

  $60 for 2 Years

  *TV, etc.* Total = _____

❏ Subscription to *Notable Quotables*, the MRC's bi-weekly compilation of the latest outrageous quotes in the liberal media.

  $19 for 1 Year

  $35 for 2 Years

  *Notable Quotables* Total = _____

❏ Subscriptions to all 3 MRC Newsletters

  $64 for 1 Year

  $120 for 2 Years

  All Three Newsletters Total = _____

  TOTAL = _____

Send to:
Media Research Center (MRC)
111 South Columbus Street
Alexandria, VA 22314
(703) 683-9733

Name _____

Address _____

_____

❏ Check Enclosed
❏ VISA  ❏ MasterCard
Card No. _____
Expires _____

# MRC Publications Order Form

❑ Additional Copies of *And That's The Way It Is(n't)*

1-9 Copies @ $14.95 each

10-49 Copies @ $12.95 each

50+ Copies @ $9.95 each

_____ Number of Copies @ _____ each = _____

❑ Subscription to *MediaWatch*

$29 for 1 Year

$49 for 2 Years

*MediaWatch* Total = _____

❑ Subscription to *TV, etc.*

$35 for 1 Year

$60 for 2 Years

*TV, etc.* Total = _____

❑ Subscription to *Notable Quotables*, the MRC's bi-weekly compilation of the latest outrageous quotes in the liberal media.

$19 for 1 Year

$35 for 2 Years

*Notable Quotables* Total = _____

❑ Subscriptions to all 3 MRC Newsletters

$64 for 1 Year

$120 for 2 Years

All Three Newsletters Total = _____

TOTAL = _____

Send to:
Media Research Center (MRC)
111 South Columbus Street
Alexandria, VA 22314
(703) 683-9733

Name _____

Address _____

_____

❑ Check Enclosed
❑ VISA  ❑ MasterCard
Card No. _____
Expires _____